W9-AQG-687

Get Started in Film Making

The Definitive Film Maker's Handbook

Tom Holden

First published in Great Britain in 2002 by Hodder & Stoughton. An Hachette UK company.

This edition published in 2018 by John Murray Learning.

Previously published as *Teach Yourself Film making*

Copyright © Tom Holden 2002, 2003, 2007, 2010, 2018

The right of Tom Holden to be identified as the Author of the Work has been asserted by him in accordance with the Copyright, Designs and Patents Act 1988.

Database right Hodder & Stoughton (makers)

The *Teach Yourself* name is a registered trademark of Hachette UK.

British Library Cataloguing in Publication Data: a catalogue record for this title is available from the British Library.

ISBN: 978 1 473 67853 8

eISBN: 978 1 473 67854 5

2

The publisher has used its best endeavours to ensure that any website addresses referred to in this book are correct and active at the time of going to press. However, the publisher and the author have no responsibility for the websites and can make no guarantee that a site will remain live or that the content will remain relevant, decent or appropriate.

The publisher has made every effort to mark as such all words which it believes to be trademarks. The publisher should also like to make it clear that the presence of a word in the book, whether marked or unmarked, in no way affects its legal status as a trademark.

Every reasonable effort has been made by the publisher to trace the copyright holders of material in this book. Any errors or omissions should be notified in writing to the publisher, who will endeavour to rectify the situation for any reprints and future editions.

Typeset by Cenveo® Publisher Services.

Printed and bound in Great Britain by CPI Group (UK) Ltd, Croydon, CR0 4YY.

John Murray Learning policy is to use papers that are natural, renewable and recyclable products and made from wood grown in sustainable forests. The logging and manufacturing processes are expected to conform to the environmental regulations of the country of origin.

John Murray Learning

Carmelite House

50 Victoria Embankment

London EC4Y 0DZ

www.hodder.co.uk

Also available in ebook

Get Started in Film Making

Tom Holden

Tom Holden has worked in television, film and video since the 1990s. He has worked internationally and taught film making and broadcast journalism at various colleges and universities. He currently works as a video director at the United Nations.

Contents

Foreword

Why on earth do you want to make a film?

What has possessed you to assemble fanciful items of technology in order to convert your thoughts into moving images? Why does the potential stress and trouble of your self-inflicted task not put you off? Wouldn't it be simpler just to keep these ideas in your head, or maybe just tell some friends? Perhaps just write it all down and be satisfied with that.

Of course, you wouldn't, because you want to make a film; you need to shoot video. It's just too important not to make into a moving picture. For some personal and abstract reason, you are possessed with the burning desire to show your story, your idea (or maybe even just yourself), to the outside world.

Those words, people and actions floating around your head can be accurately envisioned in your mind's eye. You've played it over again and again, thinking how to approach that line, that piece of dialogue, the bit when the hero jumps off the wall, or maybe just demonstrate to ordinary folk how to rewire an electrical plug.

Yet, you want to take it to the next step. The camera needs to have its juicy red record button pressed to capture it all. The microphones have to be arranged so all can hear what's being said. The lights need to be set up in order for things to be seen. Then the editing needs to be done so it all makes sense.

Does this sound like you?

Then worry no more. You are not alone.

It's hard to pinpoint the piece of us that wants to make a film – be it a three-hour epic or a two-minute YouTube effort – but millions of us around the world have this genetic mutation that prods and pulls us towards cameras and all the glittering paraphernalia of the film maker. Some of us may have had an idea floating in our head for years, honing it every day until it's been written, shot and edited all in your grey matter. Or perhaps your hobby or interests have led you to think you can demonstrate things just as well as the professionals.

We live in very exciting times when it's never been easier to realize your film and video-making ambitions. Content can be shot and edited on the smartphones carried in back pockets. Gone is the need for purchasing the expensive cameras, equipment and editing hardware of yesteryear. Uploading material to video-sharing and social media sites gives you the kind of exposure film makers of previous generations could only have dreamed about. In fact, an entire generation of people have become film makers without realizing it, such is the extent that it has become a part of daily life thanks to the proliferation and availability of video technology.

Even a humble home computer can edit an entire film, giving you the kind of movie-making capability that simply didn't exist a few short years ago. These are truly very heady times for the aspiring film maker.

Yet, to quote film maker and Monty Python member Terry Gilliam: 'It's never been easier to show more people how bad you are at making a film.' Heed his words. Just because you can easily produce a video on an iPhone, doesn't mean it's any good. Even though you may have been given a top-of-the-range video camera for your birthday doesn't suddenly mean you are Steven Spielberg. The most expensive DSLR camera doesn't turn you into a gifted expert. Without some key knowledge and basic skills, all those cameras and microphones are no more than expensive useless trinkets.

Yet, where to begin? Do you just quickly grab any old camera, wave it around while your friends look on confused as they attempt to act through a scene? Set up your smartphone in the far corner of your gloomy garage while you film the intricacies of how to change a lawn mower carburettor? Impulse is good – it's part of the energy you've got brimming out of you. It's the reason you can barely contain yourself from getting stuck in. It will see you go far on your film making odyssey. Yet, like all stories, the best place to start is at the beginning.

So how do you join up the ideas in your head and convert them into a decent, well-shot and coherent film or video? It's easy – read this book.

Tom Holden

Introduction: The film making process

Have you often seen a film or television programme and wondered how it's made? Do you watch the behind-the-scenes extras on your DVDs? Or have you simply been to the multiplex and thought, 'I'd like to do that!'

This book is a comprehensive guide to film making. Unlike other books in the genre, it does not solely focus on film making technology; to do that would be wrong. After all, cameras, lights and editing are only part of the film making equation.

You will learn how to form your random ideas into scripts, how to cast, how to choose locations, how to maybe get some financial backing, to know what to look for in a camera, how to film, how to record sound, get great images, organize your film, edit it and put it out there for all to see. You will also learn how to make smaller, less complex films like vlogs. In short, this book is a complete film making course. It is easy to follow and gives you information in digestible quantities.

By the end of the book you should have a well-rounded idea of what film making involves and be ready to get your idea up and running.

For many, film making is a near mystical art form with closely guarded secrets shrouded in a cloak of technological confusion. As consumers of the medium we only ever see the end result on television, at a movie theatre or streamed on to our computer screens. Now and again we are aware of some facets of the industry – cameras, actors, special effects – but exactly how do these elements come together to make a film?

For this reason, film making isn't quite understood by the public as a whole.

There are many reasons why a film can fail and, at worst, be ridiculed by those who witness it. It could be a bizarre story idea, poor script, terrible acting, strange props, odd clothing, bad camera work, abysmal lighting, lack of properly recorded sound, poor judgement in editing, and the list can go on.

This book will help you avoid these issues by making you aware of all the pitfalls that await you on the film making journey. One of the points it will keep making is the need to be organized, and to steer you away from the notion of just pressing the record button on a camera and hoping for the best. Although film making has a quite 'wacky' reputation, and is supposedly populated by pleasure-seeking bohemians, there isn't a film in history that did not have a diligent behind-the-scenes planning structure working for weeks, months or even years before the cameras started rolling.

This discipline and approach starts with the script. A script may come from a writer's imagination, their own experiences or a piece of history, and this simple-looking collection of words is a powerful object. It contains the potential to unleash a storm of creativity that can captivate millions and be remembered for years. Every film that ever was, is or will be starts out as some random scribbles and ideas that eventually get refined into a coherent script. But you don't have to be Shakespeare to produce a workable script: a script just has speech with some sparse descriptions of environment. So just get writing!

After writing, the next stage can be a bit of a reality check. From here on in your film can be stymied by practicalities, such as only certain people being available to appear in your film, some locations being out of bounds or certain film making equipment being out of reach. These depressing realizations can mark the start of a list of compromises between the script and what is achievable.

Unless you are filming and doing everything within a very small circle of friends, then chances are you will have to ask at least one favour from a complete stranger. This in turn leads on to another element of film making – it is a profession requiring the ability to speak to, and get along with, a wide spectrum of people. Forget about the reclusive artist/film director character; a director is a person who must interact with many different people in order to get their film completed. Rude, abrasive grouches are not well liked, no matter how much of a film making genius they may be.

Just as obtaining actors can lead you into uncharted waters, looking around for places to film can inspire latent ingenuity. Often, people interpret their script requirements very literally and feel they really must obtain a jet liner's cockpit for a scene set in a jet liner's cockpit. If you possess such an inflexible (and unimaginative) attitude, then your film may be a long time in the making. Using that example to inspire you, what other places could double up for the cockpit? There are probably dozens of answers to that question, ranging from the inside of a broken-down transit van to a quiet corner of a friend's house. However, the point serves to illustrate that being flexible and creative is a must for any film maker. You will rarely have everything you need, but anything you want is only a lateral and imaginative thought away.

Another perennial gripe of film makers is money, or lack of it. For every script that gets made into a film, there are thousands lying discarded and unfunded. Raising finance for a film is the most unpleasant, stressful and upsetting aspect of the film industry. Now this may be irrelevant for some of you as many films can be made for nothing. Vlogs and the like should be largely cost-free exercises. If your ambitions and script demand more, then the long and lonely path of film financing awaits you. The simplest form of paying for a film is to raid your savings; this isn't always possible or advisable, but many people do this year in and year out in order to realize their vision.

A more sensible and business-like way to get some backing is to apply for it through one of many financing and grant-making organizations. However, don't think you will be the only one trying to get money from the same pot. Chances are you may get nothing, especially if you are an unknown with no track record instead of a name with a reputation. The same goes for crowdfunding (see Chapter 9).

With script, actors, locations, props, and maybe – for the lucky few – finance in place, your next step is to give some thought to the technology you wish to entrust your film to. This side of film making is something that can polarize people – some see it as the most important element while others view it as a tool enabling you to simply get the film made. Most good film makers tend to fall into the latter category and some of today's most famous directors have come from a purely design or drama background. In recent years, film making technology has changed almost unrecognizably, but the methods remain the same. You don't need to be a technical wizard to make a great film, but you do need creativity and imagination. Without these two factors, no amount of expensive gadgetry can save you.

It is people who make films, not cameras. However, getting to know cameras and film making technology is something you at least need to have an appreciation of. Although sites like YouTube have opened up film making to ordinary people and allowed anyone and everyone to upload their own unique visions, it's a sad fact that a lot of it is quite bad. Often, the video images have terrible resolution, the sound is inaudible or distorted, the picture is constantly going out of focus, the shot is shaky and there are all manner of other amateur errors.

A lot of the time this is due to the film maker not bothering to take the time to figure out how the camera works. Small things like checking the brightness of the picture, making adjustments and controlling focus can make a huge difference to your images. This book will point out the things you need to be aware of in order to get a more professional look from your video camera, while still allowing you to express yourself visually.

This book will also give you a further understanding of sound recording, tripods and lighting. These may sound scary at first but are essential ingredients to your film. As this book will point out, you don't need the latest equipment to make a good film. Often, you can get away with very basic kit; the important thing is knowing how to use it.

The filming stage is when everything comes together – the script, the planning, the actors, the props, cameras and so on. As such, it can be a rather frenetic and stressful time. Unless your films are observations of inanimate objects filmed only by yourself, then expect something to go wrong – deal with it, think of a work-around, carry on and try not to lose your cool. Film making is as much about problem solving as it is about cameras and scripts. This book will try to help you to, if not avoid, then at least expect some of the pitfalls that await you.

While the filming stage remains the best-known and most redolent stage of the movie-making process, there is a closely related activity that is generally misunderstood and often ignored by the majority of film viewers – editing. If you think of film making as a production line starting with the script which becomes live action, the editing stage just follows on and picks up the process. As just highlighted, editing is misunderstood – really misunderstood. Many seem to think it is an automatic process where all the footage is put into some kind of processing machine that spurts out a finished film. Editing is an entire creative process and industry in itself. In fact, editing can be thought of as the most powerful and influential part of film making. Whole scenes can be brutally cut even though they seemed important at the scriptwriting or filming stage. The entire emphasis and emotion of a scene can be reconfigured by the simple process of removing or adding a couple of crucial seconds of footage. It is far from being an automatic, autonomous process; instead, it is a living and breathing thing that can sometimes be unpredictable. Editing can be a fascinating and absorbing activity, and this book will lead you through the basics and prepare you for your first edit.

Despite its misunderstood and mysterious nature, editing is the best-known part of post-production, which itself is an umbrella term for anything that happens to the footage after it has been filmed. Many streams of technology feed into and out of a film during the post-production process – simple or elaborate special effects can be added, graphics can be placed on the screen, music added to enhance the experience or even dialogue re-recorded to replace the actors' originals. For the multi-tasking low-budget film maker, it is important to understand these processes so that you can apply them, if need be, to your own production.

You needn't get worried about not having a Hollywood edit suite nearby because many of these things can be done with basic technology for little or no money, as this book will reveal to you.

With everything completed, surely it is time to relax, right? Wrong – there is no point making a film and then not letting anyone see it, is there now? In the 'olden days', the options for showing your low- or no-budget films were very limited. Sometimes small screenings to small crowds in sparsely filled auditoriums were the most some could hope for. For those of you making films that are of a longer duration, say 20 minutes and upwards, an auditorium screening is always a good idea if you can manage it, but luckily for today's film maker there exists a small thing called the Internet.

A potential global audience can watch your film; this power has never existed before. Yet how does one get a film from the edit stage to the Internet? Again, this will be covered in the book, as it marks the final stage of your journey.

Overall, this book is a complete film making guide that will explain and demystify all the processes involved with the production of the moving image. Each chapter will focus on a different element and bring you up to speed with the tools, requirements and knowledge needed to undertake each stage successfully.

Read on. Your film awaits.

While technical terms have usually been explained when first introduced in the text, there is also a glossary at the back of this book in case you need a reminder or clarification later on in your reading.

1

Getting ready

In this chapter you will learn:

- ▶ *what administrative tools you need to obtain*
- ▶ *the qualities you need to exercise*
- ▶ *what general attributes you need to consider*

What do you need to make a film?

No, you don't need several attaché cases stuffed full of used notes, or the phone numbers of your favourite actors (although it would help). The things you need in order to set out on your quest to make a film are much more rudimentary, and a mixture of personal qualities and physical bits and pieces.

1 A SCRIPT

This is very important as it will be a great help if you have a story or finished script that you wish to film. It is the key way in which you can show people what you want to do, what the plot is and who the characters are. You can highlight parts in the script that you are exceptionally proud of and bore people to death with them. Basically, it's the first building block in the arduous task of making a film. If there's no script, there are no characters and no story. You've got nothing to film. A script is the source of your film. It is the plan for the whole venture. Even if you haven't a clue about anything else, you will at least be able to show others what your 'blueprint' looks like.

Key idea

Scripts can often take years to develop, so don't feel despair if yours isn't quick to come by. In some extreme cases, scripts have been lifelong struggles of hardship and painstaking research before they were ready to be made into a film.

2 A TELEPHONE AND/OR MOBILE PHONE

You will have to contact a large number of people and organizations as you get things moving. These may range from friends who will take part in the film, to camera hire organizations and places where you want to film. A phone will therefore be your front line of communication. A fax machine would be helpful as well. Did you know that some production companies for TV shows and films are nothing more than a producer and a secretary in a crummy office? And guess what – they've all got phones!

Key idea

Amazingly, some films can start life from something as innocuous as a brief conversation. Communication, and communications are key to film making.

3 AUDACITY AND INGENUITY

When making a film, depending on its complexity and your ambition, you will probably have to call up complete strangers in various organizations and businesses to ask for some outrageous and cheeky favours and assistance.

I once produced a film set in 1987 Czechoslovakia where several scenes in my script were set in a Czech pub. I had to find out whether there was a Czech beer company operating nearby, so I went to my local supermarket and looked for some Czech beer. When I found that they stocked some, I went to the customer service desk and asked for the number of the supermarket's head office. I called up the number and asked for the department that dealt with purchasing alcohol. When I was connected I asked them if they could give me the number of the company that marketed the Czech beer, and then called that number. I got through to the head honcho, explained to him that I was making a film set in Czechoslovakia and asked if he could help. To cut a long story short, I was given beer, props and technical assistance worth thousands. Film sponsorship from the aisles of the local supermarket! Although I didn't actually get any cash, the support I was given put me in good stead for when I approached funding bodies – about which I'll talk later. If you don't ask, you don't get.

4 MOTIVATION AND DETERMINATION

No one is forcing you to make your first film and if you want to achieve something it's up to you how hard you try. Things won't always go to plan, and it's your call whether you want to go on or quit when things get tough. It's by no means easy, but the more you put into something, the more you get out of it.

5 CONFIDENCE

This is a personal quality you need if you are to get anywhere. There's no point trying to get a project as large as a feature film, or perhaps a five- or ten-minute short, off the ground with a negative attitude. Keep your chin up and go for it! Even when you seem to be facing a string of disasters, carry on and keep trying!

6 A FILING SYSTEM

Despite the apparent glamour of working in the film and television industry, a huge percentage of the job is given over to the rather dull task of administration. A film is a very fiddly exercise in managing various pieces of information required to make the project. If you can't keep track of things (how many will depend on the size of the project), you will not go far.

As the project progresses, you will be receiving, sending out and otherwise dealing with some fairly large amounts of information. This might include replies to your enquiries, the contact details of places and organizations that could assist you, camera rental services, drama groups and so on ad infinitum. If you are not careful, you could soon be lost under a pile of little bits of paper and yellow stickies with phone numbers and people's names written all over them. Likewise, important emails could be lost in the depths of your inbox. Sooner or later, you are going to have to get in contact with these people again and call them up to arrange a meeting or send them further details. I've been in film production offices which looked like ransacked stationery retailers – this is what happens when people aren't organized.

I'm not saying that you have to rush out and buy the latest office equipment or enrol on a management course at the local night school, but it is important to sort out a system that allows you to know exactly where a piece of information is when you need it.

A simple system is to use boxes: place copies of letters asking for assistance in one, the contact details of all the places you wish to call eventually in another, and copies of the script in another. Just make sure you keep the subjects separate before you are overwhelmed by a heap of paper. For example, don't just have one stack of details, or soon you will discover that the phone number of the guy who said he could lend you the cameras free of charge is lost somewhere under the monster pile on your desk or floor.

A lever arch file with coloured paper separator sheets seems to be the industry norm these days. It's up to you; a little common sense is all you need here.

7 FREE TIME

There's a huge number of things to do when planning a film and you will need considerable free time if you are to achieve it all. Obviously, if you have a job or are in full-time education, you could try arranging things in your lunch hour. However, guess what? The people you want to speak to will probably be at lunch as well! The same goes for calling people at weekends. (I've known people who've tried to arrange projects by calling at off-peak times only, in order to save money, but these projects never got far.)

I'm not saying it's impossible, but it does mean that you will be under a lot of pressure from your work and from your endeavours to get your film made. The solution is to have a friend, or friends, who are very, very, very excited and interested in the film idea who have the spare time to help you out. Expect to help them out with regard to the costs of mailing and faxing things, because they may not have the money to do it all the time! As the saying goes: a problem shared is a problem halved.

8 NERVES OF STEEL

By now you should be in the process of realizing that there are a lot of things to take into consideration. More importantly, if you do things right, your mind will be juggling lots and lots of information: timetables for filming, getting in contact with people, sending replies to people and organizations, keeping people informed and so on, and that's before you've even started filming. Depending on the intended size of your film, the responsibility of handling all these aspects can get a little intense. If you don't think you can handle it, then you shouldn't start in the first place.

You are the commander-in-chief of this project and, as such, you may feel at times as though your world is collapsing all about you. It's unpleasant – take my word for it – but it's of your own making and so you must cope with it. Anyone can fold under pressure; few can focus!

Key idea

Film making can be a very difficult discipline. The role of a director can be one of constant stress, sleepless nights, constant battles to keep things moving and general unpleasantness. If you plan on making something large scale and ambitious, then be prepared for such things. As a producer once said to me about these times, 'Your life isn't your own.'

9 CREATIVITY

Many people overlook this basic principle. To make a film you have to be creative. Any film, no matter how bad, no matter how sensational or successful it may have been, was made by a creative person or persons. Are you creative? Of course you are – you're reading this book, aren't you? For some reason in our modern, sterile and sometimes harsh world, creativity is something that is frowned upon. Never be ashamed of this talent – it marks you out as different from huge swathes of the population. Express this quality you have and do something with it – you may even be able to make some money, or an entire career, from it.

10 A CAMERA

Rather obvious really, but more on this later.

11 SOMETHING TO EDIT WITH

More on this later.

Key idea

During these early stages of your production, have a quick think about how and where you will get your cameras and editing computer (or editing facilities) from. They are the two most important technical issues connected with film making so you need to have some kind of idea about where they will eventually come from.

12 PEOPLE

More on this later.

That's quite a few things to take into consideration, isn't it? So, do you still wish to continue? (By the way, did you notice that I didn't mention any formal qualifications?)

Focus points

✳ Be focused on what you want to do.
✳ Feel comfortable with your creativity.
✳ Ensure you have the administrative tools you need to get started.
✳ Know what kind of film project you plan on making.
✳ Be realistic about what you can achieve.
✳ Make sure you have the time needed.
✳ Have some kind of base to work from.
✳ Have a rough idea about how to get the technical tools needed.
✳ Be prepared to ask for things from strangers.
✳ Have confidence and faith in your own abilities.

Next step

In the following chapter we will look at the foundation of all film making – scriptwriting. As Francis Ford Coppola said to a young George Lucas: 'If you want to direct … you've got to write.' The resulting film may end up being unrecognizable from the original script, but without a script to set you off on your journey, you are probably going nowhere.

2

Scriptwriting

In this chapter you will learn:

▶ *what it takes to form a story*
▶ *the 'formula' of popular scriptwriting*
▶ *the overall format for presenting a script*

In this chapter we shall be looking at the processes that will take you from the point of your story's conception to your script's unveiling. As highlighted in the previous chapter, you need to have completed your script, or at least have some defined idea about it, before you can start producing in earnest.

The storyline

It is very important to consider what your story will be about. Perhaps time-travelling cowboys, or a period piece *à la* Jane Austen, or an experimental political commentary?

Basically, the decision is yours. The only person who should have a say on whether your ideas and script are any good is you. My golden rule when I'm writing is: 'If I like it, then it's good!' That's what you should be aiming for. Everyone is different, and films and all other aspects of creative art reflect this. For instance, I love the film *The Empire Strikes Back* (dir. Irvin Keschner, 1980) – I think it's one of the best stories that will ever exist – but my aunt thinks the same of *The Sound of Music* (dir. Robert Wise, 1965) – two very different films, yet both very popular and enduring. You could be influenced commercially when you finally sit down to compose the first draft of your script, or you might just want to write something that makes sense to you. That's perfectly fine.

Remember this

The most successful scripts are those written by people who have some knowledge of the subject. What are your hobbies, what are your interests, what kinds of book do you read? Your personality and experiences should be the barometer for what kind of script you write.

Developing characters

There are, of course, a few constants that you will have to get right if you are to get your script off the ground, regardless of your 'ultimate vision'. One of these is your characters. All words spoken as dialogue will be uttered by one of your imagined beings. An easy way to get going is to play around with a set number – three, for example – and to think of a character for each number. How do they relate to each other? What is their history? Why are they in your script? What do they do? Are they male or female, the goodie or the baddie?

By doing this you can start forming ideas in your mind from which greater things will grow. You may feel that three characters is too small a number, but it is a nice mid-point to start with for the purpose of illustrating the point I'm making. Once this has been decided, it may be useful to put it down on paper in chart form as per the format opposite.

So, you see that Richard Vincent is a man, he works as a private detective and he's in the film because he's found a suitcase full of money. He's cool, sharp and a little treacherous.

and so on...

Ellie Mahonie is a woman, she's glamorous and she's in the film because she claims she's lost the money. She's mysterious and doesn't say much.

Mr Vittorio is a man, he's Richard Vincent's assistant and he's in the film because he's helping out his boss, Richard. He's nervous and clumsy.

Now that the characters are sorted out, one word of essential advice is to keep the characters consistent. I've seen many scripts where the characters not only change personalities, but after page 10 undergo a name change. It happens all the time when a character starts off as a mean, tough, gun-toting cop and a few pages later he's a bit of a pushover and doesn't really care about much. This is usually because the writer has run out of steam and hasn't thought about the story or what is going on in the head of the characters he/she has just created.

Try to get it into your head that the dialogue that you will eventually be writing is not really coming from you, but from the mouths of your characters! Therefore, the words will be spouting from different-sounding people, not just the same voice listed under different names.

Key idea

The characters in a film need to have some kind of conflict with each other to drive the story along or to create interesting scenes. There isn't a film in existence that has all the characters getting along as well as best friends. Conflict and antagonism are two of the driving forces behind a drama or a comedy.

Setting

So, with the above three examples of characters in mind, you can start thinking about a setting. The characters here could easily inhabit a sleazy city underworld full of danger and excitement, as opposed to running a quiet veterinary practice in the middle of the countryside. Characters and setting come from the same primordial soup – they are symbiotic – and this is worth remembering when you are 'populating' your world. They are acting and reacting to each other.

Put together, characters and setting have got to do something. The characters do things in the setting. They interact with the other people in the script and with the lesser individual who makes an appearance for only one line. Don't just have them hanging around reading newspapers all day long – there's a story that's pushing and pulling them over each page of your script. These aren't just words; it's an exciting marathon where anything can happen. It's all up to you.

All right, so a pushing story for Mr Richard Vincent and his pals is the fact that he's found some stolen cash; Ellie Mahonie says it belongs to her, and Mr Vittorio is trying to help his boss. So, what's going to happen? Here is one possible scenario.

Richard Vincent is in his office when he receives a mysterious phone call asking him to help out a pal of his on the other side of town. He arrives at the rendezvous and discovers that there's been a big shootout and lots of people are lying dead on the floor, including his pal. He sees a case full of cash, which he takes, then leaves before the police come. He stashes the money in a bank and coolly sits tight.

A couple of days later he's in his office again and he gets a phone call from a woman who says she needs Mr Vincent's help. She asks him to meet her in a bar. Before he goes, he tells his assistant that he's found a case of cash and that it's in a certain bank. Before Mr Vittorio can ask more, Richard leaves.

Richard meets up in the bar with the woman who says her name is Ellie Mahonie and that she's lost a great deal of money. She asks if he can help her out. Without telling her of his find the other day, he says he'll have a go and try to locate it for her. Next day Richard Vincent and Mr Vittorio go to the bank to check out the money. Richard realizes that so much money might draw attention, so he changes some of it into traveller's cheques (and why not?). Mr Vittorio is anxious to know how much is left, but Richard Vincent doesn't tell him, mentioning that it's safer if he doesn't know any more about it.

Later on, he phones Ellie from his office and tells her that he reckons the money is long gone by now. He lies and says he tried everywhere and asked all the sources but that the 'word on the street' is that it's vanished. Ellie is distraught and hangs up on him. Richard knows the money's not his, and feels a bit bad, but he's made his choice ... DRAMATIC MUSIC!

What will happen next? It doesn't take a huge amount of effort to roll a story idea around in your head. The more you play with the characters, setting and overall story you've decided upon, the easier it becomes.

Writing is a really important part of the film making process and it will help a director a great deal if they can write. It's the best way to get to grips with the mechanics of your story.

If you want to take your script to production companies and the like, they may be more inclined to listen to someone who has written a Hollywood-flavoured film as opposed to a gritty social drama set in a housing project. Remember, you are the creator, so decide what you want, stick to your guns and don't let others influence you.

How long should my script be?

That again is up to you. Just because you are setting out on a creative process as big as a film need not mean that the script has to be the size of the local phone directory. The professional rule of thumb for film timing is: 1 page = 1 minute of film time.

When you watch a film, the characters do not speak non-stop from start to finish – there will be many scenes where no one is speaking. These scenes add length to the film, which isn't always highlighted clearly in a script. If you were to read the script for your favourite feature-length film, and read all the lines non-stop, you would probably be finished in a much shorter time than the actual movie, depending on how fast you read. Size does not always equate to quality. It depends on what's on the pages!

Key idea

Who needs a script? Some brave souls among you may want to forgo scripts altogether and make a film that is improvisational. In instances such as this you will still need some kind of story outline as a starting point for each scene. Also, it may be tricky to redo scenes and dialogue if no one can remember what they just said.

What format should my script take?

This very much depends on your intended audience. If you want to make the film with friends, or a local non-professional group, then your only concern is to make it legible. However, if you want to be taken seriously or want a big and famous company to take a look at it, then it has to be done in a certain way, an example of which is shown below.

Scene 12

EXT. High Street, Bank — Day

It is raining and a black Cadillac pulls up. Mr Vittorio and Richard get out, look around the street and slowly make their way into the bank. Mr Vittorio opens the door and whispers to Richard.

Mr Vittorio

Are you sure you want to do this? Richard unbuttons his tatty coat.

Richard

Yes, get a move on.

INT. Bank — Day

Richard and Mr Vittorio enter the bank foyer and make their way to a free cashier.

Mr Vittorio

(nervous)Couldn't we wait for the rest of the crew?

Richard

Put a lid on it!

They approach the cashier. Mr Vittorio is looking nervously about the interior of the bank.

Richard puts his gloved hand into his unbuttoned coat.

```
              Richard
I'd like to open a bank account,
              please.
              Cashier
Certainly, Sir, do you have any
          identification?
Richard extracts his passport from
     his inner coat pocket.
```

The professional rule of thumb for script format is:

▶ Twelve-point Courier text on A4 paper (i.e. size 12, Courier style from the word processor, as per the script example above).

▶ Speech text to be indented by two spaces or centre justified.

▶ Character names to be indented by three spaces, or centre justified, and marked in bold.

▶ 'Exterior' and 'Interior' should be abbreviated in bold to 'EXT.' or 'INT.' and should appear immediately before explanatory text.

▶ Don't write camera moves into the script (e.g. zoom in, pan along) – that's what the director figures out after they have read the script, plus it can confuse the script for the reader.

(A television and film writer once shared the above pointers with me and then, quite rightly, said he couldn't understand how there's a whole sub-industry in books and courses based on those five points!)

The script example above is quite basic, but I hope it gives you a good idea of the general format. By the way, how would you have filmed that? You could have kept it quick and to the point, or you could have drawn it out into a suspense-filled set piece dripping with colour and danger. As I mentioned earlier, the number of words in a script can have little bearing on the final length of the film.

Tips on scriptwriting

So what tips can I give you here? One concept that professional scriptwriters keep telling people is this: *keep it simple*. A simple script usually has the following fundamental characteristics:

1 The number of characters is limited.

2 The locations are small in number.

3 It has a **beginning** (where the story, setting and characters are introduced).

4 It has a **complication** a little way into the film, when things become interesting and the adventure/story/reason for you being in the cinema begins. For example, in the original *Star Wars* (dir. George Lucas, 1977) this is when Luke's uncle buys the two robots, one of which has information about the baddies and the image of the princess they need to rescue. If he had bought another pair, the adventure and story would have stopped there and then. Another classic example of this is in the film *Witness* (dir. Peter Weir, 1985), starring Harrison Ford and Kelly McGillis. A few minutes into the film the Amish woman and her young boy are in a busy train station. While the young boy is in one of the toilet cubicles he witnesses a murder. Now if that boy hadn't gone to the toilet, then he wouldn't have seen the murder, he wouldn't be the witness and there would be no film. Think about some of your favourite films to see where this complication is. It's not always that apparent, but it's there, and without that one simple action there would be no film.

5 It also has a **middle**, when the story falls into its pace. A few other characters may get thrown in, a few adventures develop and scrapes happen, and ultimately it legitimizes the ending. The middle of the film comes soon or immediately after the moment of complication. Using the example of *Star Wars* again, it's when Luke goes off with Ben and the droids and meets Han and Chewie. They outrun the Empire, end up in the Death Star, have a few fights with the baddies and then try to escape.

In *Gladiator* (Ridley Scott, 2000) it's after Maximus has been betrayed by his soldiers and the dastardly Commodus and has to escape from Germany, gets caught by the slave traders, trains as a gladiator, has loads of fights and comes up with his plan to take command of his army again.

Even a non-action film like *Dead Poets Society* (dir. Peter Weir, 1989) keeps to the trend: after the complication (when Robin Williams' character appears) the story goes into its cruise mode with the students involved in the adventure of discovering literature, Shakespeare and creativity.

6 It then has a **second complication**. This is the bridge that links the middle and the end. Going back once more to the example of *Star Wars*, the second complication here is when Han, Chewie, Princess Leia, Luke and the droids escape from the Death Star which takes them directly to the big battle at the end of the film. In *Gladiator*, the second complication is when Maximus' plot to escape from Rome and join up with his army has been foiled, which takes him to the showdown with Commodus. Even *Dead Poets Society* has it, when one of the students kills himself. It's just a formula.

7 Finally, it has an **ending** (when the events after the second complication are resolved). The ending of the film is when all the contents of the film come to a head and are in some way resolved. Without an ending, the story would just go on and on. Some films resolve matters better than others. A popular resolving scenario is when there is a huge shootout and the baddies get killed amid huge explosions, crashing cars, earthquakes and so on.

The climax of the whole story often ends up as a major set piece where all the elements of the film – the characters and the story – are brought together in a single location (for example the baddie's HQ where the kidnapped girl is being held who has been a focus of the film so far), and it is just a great method to wrap things up rather conveniently.

Tango & Cash (dir. Andrei Konchalovsky, 1989) illustrates very well the 'big bang' way of resolving a film. Have you ever wondered why this method is so popular? Basically, it is a very easy way of sorting things out. The film has got loads of baddies crawling out of the woodwork. They're all after the good guy, so how can the film be wrapped up? Easy. Kill all the baddies. It's convenient, it's clean, it leaves the hero free to walk off into the sunset while triumphant music plays. I'm sure you can think of many, many examples of the above. However, this 'rule' isn't always adhered to. Sometimes the heroes are killed, for example, in *Thelma & Louise* (dir. Ridley Scott, 1991). We don't actually see them being killed, but it is an assumption the audience is supposed to make. In *Gladiator*, Maximus dies at the end of the film. Again, this brings a definite close to the proceedings, and though sad to some, it ends the film very well. Have you ever watched a film and felt a bit ambivalent about the ending, as if the film is not quite finished? The expected closure is not there. When I watched *The Empire Strikes Back* as a youngster,

I thought the film was going to continue as Lando and Chewie flew off. The story hadn't been resolved; things were still up in the air – it didn't make sense. At the time I was unaware of the way sequels worked.

Unresolved films tend to be unsuccessful, perhaps because the audience is a bit peeved that the story has been left dangling in the air somewhere. When you have thought about the characters, setting and basic story, it may be a good idea to jot down a timeline with the 'events' along it. The complication will usually appear a third of the way in, the second complication about one-third from the end, and the adventure/middle falling somewhere between the two. You can play around with your story in this form without having to rewrite whole pages. Just scribble down what the complication is, what happens during the adventure/middle and what the key events are, and what form the ending takes. Try it – you'll be amazed at how liberating this method can be (see Figure 2.1).

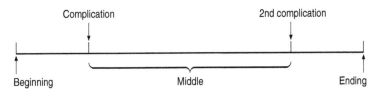

Figure 2.1

The 'keep it simple' principle is a great starting point for many film makers. I heard some of this when I was watching a documentary about the making of *Reservoir Dogs* (dir. Quentin Tarentino, 1992). Although the film is based on the Hong Kong film *City on Fire*, (dir. Ringo Lam, 1987), it was translated by Tarantino in a relatively stripped-down, no-frills way. Most of the characters are killed before they've had a chance to say much (and thus pick up smaller pay cheques) and a large proportion of the film takes place in the warehouse. Essentially, you could argue that *Reservoir Dogs* is a film about three people arguing in a large room. Simple.

Cult horror films often follow the same formula. They usually start off with some teenagers driving through the wilderness. The car breaks down and one of them says, 'Hey, let's stay the night in that old house over there', and the rest of the film takes place in the house. We've all seen them. It is worth bearing in mind that simple ideas will not involve the same hassles as a Hollywood epic such as *Spartacus* (dir. Stanley Kubrick, 1960).

Another great feature of the 'keep it simple' way of thinking is that you can get a 'less is more' effect out of the dialogue. Many people who sit down and write their first script have a tendency to write huge chunks of dialogue every time a character speaks. Don't make your scripts too wordy. Next time you watch a film, notice that the characters don't tend to say a great deal every time they speak – maybe one or two sentences. So don't think that you need to compose a page of elegant prose each time a character says something.

When thinking about your script and film, bounce some story ideas around in your head. Not all successful film makers write the screenplays to their films, but instead think up the story and recruit someone else to write it. Next time you watch the opening credits to a film you might see the following:

Screenplay by Mr X

Based on a story by Mrs Y

Thinking up ideas is easy; all it requires is letting your mind drift for a while. It usually works well with two people who are throwing ideas at each other. Eventually an idea will be finalized and you'll say: 'OK, this is it. Man gets arrested for bank robbery, is taken to prison, starts having dreams about being abducted by aliens, finds out his clone did the robbery, uses hidden power to break out of prison, looks for aliens, gives them a good beating, then becomes a manager of a restaurant.' *Voilà*!

Using other works

Look at other films, plays and books and use their ideas – thievery keeps the film world alive – but don't plagiarize. As mentioned above, Tarantino used *City on Fire*; the entry of the spacecraft in *Independence Day* (dir. Roland Emmerich, 1996) was borrowed from the first few pages of the Arthur C. Clarke novel *Childhood's End* (although the film's producers may argue differently); *Blade Runner* (dir. Ridley Scott, 1982) is based on the book *Do Androids Dream of Electric Sheep?* and is styled like a Humphrey Bogart detective film set in the future; the scrolling introduction and political situation in *Star Wars* is taken straight from Roman history books after the death of Julius Caesar, and so on. From your observation of films and books it should not take a huge amount of mental energy to think of a famous or obscure story you would like to alter for the purposes of writing a script. However, try not to make it too obvious, but be subversive, change names, setting, the time and so on.

Remember this

A little-known problem that can dog film productions is a script rewrite. Even though all the pertinent members of cast and crew may have their copies of the script, it is not unknown for certain things to be changed when the production is up and running. Confusion can spread if only some people have copies of the rewrites. In the film industry, rewrites are printed on coloured paper, so the first rewrite is on red paper, the second on blue, and so on. If you have rewritten something, make sure everyone knows what the new script is.

Finally, when you do write the script, keep it in the present tense. Novels are written mostly in the past; scripts are written in the present. So let's compare the same story written in script and novel formats.

NOVEL FORMAT

Richard Vincent slowly opened the glass door of the bar and wiped the cold rain from his tattered coat. His face was hidden under his large trilby as he peered about the dark, smoky innards of the bar, looking for the woman who had called him here.

A few drunk faces made eye contact with him as he stood inert in the doorway. The rest slurped away at the cheap spirits and beer as they half sat, half slouched at their tables or on bar stools.

He took off his hat slowly and threw it on to the nearby hat stand.

'Hey, Mack!' shouted the bartender, 'are you gonna order anything, or just drip all over my floor?' Richard looked over at the burly man and smiled curtly.

'Jerk,' whispered Richard, and then made his way across the room.

As he sat down, he reached into his inner pocket and pulled out a packet of cigarettes and put one to his mouth.

'Allow me,' said a soft female voice. Richard looked to his left and saw the face of the woman he was looking for. She lit his Marlboro.

'Sure,' he replied coolly.

'I thought you'd never come,' she said, eyeing the bottles racked up behind the bar.

'Well, I got nothing better to do,' he mumbled nonchalantly.

The heavy steps of the bartender echoed over the floor behind the bar as he walked up to Richard and the woman.

'So, what'll it be?'

'I'll have,' began Richard.

'Two large bourbons, straight up,' said the woman, smiling, with her eyes on Richard.

SCRIPT FORMAT

INT. Gionetti's Bar, Downtown — Night

The dimly lit bar is thick with smoke. A few people are sitting at tables or drinking at the bar. The glass door to the bar opens and Richard Vincent enters. He stands in the doorway and wipes the rain from his tatty coat. He takes off his wide-brimmed hat and throws it on a nearby hat stand.

Bartender

(shouting to Richard)Hey, Mack, are you gonna order anything, or just drip all over my floor?

Richard

(aside)Jerk!

Richard makes his way to the bar and sits down. He pulls out a packet of cigarettes and puts one in his mouth. A woman suddenly sits down to his left.

Woman

Allow me.

She lights his cigarette.

Richard

Sure.

> **Woman**
>
> I thought you'd never come.
>
> **Richard**
>
> Well, I got nothing better to do. The bartender walks up to the pair.
>
> **Bartender**
>
> So, what'll it be?
>
> **Richard**
>
> I'll have …
>
> **Woman**
>
> (looking at Richard) Two large bourbons, straight up.

See the difference? In a nutshell, a script is less descriptive than text in novel form.

Key idea

A novelist describes situations with words. A film maker does it with pictures!

Remember this

Let your mind wander freely when you are writing. Just get it out of your head and on to the page. You can worry about how difficult it is to film at a later stage. Writing should be an uninhibited mental exercise.

I personally find it's easier to write things in script form, so have a go yourself. Try having a look at some passages from your favourite book and then rewriting them in script format. Pretty soon you'll get the hang of it. Since the script content is such an enormously subjective thing, I'll leave you to decide how to write yours. Just remember to follow the basic format and story guidelines. Use your imagination, have fun and see you later.

Focus points

* Make sure the story is worked out before you start writing.
* If you feel comfortable with the concept, then stick to the 'keep it simple' guidelines.
* Practise changing fiction books into script formats to get the hang of things.
* Keep the characters consistent; remember they are 'real' people.
* Make sure your characters are different from each other.
* Ensure the story is interesting to you.
* Think about what the 'complications' will be.
* Revisit your favourite films, books and historical tales for inspiration.
* Get objective feedback wherever and whenever possible.
* Be proud of what you write.

Next step

So you have a fantastic, well-honed script. You're proud of it, and rightly so. But what next? You could, of course, send it to agents and producers – a potentially exhausting and soul-destroying process – but the whole point of this book is to show how you can take your script and film and edit it yourself. This will be the subject of much of the rest of the book.

3

Casting and rehearsals

In this chapter you will learn:

▶ *how to talk about and verbally present your idea*

▶ *how to co-ordinate first moves towards assembling a cast*

▶ *how to iron out problems and avoid troublesome people*

Script! Script! Anyone for a script?

Now that you have finished your script, you need to get people interested in it. The first thing to decide is how big you see this idea of yours becoming. For example, is it going to be a film made with friends and a basic camcorder, or a low-key local film involving a local drama society and technical personnel poached from local colleges, or do you see it as next summer's blockbuster? The choice, once again, is yours. However, you must be realistic. Just because you have written a script that you are exceptionally proud of does not mean that MGM Studios will be calling you for a chat.

Approaching production studios

If your ambitions do lie along these lines, then you will prepare lots of copyrighted copies, or a page-long synopsis, otherwise known as a treatment, to send out to production studios. Make sure you call the studios first to explain what the script is about, otherwise you may send your script for *Rambo 10* to a place that only makes films about safety at work. Also, you may find it impossible to get through to some of the major studios. If you do choose this route, then be prepared to wait a long time for replies, and bear in mind that production companies get literally thousands of scripts every year, each one written and sent in by someone like you with their eyes on making a fortune. Don't always expect a favourable reply, or a reply at all! I'm not saying it's impossible for your dreams to come true, but it is damned hard. You may have to call every production company and film studio in the world before someone finally says, 'I'm interested.' Even then, this may well be the limit of their support.

However, beware of the ways in which these big places deal with the multitude of submissions that are sent to them by the truck load on a weekly basis. The same fellow who mentioned the script format pointers to me, also told me of his experiences as a reader. As the name suggests, a reader reads scripts to determine whether they have the potential to make a great film or are complete rubbish. Most of the scripts that are sent in are binned or, if the company has enough money, posted back to the writer or writer's agent.

On his first day of employment with the script-reading agency, the reader's boss said: 'Your job is to make the sofa into an armchair.' All the scripts that had been sent in had been arranged into a makeshift sofa capable of seating several people at a time. The reader's job was to work his way through them all, finding the good ones.

Bearing in mind the quantity of scripts that production companies and reading agencies receive, it is impossible to read every single one from start to finish – it would take far too long. If a story doesn't jump out by page 10 (or earlier), the script is usually thrown away. It is therefore imperative to make your story interesting early on. This doesn't just apply to submitting your film script, but also to making the film.

Your submission needs to convey a story and plotline that will hook people. It may be hard to achieve the right formula to get the hook, but it is one of the things that will make the story (and subsequent film) interesting and, it's hoped, original. In short, find some names, phone them, pay for lots of postage, send the scripts out … and wait.

Remember this

Even though large studios are geared up to make films and have the best resources for getting a production moving, it still can take a long time, even years, from a script being read to it getting made into a film. Even if the film is written by a well-known actor, or by a director with a film making pedigree, it can be a long process. These films costs tens of millions to make; those kinds of decision don't happen overnight.

Going it alone

Now, for those of you who are impatient, don't give a hoot for all those big fancy film making places or simply like going it alone, then it's much easier to interest people in the project. Besides, this book is about you making your film, not someone else doing it for you!

Your first port of call will probably be within a few miles of your front door. Think about people or organizations who might be interested in acting out your script. You could try the local dramatic society, the school acting group, a local performing arts college and certainly your friends.

Look them up in the phone book and call them. In the case of the local dramatic society, they will usually be happy for you to turn up and talk about your ideas. No doubt some will be fascinated by your script; others may consider it beneath them. Make sure, however, that you are approaching the right types of group; your *Reservoir Dogs* rip-off script won't sit well with the drama group of the local kindergarten, for example.

Setting the pitch

Some of these groups or individuals may ask for written details of the intended production so they can consider it. It is therefore a good idea and a professional courtesy to have a treatment ready to give these people to provide them with some basic details of the story and so forth. In addition to the treatment/synopsis, it is vital to figure out what your verbal pitch is. For example, when you speak to people who may be able to help you, on the phone or at meetings, they may ask for some primary verbal details. Discussing the entire script may be a bit time-consuming for some people, so instead you pitch the idea to them. You hit them with what I term the 'story bullet' (more commonly called the pitch). The entire film is compressed into a few sentences that you can fire off at people as and when needed so that someone is 'hit' with an immediate idea of what the story is about.

'A kid goes back in time to save his parents' marriage', is how one Hollywood executive recalled the pitch for *Back to the Future* (dir. Robert Zemeckis, 1985) Think of a few films and practise making up your own pitches. Even the most complicated films can be condensed to a concise pitch.

An even shorter variant of the pitch is the 'high concept' of a film. The high concept is a very effective way to implant a sudden mental image in someone's head without having to endlessly explain things. The best high concept I ever heard was '*The Lord of the Rings* in space' for the original *Star Wars* trilogy.

In television, it is just the same. When phoning up hundreds of groups and organizations in the pre-production for a drama or documentary, one of the first things people fire off is the pitch or high concept so the person at the other end is suddenly hit with a mental image of what is being planned. This may sound like a less than major point, but I have seen film makers who, when asked about their film, have looked back wide-eyed and have been quite unable to articulate their ideas in fewer than several confused minutes.

Key idea

Practise the pitch on yourself. Get it down to a fine art and well-rehearsed speech. Even if you are only planning on talking to local dramatic societies, or potential film crew, it will really help the process if people know what it is they may be about to get involved in.

Getting back to the actors: it's important to be realistic with them – just as it is with yourself. Don't tell them that you'll make them famous or make them rich (you may not even be able to pay them!). Tell them what's what and don't lead them up the garden path.

Rehearsals

Arrange somewhere to rehearse. It doesn't have to be anywhere special; it could be at your house, at a community centre, at a youth club, or in a room at a school. Although this may be your first time directing a rehearsal, try not to panic. Remember, it's your script and your idea the people have come about, so try to be cool.

Arrange a preliminary workshop/read-through of the script, making sure that you have the contact details of those who you want to come along, to help ensure they turn up. Send out the parts of the script, or the whole thing, to their addresses, email it or give it to them on the day. Make sure they know where and when the meeting is to be held.

One of the 'between the lines' elements of making films and being a director is that you have to get on with a wide variety of people who will look to you to know what's going on. Although this may be nerve-racking, try to look vaguely serious about what is going on – even though it could be a zany comedy you've written – as it will make it clear that you are committed to the project. Remember, these people don't have to be here; they are giving up free time to help you out!

The first read-through is a time when things either make sense or they don't. Basically, it's the test drive. As the writer, it's up to you to make any necessary changes. A character giving a beautiful soliloquy while full of bullet holes may work on paper, but when it's being read out in the context of the situation it may look ridiculous. After the first read-through you should know what needs to be done to the script (if anything), who is most suited to the roles and who is not suited to anything. Just because you have got people reading out lines, it doesn't mean they will fit the part.

Don't be too set in your ideas about what your characters will look like, as most of the time such a person will not be at your auditions or rehearsals. You may find that you are completely surprised by someone who turns up and reads for you, so don't write a part thinking that the person who plays it should look like someone out of your favourite film or you may find yourself on a hopeless quest.

It's part of the casting process and you need someone who fits your idea about who the character is, so try to keep an open mind.

An example of the above was when I was looking for two men to read the parts of two hippy/bum/idiot students. I must have heard at least ten hopefuls and it just didn't work. Then one day a guy who looked like Billy Idol was paired with a tall red-haired man who looked like he was a Confederate army recruit – and it worked like a dream. So who knows?

USE A VIDEO CAMERA

It is always a good idea to try to film your rehearsals whenever possible. Not only does this give you, as the director, the resource to play back performances to assess them and think of new ideas, but it also gets the actors used to acting in front of cameras. Some people who turn up at rehearsals may be 'first timers', while others will be seasoned drama performers, but regardless of their pedigree not everyone gets on with cameras in the same way. Some actors may be very aware and conscious of being filmed, and this can seriously compromise their performance. It is not unknown for great stage actors to freeze the first time a camera is put on them. So, get everyone used to having cameras follow their every move. Not only will this help your actors, but it is a great way to practise using your chosen camera (see Chapter 5). Think of it as a school where you will be trying out different camera effects and techniques, choreographing your scenes, anticipating problems you may encounter while filming, and practising framing (see Chapter 10).

Key idea

If using a camera to film your rehearsals, learn to give your actors a bit of space and remember they are human beings and not mindless props in your film. Don't shove a camera inches from their face or inadvertently intimidate them. If they don't quite follow what you are doing, then explain the process to them and make them feel part of the experience instead of an annoyance. This time can be a great testing ground for your future skills as a director.

With each rehearsal, things will get better. If they don't, it usually means one of two things:

▶ You haven't fully explained the characters, the background to the story, or some aspect of the script.

▶ You have a troublemaker, or troublemakers, in your ranks.

The former isn't too difficult to clear up; the latter takes a bit more mettle. A troublemaker is usually a person who, for reasons known only to themselves, is determined to rain on your parade. They manifest themselves in different ways. They may want to change things in the script, such as the story and characters; they may want to be the main focus of the story, even though they have only one line; or they refuse to co-operate with the rest of the actors and yourself.

Whatever the reason, the solution is to show them the door. It's something you've got to do, and if you leave it too late your film could become a mess. This is a factor that shouldn't be overlooked as it can sometimes rear its very ugly head and turn your film into an unpleasant chore. There will always be, of course, moments during a read-through when suggestions will be thrown in by everyone, and you should be sensitive to these pointers. The whole point of the readings is to hammer out any problems, but, don't be railroaded into changing your script into something you don't want it to be. There are people who seem to think that it's a free-for-all where they can start sticking their oars in. On these occasions, act fast – otherwise you'll gradually be pushed out of your own creation.

Don't forget that, although you are embarking on a film, you are also embarking on a 'people' project. What you are planning and doing will eventually consist of people. This is something that sometimes scares many 'reclusive' potential film directors who have sweated out their script while locked away in their bedroom. When things have started to get going, such people have been terrified at the prospect that they will actually be dealing with people who are the vital ingredients in their film making recipe.

This is the great unwritten component of making films. You have to speak to and get on with many different people – be they potential contributors on the other end of a telephone, or people at auditions and rehearsals. Invariably many of these people will be rather creative (difficult) and it will be up to you to prevent them from getting out of control and becoming the director, and instead simply saying the lines as you want them to.

The rehearsal process is the great testing ground for this quality in a director. You will be confronted by a variety of people; some you will know, some you won't. The sight of several faces looking at you and your script is rather daunting, but just try to relax and take the problems and issues one at a time.

Key idea

You may find it helps if you give your actors some reference points regarding their roles. You could say, for example, that a certain character's style and speech is reminiscent of the way another actor played a famous role.

The first things to establish, if you haven't already done so, is who is reading for which part, what scenes you will be going through (things may not be at a stage to read the whole script), what order you will be doing things in and what props you will be using (tables, chairs, toy guns, etc.).

Again, this goes back to being organized. Having a timetable of where and when rehearsals will take place will go a long way to show people that you are organized, and it will also let everyone know what the order of the rehearsals will be.

Once the preliminary order of events has been established, just have a read-through of whatever scenes you are able to do and take stock of what is going on, for example, what people sound like, whether people are getting the context of the scene right, whether the idea is getting across, whether the accents are believable and so on. As the writer of the words, you are listening to the 'play-back' and only you can really advise people what needs to be tweaked and changed.

Remember this

Don't just observe what's going on during rehearsals. Direct it!

Don't forget, a director gives direction. Although this may seem a bit of a basic observation, many people forget this, or are too worried about raising their voices and actually directing a group of energetic and creative individuals. Don't just sit back and take in what is going on before you, explain things to people, tell them how and why this character speaks in the way he does. It is all too easy to listen to a scene that is read in a manner that makes your blood curdle and then at the end of it say, 'Yeah, that was great. OK, let's read the next one,' because you're worrying that you may upset someone. You won't if you explain things in a diplomatic manner.

It is very easy to forget that the people attending the read-throughs and rehearsals do not share your sense of empathy and 'oneness' with the script. Only you have that 'power', and it is wrong to expect everyone to get the picture as soon as they start reading what is in front of them. Things will need explaining but remember to be patient in your explanations. If something isn't coming together in the way that you absolutely want it to, then make an effort to correct it before it gets lost amid the frenetic energy and chaos of your rehearsals.

This harks back to the section on writing the script. Since you have thought of the characters, you know what is pushing and driving them, so you should impart those details to the potential cast members as and when the situation requires it. Remember that some of the people who turn up at these rehearsals and read-throughs can be very precise with their methods. Simply having a name on a script followed by sections of speech will not be enough to propel them on through the odyssey of your film making foray. And remember the other section on writing your script: these characters are 'real people', they have reasons for doing things, they have personalities, they are, above all, characters in your world. As the scriptwriter, you have the intrinsic knowledge and ability to explain everything about the script you have created.

Don't be shy – explain your 'world' and those who inhabit it.

So, once again, the script isn't just a jumble of words, names and events, it is a story that has a reason for being (no matter how bizarre you may think it is), so be prepared to explain it now and again when someone needs a bit of help figuring out why their character is the way he/she is. This is another of the great unstated necessities of film making: hone your vision before you are anywhere near filming. Never expect your actors to just turn up and 'fall into' the script that you have written – rehearsals and actors that have suffered from lack of direction and explanation will come together and produce a project that is both lifeless and boring and, in some cases, not the film that the director had in mind at all.

Key idea

Avoid situations where people are kept waiting around for a long time without doing anything. If you plan on going over the parts of your script that involve only a couple of actors, don't ask everyone to come down. They could end up getting bored or annoyed and distract from the work you are trying to do.

However, once in a while, don't be too wound up to take on board the advice and ideas that your actors may come up with during rehearsals.

Focus points

* ✳ Be organized and approachable.
* ✳ Make an effort to get on with everyone.
* ✳ Don't automatically agree with people who want to change your script.
* ✳ Make sure everyone knows what the story is about.
* ✳ Explain the characters to the actors and give them clues as to how you'd like them played.
* ✳ Don't make bad casting decisions just because you want to please people.
* ✳ Give a bit of thought to costumes and simple props.
* ✳ Give some leeway to your actors as their suggestions could improve things.
* ✳ Let people know if they are doing something wrong.
* ✳ Make sure everyone has any script updates as and when they happen.

Next step

In Chapters 4 and 5 we'll look at your essential tool as a film maker – your camera – and how to use it. As a film maker, you'll need make yourself aware of the advantages and disadvantages of the various formats, but whichever format you choose, and however simple or sophisticated your camera is, you'll need to know their capabilities inside out.

4

Cameras

In this chapter you will learn:

- ▶ *how to navigate the sea of modern cameras*
- ▶ *how to decide which camera is best suited to your production*
- ▶ *about the basic operating features available on video cameras*

There are few pieces of equipment as glamorous as the film camera. These sleek beings conjure up exotic practices and mystical know-how for many who gaze upon them. Under the cold and silent body, behind the buttons, controls, lens and viewfinder are the potential and power to capture every movement and mood, emotion and expression.

A camera is very much the embodiment of films and film making. Without a camera, there is no film. It is the most important tool in the craft of film production. Even though technology has changed almost beyond recognition over the years, and more disciplines have become integral parts of movie-making, the camera still remains the central pillar. Every piece of film making, every bit of organization, each performance, every word, the special effects and even music either flow towards or from the camera's lens. It is the hub of any film and the entire industry.

The camera operator and director of photography

The individual, or individuals, who are responsible for capturing a film's images play a very important role. They are some of the few people who channel a film's essence through their hands. Such is their importance that they are credited in the opening titles of all films. They are a director's greatest ally. In many cases, a director will work with the same camera operators and directors of photography throughout their career.

At the most basic level, the camera operator is the person who moves the camera around to follow the action and ensures its setting is appropriate to the scene being filmed. That, however, is just the tip of the iceberg. The director of photography, credited at the start of a film, is the person charged with setting the visual mood, the lights, the framing – transforming the camera work from merely recording images to capturing emotion.

On a small film, the camera operator and director of photography (also known as the DoP) may be one and the same person (sometimes as well as director). On larger productions, they can be separate. The DoP ensures the optimum lighting is set, selects which lens to use, decides whether any filters are needed and which camera functions to use, and gives movement instructions to the camera operator. Often, they may take over camera operation for some shots.

Given the importance of filming to a movie, the camera operator and DoP must ensure they have the right tools for the job – that starts with the camera.

Choosing a camera

Your camera is very, very important. You are nothing without it. You have no film without it. The more you use a camera, the better acquainted with it you will become and the more you will love it. Without sounding too weird, a good camera operator will almost treat, and look upon, their camera as a pet. The more you use it, the more you will get to know it inside and out. Such knowledge is an essential part of the film making process; competence and ability to use a camera mean the difference between a film being good and being unwatchable.

For many who have used small camcorders before, the process of pushing the red record button is the first and only consideration. For a pro, it is the very last thing they do after all the other adjustments have been made. Make no mistake, camera work is a very detailed and involved art. Those camcorders that get waved around at parties, weddings or family gatherings have the capacity to film decent images if anyone bothered to pay attention to all the functions available. In this chapter, you will learn how to get the best from any camera regardless of its cost.

If you know nothing about cameras it can be a dizzying experience trying to absorb everything about them – each camera has different functions, buttons in different places, different controls, different capabilities, a different lens, films using different formats and so on. In many ways cameras are just like cars – there are thousands of different models, but they all have steering wheels, accelerator and brake pedals and all do the same thing. In other words, despite the almost bewildering variety of cameras that exists, they all have the same functions. The trick is to recognize the Ferraris from the wrecks.

Before we delve into the labyrinthine world of cameras, it is important to get a few conventions established. In today's world of fast-changing technology there are countless abbreviations that can leave the uninitiated gasping for air. Let's have a careful look at what you can expect to see and hear down at your local electronics store or camera retailer:

SD (Standard Definition) – video that is not High Definition

HD (High Definition) – video of a higher resolution and clarity; high definition

HDV (High Definition Video) – High Definition that records on a tape

HDD (Hard Disk Drive) – a camera that records its images on an internal drive

MiniDV (Mini Digital Video) – a popular small digital tape used for recording images in either SD or HD

So that means an HD camera can be HDD, but an HDV can't be HDD or HD; however, HDD isn't always HD – got that?

CAMERA TYPES

Loosely speaking, cameras fall into three general categories according to usage:

► Consumer

► Prosumer

► Professional

Consumer cameras are the ones you can buy at your local electronics store, via mail order, on an Internet site, in a supermarket and so on. These are used by amateur enthusiasts and sometimes by the professional needing a back-up camera. Their controls are very simple and designed to be used with a minimum of fuss. The media they record on is cheap and widely available. They can also be HDD or use flash drives.

'Prosumer' is a word created to explain cameras that have appeal to both professionals and consumers. In the professional world, they are used when there is a need for the camera to be light and mobile or when the budget is limited. These cameras tend to be available only from specialist retailers. Their controls can be sophisticated, although they are much simpler than their professional counterparts. The media required to record on, such as tapes, can be bought from high-street electronics stores and supermarkets, although some may require media only available from professional dealers.

Professional cameras are those used exclusively by film and television companies and/or high-budget productions. They are also used for corporate communications by large private companies. They are big and bulky with sophisticated controls. They are the most expensive and the most capable. The tapes, discs or flash cards required for recording purposes are likewise only available from specialist retailers and can also be expensive.

Furthermore, cameras fall into two specific categories – film and video.

FILM CAMERAS

Film cameras, as the name suggests, use cartridges or reels of film. Film cameras are named after the width of the film they use. The common formats are:

▶ **Super 8 mm**

This is a grainy film, and although it's rare to see an entire production filmed using this format, many rock videos or feature films will have short sequences shot on super 8.

Super 8 mm cameras were very popular up until the late 1970s and early 1980s, when many people used them for home movies. Since then many have been abandoned in favour of modern video cameras. Because of this, they turn up all over the place for budget prices and, owing to the simplicity of their mechanisms, they tend to still be working all these years later.

A cartridge of super 8 mm isn't cheap and will last only 2½–3 minutes, depending on your camera's settings. For the price of one super 8 mm cartridge you could buy several packs of MiniDV tapes or a couple of budget Secure Digital (SD) cards.

Other important considerations are: since it's film you cannot 'record' over what you have just filmed; it doesn't record sound; the film has to be sent away to be developed; and you have to somehow get it into a digital format for editing purposes. This can all add up quickly into quite an expensive proposition. However, many low-budget film makers (this one included) just love the look and feel of this funky format.

▶ **Super 16 mm**

This format is used mainly for non-theatrical productions as a cost-effective way of making television, while still maintaining high visual standards.

The format remains a popular first choice for drama productions in Europe where its relative cheapness makes it ideal for theatrical releases as well as television since budgets tend to be lower than in North America. However, some high-profile US productions have used this format including the first season of *Sex and the City* and *The O.C.*

The format has also been used in several high-profile films such as the low-budget hit *Clerks* (dir. Kevin Smith, 1994) as well as *Leaving Las Vegas* (dir. Mike Figgis, 1995), *This Is Spinal Tap* (dir. Rob Reiner, 1984), and *Vera Drake* (dir. Mike Leigh, 2004).

Like all film, super 16 mm isn't cheap. A cartridge lasting a mere three minutes may cost the same as a consumer-level video camera. Also, don't forget there are the same developing and transfer to digital format issues and costs to be considered.

One feature of this format that makes it a bit accessible to the low-budget film maker is the availability of the cameras. Over the years there have been countless 16 mm film cameras released. These range from sophisticated professional models down to basic wind-up versions aimed at amateur film makers. The cameras at the cheaper end of the spectrum can be quite reasonably priced and are regular features on Internet bidding sites.

For the low-budget film maker 16 mm film is something many tend to aim for as it has the allure and romance of film, while being at the 'cheap' end of the film spectrum.

▶ 35 mm

This is the film format associated with high-end television productions and feature film. This format has remained relatively unchanged and has been doing the rounds in cinema for decades.

Despite the undeniable high quality this film gives, it is rapidly being eroded by the upsurge in high-definition camera usage in major feature films. There's more on this later.

The 35 mm format is a professional film format – there is no cheap version, no consumer version. It is, and will always be very, very expensive to own and operate. Even the film stock is in another price league.

It must be realized that the 35 mm format is slowly fading away. In recent years, advances in digital camera technology and post-production methods have enabled film makers to achieve images that come close to those of 35 mm. In the process thousands of dollars have been saved on budgets as HD recording media are much cheaper compared with 35-mm film stock. When confronted with the choice 'Should we get a great look and pay a fortune for 35 mm or should we save a fortune by using an HD format?', many film makers have let the budget decide for them. It's as simple as that. Watch this situation closely …

VIDEO CAMERAS

The term 'video camera' a bit of a misnomer as not all of them use video tape to record on. Despite the use of flash cards, hard disk drives, DVD and optical discs, the expression 'to video' persists very much in the way we still use the expression 'to film' even though we are not using a film camera.

In spite of this, here are the some of the most popular video camera recording media and formats:

▶ MiniDV

These cameras use small, digital video-tape cassettes. These tapes are lightweight, cheap and last for an hour or longer depending on the camera's record settings. They first appeared on the scene in the 1990s and are perhaps the most popular format of camcorder. The same tapes are also used by the newer high definition video (HDV) cameras. They can also be used in DVCam cameras, which are popular with news teams and documentary film makers.

Furthermore, some MiniDV camcorders allow you to encode your footage in either MiniDV or DVCam, just as some HDV cameras allow you to encode in either HDV, DVCam or MiniDV, giving you flexibility according to your needs. Overall it is a very versatile format with many options.

One advantage these tapes have is they are highly transportable and small. So, when one tape is full, take it out and put a blank one in. This may seem like a basic assumption, but for some other formats such a simple changeover is impossible. Also, it is very easy to archive your footage with this format – just put all the tapes on a shelf! For those of you lucky enough to afford an HDV camera, at least the tapes you need are easy to find and reasonably priced.

A disadvantage of the MiniDV format is that every now and again the tape can unfurl and create a jam, and drop-out can occur, creating a distorted image if any dirt gets on the recording heads. Also, MiniDV cameras have moving parts that will wear and create technical problems over time. Some people find it a pain when editing from this format as you sometimes have to upload the entire tapes in real time. Finally, regarding storage and archiving, the tapes can degrade over time or simply get lost (oops!).

Overall though, MiniDV tape-based cameras are prolific, capable and can be fairly affordable. That said, they have been overtaken in popularity by other tapeless digital formats.

▶ HDD (Hard Disk Drive)

These cameras record their images on an internal hard drive. This has the benefit of not having to change over tapes and risk missing something you want to film. Also, playback is conveniently broken down into individual recordings, meaning you don't have to forward or rewind an entire tape to find the bit you want. Owing to the lack of tape, you can film without having to carry an ample supply of MiniDV cassettes with you. HDD cameras can record in SD and HD. However, be very careful when buying an HDD camera as some people mistake the abbreviation to mean 'high definition'.

Editing can be slightly easier as, like flash drive cameras below, it is not necessary to play all the footage you have filmed. Instead, it is divided into the individual recordings that you can choose to import (more on editing later).

Problems of this format relate to capacity and storage. Although HDD cameras boast impressive recording times, there usually comes a point when this limit has been reached. In such circumstances, the options are either to delete some existing footage or to download on to a computer. Depending on your needs and circumstances this isn't always possible and you could be stuck.

For example, when filming on location it may not be an option to bring along a computer to download your images. Even if you could do this, downloading is a time-consuming process. Alternatively, everything you filmed may be important to you, which would prevent you from selectively deleting things. Always keep track of how much capacity you have left, measured against how much footage you think you will need to film. Since downloading on to a drive can take a long time, you need to carefully manage this aspect of your camera and filming, especially if you are filming intensively over a short period. There's more on this later.

In addition, archiving can present problems down the track – you may eventually run out of memory on your computer or hard drive. If it is your desire to archive everything, then you can become trapped in a cycle of buying external storage media. Even if you can work around this storage problem, there is always the rogue factor of a computer crash in which all your lovely images could be erased.

Finally, hard disk drives can be rather sensitive to bumps and knocks.

▶ Flash drive cameras

These cameras are another form of tapeless camcorder, but instead of having an internal hard drive they use removable drives on to which the images are recorded. As with the other formats above, they can record in SD and HD. They also have their professional counterparts, which is always a good sign.

Like an HDD camera, these do not require tape, but instead small flash drives are used to record the images. A big advantage of these cameras is that they don't have moving parts, so this means 'wear and tear' is minimized over time, unlike a tape-based format. This means that if the camera is well looked after it should give top results for a long time. Another plus point for these cameras is that editing can be speeded up using this format. Whereas tape-based cameras upload their images in real time (more of this in the editing chapter), flash drive cameras can do the same in a shorter amount of time.

However, like their HDD cousins, these cameras can present problems when all the flash drives are full and you are on location. Also, unlike prosumer HDV cameras, which can use cheap tapes, prosumer flash drives can be very expensive.

▶ HDCAM

While you are unlikely to come across this at your local electronics or photographic retailer, it is worth mentioning. This format is a professional system used in major feature films and also drama series. Although the tape stock is relatively cheap, the cameras are anything but. This system is the preserve of well-funded film makers requiring the highest digital high-definition quality for their film making.

In terms of pedigree, it is a relative newcomer to the industry, but has already filmed some very high-profile movies. *Star Wars Episode II: Attack of the Clones* (dir. George Lucas, 2002) and Oscar-winning *Slumdog Millionaire* (dir. Danny Boyle, 2008) are just two examples.

As with consumer and prosumer cameras, this system has similar and related camera formats that record images on to different media such as internal hard drives, flash memory or optical discs.

Many directors are now choosing this format to work with owing to the positive effect it can have on post-production. Unlike a film format, a digital high-definition format does not need to be developed, processed and printed before it can be edited. The media can be removed from the camera and is good to go. Also, it means it is quicker and easier to start doing special effects work as the images can be quickly uploaded on to sfx computers.

Case study: HD and digital film making – the rise and rise ...

One of the big groundswells in professional film making for theatrical release is the impact of HD and digital camera formats. When video cameras first came out decades ago, the quality was terrible by modern standards and, although used by news networks for location work, it had no place in feature films. However, over the years image quality got better and better.

By the 1990s with the use of MiniDV cameras, video camera image quality got a shot in the arm. Although still not up to the quality of 35 mm, the video sequences of *The Blair Witch Project* showed cinema what digital formats could do. *28 Days Later* (dir. Danny Boyle, 2002) used a MiniDV camera for part of the film to give things a grungy look in keeping with the mood of the film. Yet it showed that digital video systems were rapidly maturing.

Now digital HD and 4K systems are snapping at the heels of 35 mm film and things are quickly nearing a tipping point. In fact, most digital film making seems to be aspiring to get the film 35 mm look. It's quite ironic that all this modern technology is being used to replicate the look of a filming format decades old! Watch this space ...

Film cameras versus digital cameras; or, What's the big deal?

It may not be something that gets too much publicity, but not all films are shot on, well, film. Even though we liberally use the words and expressions 'film', 'filming' and 'to film' when describing the act of making a moving picture, is quite possible that no part of the process will ever come near a piece of celluloid. Why is this?

Even since the late 1990s the quality and capabilities of digital formats have come so close to traditional film formats that professional film makers and numerous big-name directors now use it as their format of choice. However, this only explains things halfway. The important consideration is that many digital formats look as good in terms of feel, richness and general quality for a fraction of the cost of a film camera format.

This wasn't always the case for non-film formats. The tape-based formats of the 1970s and 1980s were always held in low regard by many, as they didn't come close to the sophisticated feel of, say, 16 mm or 35 mm. In a layperson's terms, they looked cheap and nasty. A first major outing for these 'lesser' formats was the pop music videos of the era. While not digital, these analogue tape cameras were still a lot cheaper than film and found favour with the makers of music videos for this reason. However, their garish colour handling, smearing in bright lights and overall gaudy rendering didn't give them universal appeal. This is perhaps one reason why, soon after, music 'videos' actually started to be shot on film in order to give higher quality. However, throughout the MTV heyday of the 1980s (when they actually showed music!) the 'video' moniker remained. Ironically today, many years after these pioneering movements, the videos of Beyoncé, Katy Perry, Ed Sheeran and so on are largely shot on non-film digital formats. So, this in many ways means that they are actually true videos once more.

Skip forward to the 1990s and the arrival of digital tape formats meant, overnight, film making was revolutionized. Finally, there were tape formats that, while not 35 mm film by any means, were of very high quality and clarity as well as being easy to use. This meant many low-budget and indie film makers now had a format at their disposal that was very cheap. Instead of having to take out bank loans or max out credit cards to get a few cans of 16 mm or 35 mm film, they could buy hours and hours' worth of tape for a tiny price. The incredibly popular MiniDV tape format was a workhorse of this paradigm shift in film making. Furthermore, developments in digital editing (see Chapter 12) in turn meant that manipulating images from these tapes was easy and straightforward – no developing costs, printing, copies, intermediates and so on. The tape came out of the camera and straight to the edit – simple!

However, there was still a teeny problem that upset and irked the discerning film maker. These digital formats, while cheap, easy and liberating to use, just didn't *look* like film. Of course, when handled correctly the format would give clear, bright and sharp images, but it still had that video *feel* to it. In other words, these formats didn't have the same rich, glossy and sophisticated look of 16 mm or 35 mm. In short, the trade-off was as follows: do you shoot on a format like MiniDV, save loads of money *but* have a visual look and feel that isn't quite film, or do you somehow arrange finance so you can afford to shoot on an expensive film format?

Understandably, many film makers of the era decided on the former option. Of course, there were ways they could coax a film look from their tape formats, such as using something called a depth of field adaptor or by tweaking things in the edit, yet the fact remained they still couldn't quite replicate the classy feel of a high-end film format.

Yet, since then, each year digital formats – be they tape-based, flash memory or whatever – have been snapping at the heels of 35 mm and its brethren. The gap has been closing, narrowing and getting smaller until now we are a near-parity in terms of quality and look. Some may disagree with me and argue that there is still a long way to go, but if you visit the multiplex on any given day half the films available will probably have been shot using a digital format. Thus, in terms of non-film formats and cameras being accepted as a viable commercial format, that day has long come and gone.

This all means that a director's choice of whether to shoot film or not is a very personal one. It's a choice that, despite all the improvements in digital, still boils down to the same thing. Do I want to flexibility and cheapness of digital or the expense yet glossy look of film?

As an example of this, let's consider two film trilogies that were shot and filmed simultaneously yet using different formats: the *Star Wars* prequels and *The Lord of the Rings*. Did you know that the prequels were shot digitally while Frodo and his pals were all shot on film? In fact, the prequels were the first major release to have gone digital. One reason for this was the high number of special and digital effects in the storylines. With the principal photography of actors and sets shot in this manner, it's a lot easier to utilise these images within an editing framework which can then have effects added. Basically, it's easier to use and saves a lot of headaches, as all the processes, time and costs of transferring film to a digital format are done away with.

Yet, Peter Jackson's *The Lord of the Rings* trilogy (2001–3) was also a very effects-heavy series of films and he chose to shoot on film. Why? If the only consideration was ease of use, then surely Jackson should have gone digital, right? Well, no. In many ways, these two film trilogies are examples of the arguments that have gone on in the past between low-budget and indie film makers choosing the reasons to shoot digital or film. It still ends up as being a choice between ease of use versus the look it gives.

Jackson chose film, feeling safe in the knowledge that it would give the trilogy the rich feel it deserved instead of the slightly video-esque quality a digital format of the time would have produced. And he did so, even though it meant a lot of extra hassle with regard to getting the film digitized so it could be edited on the AVID system and have special effects work done.

To the outsider, this may seem like some abstract nuance that isn't worth worrying about. After all, people coming out of both films didn't start complaining or praising the actual image quality (some might have …). That's because, unless you are specifically looking for it, or know before that a film has been shot using one format or the other, you simply may not notice it. Maybe we *can* notice the difference, but it's something we process at the subconscious level and ascribe any perceived difference in the picture quality to the direction.

Still staying with the *Star Wars* films, let's fast-forward to 2015 and J. J. Abrams' decision to shoot on film for *Episode VII: The Force Awakens*. Why? Surely, he should have gone digital for its flexibility and savings in cost and labour. Again, the answer to this conundrum is that he simply liked the look and feel of film. Likewise, when Jackson returned to Middle Earth for *The Hobbit* trilogy (2012–14), he chose film once more.

For many film makers out there, you just can't beat the look that film gives. It's as weird, crazy and intangible as that.

The age of 4K and beyond …

There have always been standards in picture quality and resolution that many film makers have aimed for, or were expected to achieve, in terms of format and visual resolution. It was argued that anything less than a certain level of picture quality would automatically mark the production as amateur or not of a professional standard. While there has been a lot of leeway to this notion in terms of professional film makers utilizing non-professional formats for parts of their film or even the whole thing, many won't entertain this notion. Instead, they know that a combination of professional peer pressure, quality expectations and even film studio demands mean that they will only shoot on a camera of a certain picture quality or higher. In terms of current digital film making, one such current 'benchmark' format is 4K.

So, what exactly is 4K?

Simply put, 4K very high-resolution video format that provides great picture quality. Just like many other digital formats that came before, 4K is a level of picture quality that many film makers will aspire to achieve by using its camera technology. Also, its scan area is much bigger than other formats, meaning that there is more image to play around with when it comes to post-production.

It's the flexibility that 4K can give in editing that many like about the format. For example, it's an all too common problem when you finally get around to editing your material days, or weeks, after it was shot that you realize that the images are not quite right. Sure, the focus, exposure, white balance and other technical features check out, but the framing may be off, the camera wasn't set up level on the day, or you wished you had panned the camera to follow movement. In other words, your images are beset by all the usual problems created by a time-pressured and fast-paced shoot.

Owing to 4K's very high resolution and large scan, you can effectively pick up and handle the image in the edit without the problems associated with other formats. For example, if you look at your video and wish you had the camera facing a slightly different direction because it makes the framing look awkward, you can do this retroactively in the edit. In post-production, the image can be picked up and moved with a great degree of flexibility owing to its size, meaning that the edges are still outside the picture area. Or, in other words, what you see in your edit window is only a fraction of what's available. This all means that you can adjust its positioning without running out of picture. If you were to do this with a smaller-resolution format, say from an HDV camera shooting 720p, then even moving the image a small amount would result in the black edges of the frame becoming visible.

The large picture size allows you to track a subject too, so that a person walking from one side of the frame to the other can now be followed as if the camera was panning on the shot. Editing options don't stop there. The format allows editors to zoom in to a great degree without any loss of resolution. So, you could either zoom the entire shot in or create an effect simulating a camera zoom without the picture becoming grainy and noisy, as it would on lower-resolution formats.

These features make the format very popular, as they can give you more options in the edit, allowing you to add creative moves that would be impossible on other formats. Also it can, mercifully, mean that you don't have to go through the rigmarole of reshoots when you discover your images aren't quite working out as you intended. It's this latter 'safety net' aspect that many enjoy beyond and above the fact that it gives such high-resolution images.

The higher resolution also gives the format an advantage when it comes to green-screen or any kind of chroma key filming. Because the format has a much higher count of pixels, it can give you a stronger outline to work with. Often with green-screen filming, the edges of complicated shapes, such as someone's hair or a model warship, can be challenging to work with, owing to a lack of a hard edge or the complexity of its outline. This can mean that the resulting effect can be blurry around the edges, signifying the places where the outline was hard to define. With 4K, this issue is mitigated to a large degree, as you can go in close and select the pixels that mark the edge of your subject with much greater accuracy than in other formats.

Yet, as you'd expect with such a 'whiz-kid' format, these cameras are at the expensive end of the market. Even consumer versions can have a high price tag. Prosumer and professional models are even more expensive.

On top of the price, another eye-watering facet of these cameras is the memory they require. A single minute of 4K can weigh in at over 1 GB of memory. So, not only is this a potential issue for the computer you will be editing on, but it's also something to think about when you are actually shooting. If you are buying a consumer or prosumer 4K camera that takes SD card memory storage, these will need to be high-performance ones in order to handle the files being written on them. This could mean that your SD cards could blow a hole in your wallet owing to their expense. The high-end, high-speed cards made by the big brands don't come cheap, yet if you skimp by relying on lower-speed, cheaper cards, you may find that they simply can't handle the video being shot or the files may get corrupted in some way.

This issue also has a follow-on when you are filming. Whereas other camera formats able to use cheap SD cards or even MiniDV tapes can simply load in other card or tape owing to their low cost, this may not be an option with 4K. You could end up in a tricky situation where you have filled up your SD card or cards and need to think about how to free up some space in order to continue filming.

This is covered a bit more detail elsewhere in the book.

Yet beyond 4K are 5K, 8K, UHD (*Ultra* High Definition) and all manner of exotic super-quality formats. Essentially, things will get better and better, resolutions will get clearer and clearer, picture sizes bigger. Ultimately, however, all this shouldn't change how you make a film in any fundamental way.

Cameras – a closer look

As technology has moved forwards, many cameras have been blessed with some very sophisticated and helpful features. On the same note, many have been cursed with an equal number of superfluous and useless features, too.

First, some of the useless ones: the effects, features and buttons that will dazzle people walking casually past the window of an electronics retailer, but which have the professional laughing or shivering with revulsion.

- ▶ **Sepia, black and white, or 'art' effects** – like many effects, these are things best left to the editing stage where they are easy to add or remove. If you choose to impart these effects to your footage then you will be stuck with them.

- ▶ **Wipes and fades** – again, these effects simulate things that are best done in the edit. More information on these topics is given in the editing chapter.

Overall these camera and filming effects should be regarded as nothing more than gimmicks. A professional camera operator will never use them and a professional camera won't even feature them – it's that simple.

The important controls you should look for in a camera are these 'big three':

- ▶ White balance

- ▶ Focus

- ▶ Exposure

Any camera with these is a good start. So, what do they represent?

WHITE BALANCE
White balance is a function that helps the camera set the correct colour tone for a shot according to the lighting situation.

To look at this function more closely it is important to realize that there are two basic types of light: natural (sunlight) and artificial (light bulbs, etc.). Unlike the human eye, a camera can handle only one type of light at a time and has to be 'told' what light it is currently filming in. If you have the ability to control this function, then your footage will have good and true to life colouration. If you don't use this function, you will often produce images that are tinged with strong hues of orange or blue.

Many modern consumer cameras have white balance settings that are (supposedly) able to distinguish lighting conditions such as cloudy, bright sunshine and overhead 'strip' lighting. However, so long as your camera has the ability to set its white balance to artificial or natural, that should be more than enough. Also, if you are able to set its white balance manually, this is another bonus. Put simply, this is when you show your camera a white object, such as a piece of paper or a wall, and tell it to 'go fetch'.

Remember this

Many cameras, even consumer versions, have the ability to save and remember the white balances for various locations and conditions. For example, if you set the white balance for your outdoor location and then another for something inside with artificial lighting, you can assign each of these a number and then revert back to them depending on where you are. This can save a lot of set-up time when filming.

FOCUS

Focus is the most straightforward function to understand. Something is either in focus or it isn't. Therefore, your ability to control focus is a key ingredient of film making.

Consumer cameras tend to have simplistic lenses when it comes to focusing issues. For them, most objects over a certain distance from the lens will be in focus, or, to put it in photo-speak, they have a deep depth of field. In terms of your focus controls, this can mean that focusing is never really a huge deal. It's only when you want to zoom in and then focus that you have to use the focus control. Likewise, trying to track something that is constantly moving, such as a car or a person running, can get a bit tricky as you may lose the focus.

For more sophisticated lenses on prosumer and professional cameras, focusing can be a much bigger concern. Owing to the way their lenses work, they have a shallow depth of field and so at times only one object they are filming is in focus while the rest are blurred.

On movies and drama serials there is a member of the camera department known as the focus puller. It is this person's job to ensure that the lens is focusing on the correct thing at all times. In practical terms, this means there is someone hovering near the lens throughout the shoot ready to adjust the focus wheel according to the situation.

EXPOSURE

This control is something that can often catch out the novice camera operator. Exposure is the photographic way of saying how bright or dark a picture is.

Exposure is perhaps the most fluid consideration for your camera work as it is often changing from shot to shot, depending on where you are, what the weather is like or what lighting you have. In spite of these challenges, it is very important to your film making and often exists within narrow margins of tolerance. If you get things wrong your picture could be dark and difficult to watch, or it could be too bright and full of flare.

Getting the right exposure is very much a skill and can sometimes be quite subjective. This is made more acute with consumer video cameras as their f-stop tolerance can be very small. F-stop is photo-speak for controlling the exposure of your picture – some cameras actually have numerical f-stops in their viewfinder telling the operator what the exposure is; others may just have a simple bar or indicator. Unlike film, which can handle several amounts of brightness and shadow at once, video systems can handle only a couple. Therefore, when filming someone's face, in order to get the exposure correct everything else in the picture may be overexposed. Alternatively, if filming a very bright object, you may have to adjust the exposure so that everything else is lost in shadow. This is why exposure is so important; get it wrong and you will ruin your footage.

During the filming of *Miami Vice*, with Colin Farrell and Jamie Foxx, the production had an f-stop issue with their HD cameras. Owing to the low f-stop tolerance of the system being used, when shooting a scene against a large sunny window, it was necessary to illuminate the cast with very, very powerful lights so the light was equalized. In between takes, a protective shield had to be placed in front of the actors to protect them from the intense heat.

Remember this

It is common practice for a professional camera operator to briefly flip the camera controls on to 'auto' for a moment or two then put them back to 'manual'. This way a good idea of the correct exposure is given and then 'locked' into the camera. With consumer cameras, you should be able to do the same thing. The danger in doing this is that sometimes an unsuitable exposure may be given – for example, if you were filming someone against a window, the camera would expose for the outside light brightness and turn the person into a silhouette.

Buttons and menus

With the above three controls in mind, the next consideration for selecting a camera should be how easy it is to control.

As a rule of thumb, consumer cameras have many of their controls accessible via an internal menu. A professional camera has them on the outside in the form of switches, buttons and so on, whereas a prosumer camera has a mixture of both.

In striving for streamlined camera shape and design, most of the cameras coming out at the moment have their controls almost hidden away in the bowels of their microchips. Now, this isn't really a problem as, after all, you can still get to the controls, right? The only inconvenience such an array can create is the speed at which you are able to adjust your camera's settings.

There are few things more frustrating than trying to adjust exposure or focus mid-shot via several internal menus, and then have the thing you were in the middle of filming finish! Although this can be a superficial consideration when weighed against cost and mobility, it is worth thinking about.

Combine this with the small size of these cameras and it can be like using a calculator while wearing boxing gloves. Many a time I have seen people get very frustrated as they struggle to make an adjustment in time.

Also, some camcorders that have both viewfinder and flip-out screen require you to open up the latter in order to make your adjustments. If the sun is bright you may have trouble seeing what's going on, and if it's raining you will have to remove whatever cover you are using or go inside.

Thus, it is ironic that sophisticated professional cameras are often easier to use owing to the ease of access to their control interfaces. Despite the huge and daunting size of some cameras, it is refreshing to know the exposure control is easily accessed, likewise the focus and white balance controls. However, this has to be weighed up against the fact that many of these professional cameras cost more than a new car.

Key idea: Camera joy

Canon Inc. has many cameras featuring a joystick control on their flip-out screens. It allows the user to make relatively quick picture adjustments and is an interesting compromise between internal menu and external controls.

Intermediate/advanced controls

With the above 'big three' in mind, there are some other camera settings worth thinking about that can have a strong influence on your style of filming.

SHUTTER SPEED

This setting controls the speed at which your images are being captured. For many people who buy consumer camcorders, and even some prosumer cameras, this setting is often viewed as a bizarre and unimportant annoyance and is ignored, to the detriment of their footage.

Shutter speed tells the camera how to process the movement it is capturing. For example, a person running can have the movement of their limbs captured in detail with an almost heightened sense of movement or, conversely, have that same movement drawn out and blurred.

For those cameras with a shutter speed control, the normal setting is 1/50, meaning that the camera is capturing 50 frames per second. When a camera is at this setting, things will look very much how our own eye views movement in the world.

When this number is increased, for example to 1/250 or 1/400 and beyond, the camera uses a higher shutter speed so that invisible details of movement are captured. Water droplets can be seen spraying from a garden hose, the erupting sand in a long-jump pit becomes clear and the karate moves of two men fighting take on a new feeling of danger and immediacy. This is what high shutter speed allows you to do.

Contrary to this is low shutter speed. Generally speaking, this is any speed under the 1/50 reference point. Unlike its speedy counterpart, low shutter speed distends movement and blurs objects moving through the screen. The effect is that someone running across the shot appears to the trailing a ghost behind them. This effect is very popular to emphasize disorientation or in spooky flashbacks.

Setting shutter speeds really low to 1/6 can give some spectacular effects. Setting the speed to just 1/25 can give the look and feel of film; however, this low shutter speed has poor ability to deal with motion, which is a drawback.

Some consumer cameras that feature the ability to control shutter speeds may in fact call it something else, such as 'sports mode' for high shutter, or 'digital effects' for blurred, low shutter speeds.

One other important point about shutter speed is that, even if you don't want to use it at particularly high or low speeds, you should still make sure it is set to 1/50. The reason for this is that many cameras use the shutter speed to control the brightness of an image when the camera is turned on. Therefore, if you use your camera in bright and sunny conditions, the shutter speed may have automatically adjusted itself to a high shutter speed. In turn, this will mean that your footage has a sense of heightened movement, which might not be what you want.

Two important factors to remember when using shutter speeds are:

▶ increasing shutter speed will darken your image

▶ reducing shutter speed will brighten your image

Therefore you will have to adjust the exposure accordingly.

GAIN

Not many consumer cameras feature a manual gain control. For those cameras that do, it is another ally to your film making. Gain is a function that boosts the brightness of the image at the expense of the picture's clarity. It doesn't increase the amount of the light the camera receives, though – the best way to think of it is like turning up the brightness on a TV set.

Strictly speaking, gain is an emergency function. It is a way of artificially boosting the brightness of your footage when the lighting is poor, for example, filming at dawn or dusk, or under dim streetlights at night. The drawback to using this function is that the picture becomes very fuzzy with grain and interference. Gain is measured in dB, and when you want to increase the gain you adjust the function so that the dB increases to +6, +12 and so on.

Until very recently, you would only see gain being used professionally in factual pieces such as news reports and documentaries. However, while gain came into being as a way of getting a slightly better picture in poor light, many directors quickly realized that adding a bit of grain and noise to a picture makes things look gritty and rough. Often this can heighten the mood and emotional impact of a scene. In the TV remake of *Battlestar Galactica* (2004–9) it was quite common for a high gain effect to be used in certain scenes for added emotional effect.

Key idea

As highlighted earlier in this chapter, using film stocks can be very expensive. However, if you combine certain low shutter speeds with a high gain, the resulting look is not too dissimilar from an old reel of film going through a projector. Also, if you render the image black and white while editing (see Chapter 12), the effect can be quite convincing.

Sound with vision

Although cameras are a visual tool, spare a thought for sound as well. If you plan to have people speaking in your film, then you need to be aware of your camera's capacity to record sound. All cameras will come with some kind of in-built microphone, but the audio quality they produce can be poor. For this reason, it's important to check to see if a camera can have external microphones plugged into it. The simplest microphones are usually ones that slide into a 'shoe' at the top of the camera. Although these improve the quality a little, they should not be used in any way for recording speech.

Ideally, your camera needs to have an XLR input or a microphone jack. We will look at microphones and sound recording in more detail in Chapter 7.

Other camera systems

As technology proliferates, there are now more and more devices capable of capturing moving images. Mobile phones, flip cameras, iPods, digital photo cameras and so on now boast features that allow them to be multifunctional information storage and image capturing apparatus.

However, despite the advertising and marketing claims surrounding these cameras, the quality of the recorded images can vary widely, especially when viewed on a large screen. Owing to this technical issue, and a frequent lack of manual controls, anyone thinking of filming an entire presentation using one of these devices should think very carefully about each format's capabilities.

DSLR CAMERAS

The Digital Single Lens Reflex camera came into film making by accident. Yet, it has taken low and high budget productions by storm.

Why is this? This camera is the meeting point between a system that offers all the cost savings and flexibility of video combined with the look (or near look) of film. It's the thing that many out there had been hoping for, for years; a camera that doesn't quite break the bank and gives quality to compete with major productions.

How did all this come about?

Like its analog film loading antecedent, the DSLR was made just for taking still images. Its shape and design was likewise based on the plain ole' SLR cameras with the large lens at the front giving the distinctive depth of field that many considered a benchmark for pro photography. Its body could be used with a variety of lenses such as zoom, wide and so on, giving the user flexibility in the pictures they wanted to take. As such, it was the preferred camera type for press and news gathering in the pre-digital age.

Skip forward to the early 2000s, and digital counterparts started being produced and marketed that more or less made the analog cameras obsolete overnight. No longer would press photographers have to take out their reels of film, get them developed and then somehow send them back to base to be printed and published. Instead they could be downloaded and emailed or otherwise sent over the internet. Simple.

Yet, that's only a small part of the story. A seemingly innocuous feature of these new DSLRs was the fact some came with a video function just like many other digital stills cameras. As well as taking stills, you could turn the selector wheel to video and shoot some moving images. The telling difference was, the quality on the DSLRs wasn't pixelated or low res that fell well below even the most basic domestic video camera, far from it – the quality was superb!

The quality was amazing.

All of a sudden people in the know cottoned on that using DSLR cameras gave you a kind of picture quality that resembled certain stocks of 16mm film. It was glossy, the lenses gave great depth of field and it almost 'felt' as you were watching a genuine piece of celluloid. After a while the secret was out, and almost everyone in low budget was getting in on the action.

No longer would you have to max out all your credit cards, remortgage the house and sell your car to get a few feet of film; you could pay a respectable price and get a complete system (minus the lenses, they were extra – can't have everything …).

No longer would you have to fiddle about with trying to fit your Depth of Field adaptor to your MiniDV cameras, and then hope and keep it in place during the shoot.

No longer would you have to worry about filming something on BetaCam, DVC-Pro or MiniDV and hope you could achieve a decent faux-film look by rendering things in the edit.

Quite simply, it was revolution within film making and low budget seemed to be its niche.

Yet, despite the interest from film makers the manufactures, Canon, Nikon, Sony, etc. still kept producing plain old DSLR cameras with seemingly little mind that they were just as popular with film makers as they were with still photographers. The functions and controls were all designed around someone taking photographs and not moving images. Therefore it could be tricky to hold and shoot with as you went about your film making. Also, depending on the lens you had, it could be very heavy at the front and tend to droop forward if you were shooting hand-held, unlike larger video or film cameras that you could partially rest on your shoulder. Not all of the models had microphones. Those that did may have only had a little basic one inbuilt to the main body that didn't give great quality.

As time progressed some models incorporated mic inputs, meaning you could at least use something like a 'beach box' XLR adaptor allowing you to use professional mics, or even a simple jack-plug microphone.

A whole sub-industry in film making sprung up around DSLRs to accommodate film makers choosing this format. Suddenly there was much talk of 'The Rig' or the attachments and gadgets you fastened to it in order to enhance and aid your film making. This usually consisted of a wheel, often known as a stabilizer, with a bar across the lower third you could fix your camera to. Thus instead of holding the camera, you held the stabilizer giving you smoother camera moves and generally making the DSLR easier to handle. Plus you could add a microphone on the top which plugged in to the camera, or a light and so on. In some ways rigs almost resembled the one-man-bands of old, with the number of things you could add.

Soon shoulder rigs appeared giving the camera operator the familiarity of a larger video camera by resting part of the rig on the shoulder and having two hand grips out front. Extra functionality like focus wheels enhanced things further and generally allowed the operator to use the DSLR like a larger video camera. Plus it all looked rather cool and impressive!

In many circles shooting with a DSLR rig became de rigueur.

As the scene matured it was the turn of the manufacturers to finally cotton on to things and manufacture purpose-built video cameras. As an example of this, Canon released their C-300 video camera replete with XLR inputs and all the gubbins that a pro film maker looks for. However, its price was rather high and as a result many still gravitate towards plain DSLR models like the Canon 5D.

In conclusion, DSLR cameras give great results, have the option to use a wide variety of lenses to suit your needs and have a huge selection of accessories available. It's for this reason they are still very popular with low budget film makers. Make no mistake, while reasonable priced compared to higher end formats, they are still a touch more expensive that basic video camera models available from your local electronics store. As such, for pricing reasons alone it may not be a great format for someone who wants to 'test the water' or who has no prior photographic of video experience. Plus don't forget the lens they come with (if they come with one at all) probably won't suite all your filming needs, meaning you may need to buy one or two more. This isn't cheap. Also, combined with the fact the operation can be a touch more complicated than a regular video camera and the video may need some transcoding before it's brought into an edit, this makes it a slightly less forgiving format than others.

However, for those searching for the Holy Grail of a film looking video format, there is no better.

SMARTPHONES

There was a time when the ability of a cell phone to record video was no more than a novelty – a curious extra that complemented its core important ability to make phone calls and text messages. After all, the simple, low-resolution video would soon overload your phone's limited memory, meaning that you would soon have to delete whatever you had filmed. Surely this would never catch on or tweak the attention of serious film makers?

How times have changed.

Nowadays, not only can a decent smartphone shoot full HD or 4K video, it can also edit and upload those same images. In fact, an entire generation of film makers have practically grown up shooting on these devices and using it as their camera of choice. It further muddies the already-murky waters when it comes to discussions about camera formats and what you should be using to shoot your film on. Smartphones have added yet another capable camera format into the fray to bite at the heels of the established professional formats.

While many film makers would never consider using a smartphone, they do have many advantages over larger established professional formats. First of all, they are almost everywhere. Chances are a walk down your local high street will have you side-stepping smartphone zombies glued to their screens as they WhatsApp their pals or while away the time on some other social media activity. More importantly, they are widely available at the retail level too, meaning that you can get hold of them almost anywhere. It's a very competitive market, with stores and companies doing deals left, right and centre to pique your interest.

Nor to be ignored is the fact that most people know how to use them. A smartphone is not some exotic piece of technology akin to a high-end video camera that people struggle to handle properly. Far from it, you pick it up, you hold it, you film something – it's that easy. Even if we've never filmed with a smartphone before, we could probably figure it out rather quickly. Again, this is in stark contrast to professional video cameras that have power switches, buttons for filming and playback mode, menu options, removable media and various other bewildering controls and dials. The touch screen set-up of a smartphone means that you can do everything with the same finger!

Key idea: Hold your smartphone horizontally

If you are filming with a smartphone, hold it horizontally. Owing to its palm-friendly design, these devices are supposed to be held and operated while in the vertical position. The trouble with that comes when you start to shoot some video. When played back the frame is a narrow vertical strip with thick black bands either side. However, if held horizontal the video nicely fills out the screen and looks normal on playback.

It's highly mobile – after all, it is a mobile phone. It can be placed in your pocket and tucked away easily and safely as you go from location to location. This means that there are no huge soft carry bags or accessories to haul around and tire you out.

It's small and it's discreet. There are times when you may not want to draw attention to yourself. Perhaps because you are filming a street scene and you just want people to walk around like they normally do, rather than gawking as sometimes happens with large cameras and crews. Or perhaps you are somewhere where professional film crews are not allowed to film yet private citizens are. (Please note, I'm not encouraging underhand behaviour here; I'm just pointing out one of the legitimate advantages of a smartphone's size.)

Remember this

Cheap accessories like 'selfie sticks' can work well as a kind of bargain-basement Steadicam rig for shots when you are walking alongside someone or filming downwards.

You can edit on it. Something like an iPhone will have Apple's basic video editing application iMovie installed on it or at least available via the App Store. Therefore, there are no hassles with transferring your clips to another computer for editing: it can all be done on the same device. Then, of course, you can upload it all from the self-same device. What's not to like?

Oh, not forgetting that you can call people up on it.

Yet, there are some things to consider with these recording devices. The number-one bugbear of the professional when talking about smartphones is the lack of control you have over the recording. Some, while providing great resolution video, have no manual controls whatsoever, meaning that you cannot adjust exposure, focal distance, white balance or shutter speed. This alone is enough to turn many off using smartphones. An absence of such controls means that you will be compromised when setting up your shots, as you will have to work around whatever picture your smartphone's video sensors are giving you. This may mean that shooting a scene with lots of movement could constantly give you fluctuating picture brightness as well as focal issues. By contrast, if you were shooting with a higher-end pro camera you could set the controls before the shot to maintain a consistent picture.

The sound quality can be poor, too. While there is an inbuilt mic, the sound quality can be less than great unless you are actually talking into it. After all, this is primarily a phone and the mic is designed for use in very close proximity to the user's mouth. Therefore, if you are hoping to film a scene with a couple of people talking in a busy environment, the audio quality may come across all echoey and distant, just like any other on-board mic. Also, depending on how you are holding your phone, you may be accidentally covering the mic with your fingers, muffling or entirely cutting off the audio. The handling noise, too, could affect the audio quality. While many smartphone film makers use the earphone mic set-up to record audio, this will work only if someone is talking directly into the mic. It works best for factual shoots, as it's no big deal if the mic is visible. For any kind of fiction shooting, this method is impractical as the mic cable will be in shot. Therefore, some kind of separate audio recording device would need to be used, which in turn complicates your filming and editing.

Key idea

In 2015 the BBC News technology program *Click* filmed an entire episode on smartphones to prove the capability of such devices. In spite of the high visual quality the program makers had to use separate audio recording devices due to the limitations of the phones.

Another issue with smartphones is editing. While it's good that you can assemble your films on the same device used to shoot it, things can soon get confused and fiddly. For example, if you plan on shooting and editing a ten-minute short film, this may require you filming hundreds of shots. This is fine and dandy if you have no memory issues. However, trying to keep track of those shots within your iMovie browser, for example, can be very challenging. Trying to find the clips you need on a section of a small screen can be frustrating and it's easy to lose track of things. Any professional editor will tell you this is no way to edit, as it's important to have your clips arranged in a logical and easily searchable manner. This isn't the case with smartphone editing. Everything is lumped in the same place, making it hard to find what you are looking for, or even recognize the clips you have selected.

Equally, it can be hard to see your edit timeline in its entirety or at least to a level where you know what is what. It's worth remembering that most professional film and video editors will be working from at least a couple of full-sized computer monitor screens, comprised of the editing application's clip and output viewer screens plus an external TV monitor. With a smartphone, well, it's just the screen – and a rather small one at that. All this makes for a very challenging edit for anything consisting of more than a few shots.

What's more, there may be no ability to adjust picture brightness, adjust colour for shots with poor white balance, or boost the audio. Beyond a few pre-set effects, there may not be much you can do to enhance your picture and audio quality.

Be warned!

This shouldn't distract from the fact smartphones are seen by many as a bona fide film making camera. This is underlined by a handful of established directors using them and the numerous gadgets and accessories out there, such as hand mounts, stabilizers and clip-on zoom lenses, aimed at enhancing their capabilities. Also, several news channels around the world do rely on them for news reporting. It's perhaps in this context that smartphones are the complete package. You can film a report on them, edit on them, then, via the web, file your report by mailing it back to HQ for broadcast. This is all in stark contrast to 'regular' news crews requiring a full filming crew, outside broadcast van with editing suite, and some kind of satellite or microwave link for transmitting the final report.

GOPRO

'Yeah! GoPro' – we've all seen the ads. You can strap them on your head and film yourself base-jumping off the local rock formations into rapids. That's all they're good for, right?

There was a time early on when this camera range seemed a bit on the limited side and marketed solely at the extreme sports crowd.

As with smartphones, they have evolved far beyond their original remit and become altogether more capable. And, like many other 'non-traditional' cameras, they do offer the low-budget film maker a great deal of flexibility. Also, like smartphones, they are small, meaning that they can easily be used in situations that would spell the death of, or be impossible for, a large professional format.

Aided by their impact-proof cases, they can be sent into dangerous situations such as being fastened to the hilt of a sword so as to give a sword's-tip view of a medieval combat or being strapped to the side of a dirt bike going over sand dunes. This means that they are popular for drone filming owing to their size, low weight and picture quality. In Peter Jackson's second *Hobbit* film, *The Desolation of Smaug*, GoPro cameras were used for the 'barrel chase' scene.

Yet, there's nothing wrong with using them for more sedate scenes, too. Just like smartphones, there can be some drawbacks with this format owing to limitations with the manual controls and audio. However, they do give very high picture quality and should be considered as a low-budget option for the aspiring film maker.

As with smartphones, the range has evolved since the first models were released and now the cameras do come with more controls and audio options. However, since the GoPro was designed primarily as an action camera that was supposed to be attached to surfaces with suction mounts and so on, it can be fiddly to use. Finding a way to mount it effectively on a tripod could mean that you are relying on some kind of Gorilla Grip and crouching down to use it, or putting it all on a higher surface like a table in order to film at head height or similar. Also, some are put off by its very small, almost matchbox size. In some circles this automatically classes the camera as a kind of toy or gimmick. For others, though, the small size allows the camera to be used very energetically. Not to mention that it can be easily placed in your pocket or small carry bag.

In short, as with smart phones, there is absolutely nothing wrong with using this type of camera. It just means that you may need to be a bit more creative with your film making in order to bring out the camera's best features.

Remember this: A final word

Any talk about camera formats can get confusing. The bottom line you should consider is this: can my camera film clear, high-resolution images?

If the answer is 'yes', then you are doing well.

One area in which less capable and lower-res 'cameras' hold the absolute advantage is when you want to convince your audience that what they are seeing is 'real' and 'dangerous'. Think about it – whenever you watch some news or YouTube amateur footage of a disaster, catastrophe, civil unrest, or something else unpleasant, the footage can sometimes be very fuzzy, out of focus, very confused-looking and generally difficult to watch. Mobile phone, iPod cameras and the like really come into their own here.

If you are trying to film a mock disaster and make it look real, the psychological impact of using one of these camera systems on your audience is immense. As soon as the viewer sees this kind of footage, they will automatically associate it with seeing news footage, or poor-quality clips off the Internet, and in turn will consider it to be realistic.

The film *Cloverfield* (dir. Matt Reeves, 2008) played on this effect. The footage was made to look as though it had all been shot on a small, low-quality camcorder constantly shaking and being used by people in a panic.

In a way, this effect can cause people to imagine things they can't necessarily see. By only having small pieces of distinguishable footage, the audience crave to see more or fill in the blanks with their own preconceptions. In this regard, horror films are a perfect platform for this kind of camera psychology.

The 2009 horror films *Fourth Kind* (dir. Olatunde Osunsanmi) and *Paranormal Activity* (dir. Oren Peli) both relied heavily on using similar camera techniques. Much of these films' look and feel related to footage of spooky happenings involving ghosts and aliens, supposedly shot on surveillance and other traditionally low-quality cameras. By employing this technique, the film makers were playing on the fact that an audience confronted with such footage will associate it with being real – and for a horror film, a director couldn't wish for more.

Also spare a thought for older video camera formats, such as VHS, which can now be picked up for pennies. As with the systems above they can provide a very convincing cheap and old look, as if the footage was filmed decades ago – useful for faking an old news report or 'lost footage'.

Closing thoughts on cameras

Navigating your way through the labyrinth of cameras, formats and technology can be a dizzying experience. For those of you with little or no prior camera knowledge, it can often be difficult to decide what system, make and model to choose.

DON'T BE MISLED BY TECHNOLOGY

Many people will purchase sophisticated camera systems in the misguided belief that they will make great films for them, even though they know very little about operating a camera. I have known people who have purchased incredibly expensive and modern camera systems with which to film incredibly simple presentations. The results have been embarrassing to watch. It was almost as if these people expected the camera to do the work for them. Nine times out of ten, people just leave the camera's setting on automatic and merrily film away without a thought about the poor-quality footage they are producing (more on this in the next chapter).

GET SOMETHING YOU ARE COMFORTABLE USING

Since your camera is an essential part of your film making arsenal, it is very important that you feel comfortable handling it and using its controls. If you are looking at cameras in an electronics store and there is something about a model you don't like, such as a button in an awkward place or a control that's hard to reach, then look at something else. After all, you are the one who is going to be using it.

HOW EXPENSIVE IS IT?

A basic consideration, but it's important to put a cap on your technology spending. If you blithely go towards the latest technology and model then you will end up spending a considerable sum. If your budget is limited, then give a thought to some of the 'older' digital formats such as plain old MiniDV. These cameras are very capable, producing great images, and have some decent features ideal for the low-budget film maker. Also, some of them tend to be rather cheap.

CAN I GET THE MEDIA FOR IT EASILY?

This may seem obvious, but there's no point investing in an affordable camera (or otherwise) only to discover that the tapes, discs or drives for it are expensive or hard to come by. After all, in the course of making your masterpiece you may need a large supply of these things.

HOW MOBILE IS IT?

Depending on how strenuous your film is, and where you need to go, having a camera system that is easy to carry around is a handy thing to have. To be honest, most cameras you can purchase on the high street can fit into a large coat pocket. However, when you've accounted for all the accessories you may need to take with it, it can sometimes be a shock to discover you need a wheelbarrow to carry it all around!

Above all, don't develop a complex over the camera you have chosen, or look longingly at the next generation, or automatically upgrade to the latest release and so on. Ask yourself these simple questions: does it record images, can it record sound, and can you edit from it? If you can answer 'yes' to these three questions, then you have a decent camera.

Focus points

* Try to get hold of a video system – they are much easier, and cheaper, to use than film.
* Decide on the format you want to use – and stick to it.
* If using a non-tape format, ensure you have ample storage for your footage.
* Know where all the controls are and learn how to use them.
* If you plan on using plug-in microphones, make sure the camera has the appropriate inputs.
* Don't worry that you are not using a state-of-the-art camera system.
* Give some thought to using mobile phones, iPods or similar formats if suited to your film's script.
* Check that the format you are using is going to be compatible with the edit system you will use.
* Think about how your camera's capabilities can impart a special mood and style to your film.
* Always use the manual settings – they can help you achieve better results.

Next step

You need to know how to look after your camera – it is often a very expensive piece of equipment, and you've probably grown to love it like a good friend. In return for your care, it offers you some effective techniques and tricks of the trade.

Using your camera

In this chapter you will learn:

- ▶ *how to look after your camera*
- ▶ *some basic and effective camera techniques*
- ▶ *fantastic and easy film tricks and 'cheats'*

Anyone know how to use this thing?

A script, camera and people are the essential components of making a film; look on anything else you manage to get hold of as a bonus. Therefore, it is imperative that you learn how to use the camera you have chosen to the limit of its ability. The reason for this is that technical details, such as camera operation, can be learned – it is an objective quantity. However, creativity, which of course you already have, is something you cannot learn. You either have it or you don't.

Making a film is about combining creativity and technology, so it is vitally important that you learn to use your camera. Being able to combine your creativity with the know-how to use a certain camera format will make you very formidable when you are creating your film.

If you don't know how to use a camera, you will find yourself severely limited when the time comes to start filming. You may have to rely on someone who may not be creative and is more interested in the latest technology. Also, you may find it incredibly difficult and frustrating trying to communicate your vision of how to film a certain scene or shot to the operator. Some people just view a camera as a neat bit of kit, others see it as something to help make something entertaining and enjoyable to look at.

Learning camera skills

One of the massive mistakes a new camera owner/operator will make in the early days of getting their camera, or possibly throughout their entire time with it, is to use the camera without paying any attention to the camera's settings and features.

Each time a new camera model is marketed, one of the key features mentioned is how fantastic its automatic functions are. Everything from adjusting the brightness of the picture, the focus and even steadying the image are all handled by the inner workings of the camera itself. Now, this is a very appealing thing for a consumer looking to buy a camera. After all, who wants to bother with adjusting the intricate functions and features on a camera? The answer is, you do. If you are to be a serious film maker at any level, then you need to look beyond these 'tricks' and get to know your camera in a bit more depth.

In the previous chapter we took a look at the 'big three': white balance, exposure and focus. We learned what they did and what effect they have on your footage. The important point to get across is that they must be adjusted manually at all times. As a camera operator, it is your (or whoever is doing it) responsibility to ensure the best quality footage is obtained at all times. Therefore, these three functions need to be understood and learned for the type of camera you have.

Even the most basic consumer camcorder has these features, yet it is amazing that very few people ever bother with them. Before each shot you must take stock of what kind of lighting you are in, what the brightness level is like and which part of the picture needs to be focused on. If not, your footage will forever be changing in brightness, going in and out of focus and possibly changing colour depending on the white balance considerations.

Being aware of these considerations will also have an impact on your filming. Whereas a clueless amateur camcorder user may simply follow someone walking around a house and in the process take a shot lasting several minutes, a person who knows their camera's functions will consider the filming set-up in a different way.

For example, they will know that if they go from inside to outside the exposure will have to be adjusted from the dark interior to the bright outdoors. Also, they will have to adjust the white balance. Realizing this, they will then know to film the interior section in one shot, or a series of shots, and then adjust the camera's setting for filming the outdoor shots. By filming in such a way, there will not be the sudden changes in brightness and white balance that will make the footage look amateur and plain awkward to watch.

When you are aware of what your camera can do, you will in turn know that certain conditions have requirements you need to factor in.

Key idea

One of the most important factors in relation to filming in any given location is usually the light. Knowing what levels of light your camera can and can't handle is very important.

Getting to know your camera

As you will keep hearing throughout this book, there is more to using your camera than switching it on and pressing the record button. All cameras, from consumer camcorders to professional models, come with instructions. It's always a good idea to look through these instructions just in case there is anything you don't understand or in case there are any operational idiosyncrasies.

The next step is to use your camera in a series of test exercises to help you understand how you and the camera work together. I have often seen several people use the same camera over the course of a day, and each individual's ability with using, and simply carrying, the camera differed wildly. In other words, get comfortable using your camera.

POISE AND HOLD

The simplest, yet most overlooked, consideration is holding your camera while filming. Although we will talk about using tripods later, sometimes it is necessary to film 'hand-held'. Now, it's impossible to film in this manner without having some degree of shake and movement. The trick is to make any movements slow and smooth instead of panicked and rapid. You may wish to lean against a wall, hold one elbow to steady the arm holding the camera, or cup the camcorder in both hands to steady it. Whatever works best for you – use it. Also, don't forget to breathe when hand-held filming. Many inexperienced camera users stop breathing when they press the record button and then only exhale when they stop recording. Holding a steady camera is all about being relaxed; you won't be if you are gasping for air.

An exercise you could try is to film a distinctive object a certain distance away and see how long you can keep it in the centre of your viewfinder or flip-out screen.

PRACTISE FOCUS

Selecting various objects in front of you and adjusting the focus for each one is a great way of getting the hang of focus. You could set a few things down on a table at varying distances away from the lens and take turns focusing in on each one. Next, you could put two distinctive objects in an off-kilter line in front of the lens (two candles for example) and pull focus from one to the other. This is a film making stalwart, and if you can master this technique you are half way to being a great camera operator.

Pull focuses can also be practised over a greater distance. Try doing one that goes from a nearby wall to a city skyline, for example.

Just be aware that many consumer camcorders have simple lenses. Therefore, you may need to either zoom in slightly to start adjusting focus for objects at different distances from the lens, or physically place the camera very close to the nearest object, for this focus exercise to work properly.

FAST DRAW EXPOSURE

Try quickly moving the camera from the inside of the room to looking at the window. See how fast you can adjust the exposure so that both views are correctly exposed. Also, try doing the same again, but this time adjusting the white balance if there is bright artificial lighting in the room.

LEAVE THAT ZOOM BUTTON ALONE

The zoom controls on a camera are very tempting to use. On a consumer camcorder (and many prosumer cameras) they are positioned near to where the fingers of your right hand rest. It is therefore easy to feel almost obliged to use them constantly. Don't!

In professional film making and camera operation, zooms are not very common. You may see only a handful in any given production, and where you do they have some meaning and purpose. If you use the zoom all the time, your footage will look crazed and amateurish, and be disorienting.

Try to be a responsive camera operator. When filming actors and people in general, things can get very animated. Often someone will move out of frame slightly or tilt their head. The wrong thing to do is to wait for them to re-enter the frame or to suddenly 'jerk' the camera to get them back in shot. Try to be smooth with your camera movements, and if someone does exit the frame, try to anticipate this and move gently to accommodate.

Key idea: Camera zombies

When someone first picks up a video camera and begins filming, it is common for them to mutate into a 'camera zombie'. A camera zombie is a person who holds the camera close up against their face and then walks around slowly filming everything as if they are scanning the world around them. Normal cognitive abilities are forgotten as the camera seems to act like some kind of tranquillizer. The user becomes a docile creature relying on the camera to process what is around, instead of using the camera to create something exciting.

It is only natural for a beginner to use a camera in this way, as this is how humans process the world. Every day since childhood our eyes have been recording things around us in long swathes. However, when we pick up the camera we have to 'unlearn' this habit. Good camera work is quite the opposite; only small interesting pieces of the world are noteworthy to the film maker.

Looking after your camera

Once you have obtained your camera and learned some basic techniques, there are a few things that you should get into the habit of doing.

GUARDING YOUR CAMERA

An important rule to remember is to keep an eye on your kit at all times. It's not surprising that cameras and the associated paraphernalia attract a lot of attention from passers-by and those in the area. Not all of this attention is favourable. There has been many a film crew out at night filming a documentary who have turned around to find that the tripod is missing or there's no camera. Owing to the legal and bureaucratic nature of television and film companies today, there's usually some form that has to be filled in before a crew can go out. One of the risks on these forms includes 'theft' – it's a major threat in cities and other places.

I know of one tale of woe concerning a film crew who were making a gritty film about life on unemployment benefit and poor housing on a notorious British housing project. The director thought he knew it all and disregarded the warnings of the local fixer (person who sets up and arranges things) by retorting, 'Don't bother me. I've been to Beirut, I've been shot!' As the crew were introducing themselves to the owners of a property, the van they had come in was broken into and all their gear was stolen. All this happened in the space of one minute from a distance of about 50 feet / 15 metres.

TRANSPORTING YOUR CAMERA

Use the carry case that comes with the camera. If your camera didn't come with such an accessory, then try to improvise one from something. I don't need to tell you that a camera is one of the most important things when making a film – look after it. It's often tempting to carry the camera clutched in one hand as you go from place to place, or have it slung around your neck like some obscene medallion. Such treatment will shorten the life of your camera. Remember that modern cameras are made up of largely fragile and precisely made components. Jolts, bumps and drops can stop them from working.

There is probably some bag at home you can use, otherwise a cheap camera case from a photography store or Internet shop should suit your camera's needs.

BEWARE OF THE ELEMENTS

Protecting your camera against the elements is another thing to consider if you are planning on filming outside. Cameras do not like water, especially video cameras. All it takes is one drop of water to ruin things and effectively scupper your plans. The best way to avoid this is simply not to go filming when it starts to rain. However, there may be times when this is not an option and you will have to obtain some kind of protection.

Since professional camera rain and water protection 'jackets' cost a fortune, and they don't exist for domestic cameras, the tried-and-tested method is to use a decent quality and sturdy plastic bag. Although crude and a bit messy to use, it is very effective. Just place an appropriate-sized plastic bag over the camera 'poncho style', then cut holes for the lens and viewfinder. Use some electrical/duct tape to seal and waterproof the joins. I once used this method while filming a car rally one rainy day, wedged between two international news camera crews, and although my waterproofing method looked embarrassing in such prestigious company, it did the job brilliantly.

The drawback with this method is that it can be awkward when you need to change tapes (if using a MiniDV camera, for example). This is a procedure best done inside, as the pervading dampness in the air can get into your camera and jam the mechanism for a while.

Remember this

Avoid rain, is the lesson here – even the slightest hazy drizzle can build up on your camera's plastic exterior and turn into a mini torrent that invariably makes a beeline straight for the master electronic circuits.

Still on the same subject, one way that rain conspires to ruin filming is by leaving droplets on the lens. In the madness of filming, these tiny conspirators are very hard to notice. Although the larger of them can be seen and carefully wiped off the lens with an appropriate material, their smaller brethren are invisible both on the lens and in the viewfinder. Therefore, when you look back at what you have filmed on a television, there will be a drop awkwardly covering the left eye of your lead actor or hanging mysteriously in the air above your actors like a surreal spacecraft. They really can spoil things. This is one of the reasons why people use monitors (see Chapter 6). To guard against rain droplets getting on the lens while filming, it is advisable to use a hood.

Another environmental problem is filming somewhere cold and damp when condensation forms on the lens. This is easy to remove, with a careful wipe of the lens or by letting the lens 'breathe' for a few moments. The only reason I mention this is because it formed on my camera lens when I was filming a restaurant scene in a half-derelict cellar and I thought the camera was suffering a major fault.

Last on this list of dangers to your camera is bright sunlight. Although it is the friend of all film makers (see the section on well-lit scenes in Chapter 6), I have known a few small cameras to literally be cooked and effectively destroyed by the heat of the sun. Many cameras are black= or dark-coloured, and this is a disadvantage when it is very sunny as the camera will become progressively hotter. It is not unheard of for the heat to reach levels where it has buckled and warped a spooling mechanism, melted a tape or simply 'fried' some circuit. So once again, cover your camera with a suitable material (e.g. a white cloth) if you consider the weather too hot.

Key idea

If using tapes, discs or media that can be written on, ensure that you label them clearly before you start filming. All too often, impetuous film makers will start recording images without taking the time to accurately write basic information on the discs or tapes. This means that things can get lost or forgotten in piles of blank media, which has to be sifted through and viewed just so you can find what you are looking for.

Camera toys

Wherever there are cameras, and camera shops, there will always be camera toys, or accessories as they are more commonly known. Some of these accessories are freakish contraptions that have no place in the kingdom of cameras, whereas others can be helpful aids to your film making.

It is sometimes jaw-dropping and hilarious to see enthusiastic amateurs piling various add-ons on to their camera until it is hidden under a heap of gadgets, wires and extensions that have little use other than to make the camera look like a hot-rod. Avoid this.

So what things are available and why do you need them?

TRIPODS

Everyone knows what a tripod is, but not everyone uses them, either through ignorance or laziness. Tripods are the accessory to give you steady shots, pans (going side to side) and tilts (going up and down). Decent tripods can be incredibly cheap, whereas a professional one will be surprisingly expensive. When choosing a tripod make sure that it can be set up without slowly sliding down again and that the head can move smoothly either vertically or horizontally. Also, make sure that it is tall enough to suit your needs. Generally, it should be high enough that when fully raised with a camera attached it is almost at head height. Look for spirit levels as a feature of the tripod so you can tell when it is level.

DEPTH OF FIELD (DOF) ADAPTOR

One of the big gadgets that has turned heads and transformed humble camcorders into something more capable is the DoF adaptor. This is an add-on lens that enables you to achieve shallow depth of field shots. The DoF adaptor is a device designed to make your footage look slicker and movie-like. Owing to the limitations of some camcorder lenses and image chips, it is sometimes hard to get a shallow depth of field (see Chapter 4).

The film *28 Days Later*, which famously used a MiniDV camera, also used a (rather large) DoF adaptor.

WIDE-ANGLE LENSES

As accessories go, these are perhaps the most practical item to get hold of. In fact many film makers tend to buy one of these above anything else. As the name suggests, a wide-angle lens will increase your camera's field of view by a certain proportion depending on its specification. They can be very useful when filming in a confined space and for showing vistas of the countryside or cityscapes. Their one disadvantage is something called 'vignetting'. This is when the lens gives such a wide view it actually makes the edges of the lens itself visible.

SHOULDER PODS

Shoulder pods are another gadget some film makers choose to use. A shoulder pod is a platform that can be shoulder mounted which the camera is then fastened to. Not only does this give smoother and steadier hand-held filming, but pods can often engage with the LANC jack in certain cameras so that zoom, focus and other functions can be controlled by keys on the hand-holds of the pod.

Many modern camcorders are rather small, and one disadvantage of their size is that some people find it difficult to get a decent steady shot when filming hand-held.

Key idea

So you think you have a cool camera? Then take the Google image test! When thinking of choosing a camera, it is sometimes useful and fun to do a Google image search. If a picture of it turns up with various pro/prosumer accessories attached to it, then chances are enough serious film makers rate it highly enough to warrant such add-ons.

MINI STEADICAMS

These are small pistol-like devices attached to your camera as a tripod would be. They are balanced to give a smooth motion when being used hand-held by a camera operator walking to follow actors or going through the rooms of a house.

LENS HOOD

A lens hood is a simple and generally always usable accessory. It's usually very cheap, too. It is an inert attachment screwed on to the lens. Its purpose is to shield your footage from stray light and it also gives a little bit of protection to the lens in light rain conditions.

A FRENCH FLAG

Despite its name, a French flag is not from France, nor is it a flag. Essentially, it is a larger version of a lens hood; however, it can consist of up to four separate 'fins' that can be adjusted to various angles in order to shield the camera lens from flares of light that may otherwise creep into frame. For consumer and prosumer cameras, French flags are available that consist of only the top fin.

MATTE BOX

This is a follow-on from the French flag, but it allows for large-sized coloured glass or plastic filters to be held in place just in front of the lens. These filters can be easily and quickly put in place or removed.

Key idea

The French flag and matte box can be large and heavy contraptions. On professional movie cameras, they are held in place by rods extending from the top of the tripod. On consumer and prosumer cameras, they are usually light enough to be screwed to the lens thread.

VIEW SCREEN HOOD

A nice and simple accessory is the view screen hood. When filming in bright conditions, it can often be hard to see clearly what is on the view screen due to the sunlight being reflected. The view screen hood fits on to the flip-out view screen and provides cover and shade, enabling you to see what is going on. Although many cameras have a view screen and a viewfinder, many modern consumer camcorders have only the screen. Therefore, on a sunny day you don't have the option of looking through the viewfinder. For this reason, it can be a very practical thing to have.

As with many things in film making, get these gadgets only if you think you really need them. Buying all of these tools and toys can be very expensive. However, some of them can be easily improvised from household materials.

Those amazing film makers with their flying machines – drones

One innovation that has been embraced and fully exploited by the film making community is the drone. The ability to place a high-resolution video camera on a small flying machine that can hover, move horizontally, vertically and in all other directions is a boon to the film maker.

Key idea: What is a drone?

In film making a drone is a small four rotor bladed remote controlled flying device that can have a camera attached to it. Depending on the sophistication of the drone, the camera can either be in a fixed position or on gimbal that can pan and tilt. The drone is operated by a person on the ground.

Before drone technology, the available options for getting high-altitude moving shots, or a smooth tilt-like shot up a tall building, either meant that you had to hire a helicopter or a cherry picker. These are very expensive things to do and only big-budget productions can afford a specially adapted helicopter with a special filming pod under the nose that could fit a camera in it. Even then, the shots may suffer from jitter as a result of the mechanical movements of the aircraft. Plus, if you are trying to film relatively close to the ground, the downdraft from the rotor blades can blow away, endanger or severely disrupt whatever was below, including actors, props and lights. Not good.

Even the comparatively cheaper option of using a cherry picker may give poor results, as there are limits to the places it can access. In addition, the shake and wobble as it gets higher and further extended can compromise shots. And of course it can only go so high. Having filmed in them many times, standing in a swaying cab a hundred metres above the ground while trying to line up shots, I can say that it wasn't my cup of tea.

For these reasons, and more, drones have found a very wide niche within film making. Gone are the days when you did have to hire a helicopter to get that lovely shot over the countryside; instead, you can buy a drone, hook up your GoPro (or whatever) and merrily film away for a tiny fraction of the cost of renting a chopper. No need for an airfield, fuel costs, technicians to fit the camera into its gimbal, a pilot and flight plans. The flexibility of drones in film making speaks for itself.

Yet, it's not only as a cheap helicopter surrogate that drones can be useful. They can also dispense with the need for other exotic pieces of film making kit such as cranes, jibs, dollies and other devices designed for giving some smooth and interesting camera moves to a shot.

For example, if you had a scene in a film where two people are walking along the edge of a cliff, a drone could fly over the drop and smoothly track the actors as they walk. Quite possibly this could be a stunning shot and one unachievable by other means. Not to mention the fact that no one would be endangered, as the dangerous job is being done by a machine. Likewise, a shot with someone running up the fire escape on the outside of a building could be filmed with a drone. Instead of a crane or cherry picker being used, the drone could fly vertically, matching the rate at which the actor is running upwards. What's more, you can film high-altitude cityscapes or panoramas of the countryside, thereby providing your production with some epic images (if the weather is clear).

As drones have become more and more popular, many jurisdictions have brought in laws and other controls that oversee their usage. For example, you can't use them within a certain distance of airports, or you may need a licence to operate them within certain municipal districts. If the drone is over a certain size, it may be banned altogether. There are also considerations about privacy, if you plan on flying near buildings or public places. Some countries are even rolling out plans for drone pilots to be qualified in order to fly them. For this reason, you may need to do some research, depending on where you live, to learn what operating restrictions exist.

Drones do require the weather to be relatively calm to get the best results. Specifically, owing to their relatively small size, they can be particularly susceptible to wind. If you try to operate one in high wind, not only will the drone itself be jerking around in the sky as you try to control it, but the camerawork will likewise be jerky. Furthermore, very strong winds can simply blow the drone outside the range of the remote control, meaning you and your crew may have to spend the rest of the day looking for it.

Remember this

Let's not forget that drones do have the potential to damage property and hurt people if there is an accident. Something you need to be very careful of.

Do bear in mind that the kind of camera you get for your drone could be of considerably different quality from the one you are using on the rest of your film. While the latest GoPro camera, or better, fitted to your drone would give some good results, it may well be that your budget only allows you to get a basic model with a correspondingly not-so-high-quality camera. Therefore, while your drone work may be ambitious in terms of flying it around your actors, or above the countryside, the resulting footage may be poor in terms of the resolution and definition. This could be a difference that could really jolt with the rest of your film if you cut back and forth from something shot on a high-end Sony 4K camera and to a video shot on a budget RunCam drone camera.

Key idea: Do you really need a drone?

A final word on drones is to consider whether you need one or not. They've been so popular that they've almost taken on a kind of novelty must-have factor. They can give some spectacular results, but is it essential for your film? Just because they are an option doesn't mean you have to use one. After obtaining a drone, you may find yourself putting lots of gratuitous aerial footage in your film for no good reason. What's more, if you can't guarantee footage of the drone's camera will match the quality of the rest of your production, you should critically assess what advantage it will bring to your film.

Key idea: The grip

Who is the grip? Who is this mysterious film making technician with the bizarre job title? Now all shall be explained.

The grip is the person responsible for ensuring the camera is properly and safely on its mount. At the simplest level this means that the camera is put on a tripod. However, don't forget there are many complicated camera mounts – moving cranes, wheeled dollies, things with gyroscopes, cameras attached to the underside of helicopters and all manner of challenging situations. Sometimes their work is near enough construction and engineering combined. So, next time you see a smooth shot in difficult circumstances, thank the grips.

Basic filming techniques

USING A TRIPOD

When using a small camcorder, you can attach it to the end of a tripod, as per usual, and create quite an interesting film 'tool'. I discovered this trick by sheer accident one day and found that this set-up allows you to use the camera like a simple crane. For example, you can fix the tripod to its maximum extension and then hold it by the 'feet', which allows you to have the camera a considerable distance above your head (see Figure 5.1). With this you could film over a tall wall, in the branches of a tree, or you could just spin it around, depending on what you wanted to do. It's like having an 'eye' on the top of a pole.

Figure 5.1

You can manipulate it, twist it and swing it around to get an incredible range of views and shots that would otherwise require some very specialist and expensive equipment. Even then it would be rather slow-moving compared with this method. You can also suddenly and dramatically increase the height of the shot, by holding on to the base of the tripod and shoving it into the air – making sure that the camera is pointing at your subject, of course. For example, you could have a shot of a man walking down the street and raise the height of the camera as he's moving along (see Figures 5.2 and 5.3). Such a suddenly moving shot would be very powerful and would give your film a really strong style. Using this method you could also film a fast, frenetic party by swinging, increasing height, shoving in between people and so on. This method can add a new dimension to your films.

Figure 5.2

Figure 5.3

Video cameras that have flip-out view screens really come into their own with these techniques as you don't have to rely on the viewfinder to see what you are filming. Perhaps you can think of some other moves using this method.

Not only is there the energetic shot element to this 'camera rig', but it has the advantage of being a steadier way of filming. When you hold the camcorder in both hands and clutch it close to your chest, every step and move you make will result in a very shaky and bumpy picture. Using this 'crane' method, you create a much more fluid picture. For example, say you are using the camcorder to film someone from the side as they walk down the street (see Figure 5.4). If you were holding the camera close to your chest and squinting intensely into the viewfinder, not only would the shot be rather bumpy but you would also risk falling over or walking into a lamp post. With the camera on the tripod, you can hold it by the 'neck' and just point the camera at the subject while alternating between looking at what you are filming and where you are going.

The shot will tend to be steadier as your elbow acts as a kind of 'damper', with the tripod legs acting as a 'counter-weight', so reducing the shake. With some practice you will soon learn what your camera's field of vision is and improve your method for keeping things steady.

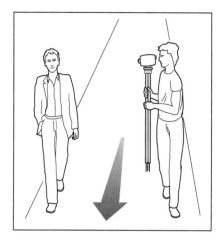

Figure 5.4

Another great trick is to 'walk the camera'. Most camcorders should come with a shoulder strap for carrying the camera around. If you hold the middle of the camera strap in one hand and walk with the camera close to the ground, it produces a great visual effect similar to the point of view of a roving animal or baby crawling across the floor. Or perhaps in your film it could be the perspective of a small remote-control device scurrying across the floor of a top-secret installation.

USING COLOURED FILTERS

Another tip to make your camerawork more interesting is to use coloured filters – easily obtainable from your nearest quality photographic shop. They can either screw on to your camera's lens using the existing thread, be attached by use of an adaptor or be placed in the matte box as mentioned before. Even simpler (and cheaper), you could just hold some flat, coloured plastic sheet in front of the lens.

Using filters adds a sometimes surreal or moody effect to a shot. For example, imagine if you were in a disused quarry and you were to hold a piece of red-coloured glass in front of your eyes – you'd have an instant alien planet. Or if you were in a wood and did the same with dark-blue glass – you'd have a night-time effect just like in an old film.

Not all filters are one uniform colour across the glass; some are graduated. These filters have a coloured strip at the top that fades in colour down the glass. So, if you were to film something with it, such as a landscape shot of a field, the sky would be tinged with a certain colour, while the ground would be normal, leaving the buildings or actors you were filming untouched. Have a look at any Jerry Bruckheimer-produced blockbusters (*The Rock, Con Air, Gone in 60 Seconds, Black Hawk Down*) to see how cool and delicious graduated filters can be when used in some shots. There is actually a quarry I know of that, with the use of filters, has been used for several different alien planets (for the same television series) as well as a Roman gladiatorial arena.

TRICKS WITH FILM

To give a shot a bit of bite, try out something known as the 'Dutch tilt'. This is a very simple and effective camera technique achieved by using a tripod with one leg shorter than the rest – or by just resting it on the ground and tilting it. This has the effect of making everything seem to be at an angle (the steepness will depend on how you have set up the camera). This can make things look creepy, disturbing, unnatural and downright funky. It is also a good way of exaggerating the height of something. If you have a tilt looking upwards at a building, or even a person, the effect will be near giddying. Simple and effective. Try it out.

Staying with tilting cameras, a clever and funny way to simulate someone climbing up a steep cliff, or the outside of a building, is to place your camera on its side on an appropriate surface. This will make the ground appear as a vertical surface, and you can then have your actors stooping forwards, pulling themselves 'up' on a rope. Anyone who has watched the 1960s series *Batman* will have seen this in most episodes. Be careful, however, not to arrange the shot so that trees are growing horizontally out of the 'mountain'.

If you want to create the impression that someone in your film is being watched or stalked, film through some bushes or tree leaves. This will automatically feel as if someone is hiding and spying on a character.

Finally, there comes one of my favourite tricks: move in, zoom out, aka 'The Trombone'. You may have witnessed this slightly unsettling effect in a few films, but one of the most famous examples is in *Jaws* (dir. Stephen Spielberg, 1975), when Roy Scheider's character is on the beach and there are shouts of 'Shark!' from the water. The camera rushes up to him, but it appears as though the background is expanding.

This effect is achieved by moving the camera directly towards your actor, while at the same time zooming out with your camera. It's an effect that even the cheapest camcorder can manage. It takes a bit of practice and helps if the move towards the actor is smooth and in a straight line, and the speed of the zoom out equals the move of the camera. Simple and free.

Get to know your camera, experiment with it and make sure it works hard for you!

Remember this: I didn't film that!

A surprise awaiting you when you start your edit can be the strange realization that your footage contains things you can't remember filming. For example, a shot of an actor may have part of a tree visible which you are certain you framed out. This is simply that your camera's scan is actually larger than what appears in the viewfinder or flip-out screen. This only becomes noticeable when played through a computer and will be invisible if played through a television. For Internet uploading it can be a big issue, so always try to compensate for this extra margin of picture if possible.

Focus points

* ✳ Respect your camera; without it you have no film.
* ✳ Become comfortable holding and filming with your camera.
* ✳ Ensure that you have enough recording media for each day's shooting or that you have a way to download.
* ✳ Make sure your batteries are fully charged.
* ✳ Carry the mains power lead if filming inside so you can use any sockets available.
* ✳ Check your camera before each shoot to guarantee everything is working.
* ✳ Always try to be creative with your camera work.
* ✳ Always give serious consideration about when to use and when not to use the tripod.
* ✳ Think about what tricks and effects you can get from your camera.
* ✳ It is you who makes the film, not the camera.

Next step

In Chapter 6 we turn to the issue of light and lighting. Without light you will have a bad looking film, and poor lighting can ruin an otherwise good scene or entire film. However, excellent results can generally be achieved using relatively simple means.

6

Lights and lighting

In this chapter you will learn:

▶ *about the different types of lights available*

▶ *how to achieve superb lighting effects with minimum resources*

▶ *a few basic safety tips for you, your cast and crew*

This room's rather dark!

Not only will you need a camera to film your masterpiece, but you will also need some kind of illumination. You don't need huge lighting rigs, and it's quite possible that you already have a suitable light in your house that will effectively illuminate what you are filming.

Depending on the light sensitivity of the camera you are using, and the mood you want to achieve, there are lots of ways to improvise. I would suggest starting off with as much light on set as possible and then, if required, work your way down. For example, if you have bright lights that are blinding everyone, all you need to do is turn them round or switch a couple off to obtain the desired effect. However, trying to squeeze more power out of a candle is impossible.

Key idea

If you think you won't be able to afford strong lights for your indoor scenes, identify locations with large windows. In the absence of strong artificial lights, having plenty of daylight is the next best thing.

Lighting your set

Most camcorders and smaller film cameras have built-in lights, or slots for external lights, that you can use to illuminate what's directly in front of the camera. However, if the light is built in, it will drain your camera battery much more quickly than normal. It can also give the game away because the light will be shining merrily away on everything the camera is pointing at. Thus the audience will think, 'They've got a light on that camera.'

There is a flip side to this, however: a camera light does have an 'artistic' use as it's a good way of simulating someone's view as they walk slowly through a dark and deserted building at night, for example, with the light acting as a torch on a hard hat. Give it a go.

As a general rule, household lights tend to be ineffectual for video cameras. Although things may look bright enough to your eye, the view through your camera's viewfinder may be a dark, hazy sludge with shadows moving around. It's important to recognize what lighting will work, and what won't, with your camera. However, there are plenty of ways to increase the quality to half-decent levels.

Bedside and household lights can be very useful and you can change their brightness by fitting them with different wattage bulbs. Do check the maximum wattage information, which should be somewhere on the appliance, as some bedside lights aren't always happy with a high-wattage bulb and you could end up with an unanticipated 'special effect'!

Experiment using different coloured light bulbs, which can drastically alter moods (just as filters can outdoors). A red light can make things either erotic or evil, and a blue one will create a cold and haunting atmosphere.

Some good, reasonably priced all-rounders, which won't break the bank, are the powerful 300- or 500-watt halogen lights. They are available from most lighting retailers and hardware stores, and they produce good results. They can come with stands making them ideal for film sets as you can adjust the angle of the light. Although when you switch them on indoors you may find the light to be too intense, you have to realize that many small camcorders need a lot of help with light. They will immediately improve the quality of your footage by illuminating your actors instead of having them as half-lit shapes in the general gloom of your shot.

Remember this: Warning!

500-watt halogen lights (and higher wattage) get very hot, so if you want to adjust the angle of the light use an appropriate tool or a pair of safety gloves.

These powerful lights not only present handling problems, they can also make it very uncomfortable for the people on set. Sweat pouring down someone's face can cause unpleasant aesthetic problems in close-ups and, more importantly, some people have an unfortunate tendency to faint under such lighting. You would be surprised how many people pass out every week in television and film studios.

In addition, 500-watt halogen lights are very bright, so if you are in a small room filming an intimate romantic scene, the presence of such a powerful light might suggest to the audience that a hydrogen bomb has detonated nearby. Angling the light beam can correct this or you may want to bounce it off the ceiling or adjacent wall.

Depending on the kind of lights you want, pay very close attention to its needs. For example, a 500-watt light will not use a regular fuse. If you get things wrong you might plug it in and be met with a loud pop, a blue flash, a melted bulb, a blown fuse box and the irate comments of whoever owns or manages the building you are filming in. Try to get someone, preferably with a modicum of electrical know-how, to help you if you have your heart set on the more powerful lights.

Key idea

A good way to establish whether you are using too much light is to see if your actors squint and shade their eyes during a take.

Remember this: Safety tip

If you end up with a set of powerful lights, think about investing in a circuit breaker. This will prevent you overloading and blowing up a humble domestic electric system as it will cut out before an accident happens.

WHAT THE PROS USE

Basic lighting used for professional productions are products known as 'redheads' and 'blondes'. These are small-sized portable lights of a few hundred watts' power that are placed on tripod stands, which can be raised to varying height. Redhead lights have a red outer casing, while blonde lights have a blonde/yellow casing. Blonde lights tend to be more powerful, although both are used widely for the same lighting situations. They have 'barn doors' on them – these are metal doors that resemble flat rose petals, so that light coming from the bulb can be lessened or increased depending on their configuration. Coloured transparent paper called gels can be attached to these barn doors with bulldog clips to adjust the colour of the light. Also, pale, paper-like 'spun' gel can be placed over the lights to soften the effect and make it more diffused. As with 500-watt lights, these barn doors get very hot, so be careful when handling them! Some community camera suppliers hire out these portable lights at reasonable daily rates.

The choice of lighting available on professional productions doesn't stop with these portable lights though. Exotic things such as 'flying moons', which are large circular orbs hung high in the air to give illumination at night, are just one of the many things in the professional lighting department's arsenal.

Key idea: The gaffer and best boy

Who are these people? These two job roles relate to the electricians on a film set who deal with setting up and hooking up the various lighting arrays. The gaffer is the head of the electricians while the best boy is the second in line. I find it is a big morale booster to people on an otherwise small production to find out that they are in fact the gaffer or best boy instead of just 'the lighting guy'.

'THE LED IS YOUR FRIEND'

Recent developments in lighting and illumination technology have given the world some very useful new toys to play with.

For the low-budget and aspiring film maker, this means that there is no longer the requirement to either have low-quality improvised lighting or expensive and energy-hungry professional equipment.

As discussed, while some lighting found around the house may be just about OK for a vlog, it doesn't always cut it for video productions. They are just not strong enough to effectively illuminate a set. Likewise, professional lighting such as redheads or something from Arri (the world-famous German film equipment company) are very expensive to buy (although cheaper to rent if available), plus they can get dangerously hot. Furthermore, some of the more powerful lights may need qualified technical handling instead of just plugging into the nearest wall socket. So where does this leave you?

In exactly the same place as all other cash-strapped film makers – improvising and hunting around for cheaper alternatives.

One boon to such people is the range of LED lighting systems available today. Their versatility is such that they have been incorporated into pro lighting systems giving a very bright light without the heat of their halogen counterparts. However, such kits can be expensive. Luckily, many smaller alternatives are available that can fit on the top of your camera and give you decent illumination for subjects nearby your lens. Now, this is fine for vlogging, interviews and even, maybe, some dramatic scenes. However, if you want to light a scene, or at least a room, you need to think a bit differently.

A method you may consider is the use of LED light strips, as these are widely available in hardware stores and discount stores as well as many supermarkets and everywhere else in between. Importantly, they are very reasonably priced. While perhaps unorthodox, they can give the film maker some brilliant illumination. There is nothing wrong with taking a few strips of these lights and attaching them in parallel to some flat object such as a small square piece of wood or hard cardboard so that you can construct your own lighting rig.

As mentioned, these lights don't suffer from the same heat issues as halogens, so they won't suddenly burst into flames or start melting things midway through your shot. Also, depending on what product you get, you may be able to dim them and alter their colour – the latter, of course, could help you with white balance issues in certain filming environments so that you don't need to resort to using gels on the lights.

Key idea

Construct things to suit your budget. You may be happy with light strips arranged on something the size of a piece of A4 paper, but perhaps your aspirations are to build a behemoth key light on a roofing panel. The choice is yours.

Of course, you still have to think of a way to secure the lighting rig. Maybe you can simply prop it up on a table so it's the right height or leave it leaning against the wall sitting on the floor. Needless to say, if you want to mount on a tripod, then you'll have to build or improvise something else.

Take a look on YouTube for various tutorials showing how low-budget film makers have put together some great lighting rigs from LEDs.

THREE-POINT LIGHTING – THE CLASSIC SET-UP

A lot of film lighting revolves around the three-point set-up. It is a benchmark way of lighting people and is a great starting point to develop and experiment with other lighting effects. It gets its name from using three lights. These are called:

▶ the key light

▶ the fill light

▶ the backlight

The **key light** is placed a little way away from the camera and is pointed at the actor's face. The **fill light** is positioned a similar distance away on the other side of the camera. The effect of these two cameras is to fully light the actor's face and minimize any shadow. Finally, the **backlight** is placed out of the camera's view behind the actor. This light will create a 'halo' around the outline of the head and separate it from the background.

Key idea

A lot of film making uses the three-point lighting technique – from news reports, to horror films, to romantic comedies. It is the cornerstone of lighting your actors.

Once you have become familiar with this technique, try using only a couple of cameras and play around with the positioning (see below). It will produce some startling results.

Lighting effects

Lighting is something that all too often gets overlooked. First-time camera users have a tendency to start filming without having taken much stock of lighting requirements. If filming has taken place with low lighting levels then your footage will look hazy and grainy. It may also mean you experience focusing problems as you can't see what you are filming. Light is a vital ingredient in the film making recipe and, just as in any recipe, there are loads of ways to spice things up. Simple experimentation can produce some rather stunning effects.

The lighting effect for a particular scene is up to you. Do you want long shadows? Do you want it bright, or dark and dismal? As director, it's your say and you make all the decisions. Here are a few money-saving and improvised lighting effects that may inspire you to think of and dream up some of your own:

▶ **Simulating a group of people watching television.** Have a bright blue light shining on your actors and then quickly wave a piece of paper in front of it to simulate the changing pictures of a television. The light from a real television is rarely bright enough for filming.

▶ **Making a fire without a matchbox or gasoline.** Shine some powerful coloured lights, preferably orange and red, at your actors and then (like the effect above) wave some paper in front of it. The effect will produce flickering fiery light on your actor's faces.

▶ **Lightning outdoors.** Obtain aforementioned 500-watt lights, or something more powerful if possible, and then cover the light with a non-flammable material to make sure there is no 'light leakage'. Then, when you want lightning, uncover the light and then cover again as per the desired duration. Covering and uncovering the light is much preferable to switching the power on and off as this risks blowing the bulb. Be aware that lightning is usually accompanied by rain – water and powerful lighting don't really mix very well ... Also, light disperses rather quickly outdoors so your light will have to be relatively close to whatever you are filming to be effective.

▶ **Lightning 'indoors'.** Have the same set-up as above but place the light as close to a window as possible, while still allowing someone to cover and uncover the light. The lightning will shine through the window and into the set/room you are filming in but, since it is indoors, you won't have to worry about creating 'rain'.

▶ **Someone looking into shimmering water.** Shine a bright light on to a sizeable piece of reflective material, such as cooking foil, which has been crumpled and therefore reflects the light very unevenly. Then angle the reflective material so that the light bounces up into the actor's face and move it around slowly and rhythmically. The result will be that the actor's face is 'painted' with sparkling and moving points of light. One thing to mention here is that this trick is only effective on sunny days (otherwise where would the reflected light come from?) but can cause a problem as the lighting you are using may get lost in the natural sunlight, so you will have to keep the lights and the reflector quite close to the actor's face. However, using this effect on a cloudy dull day would look very supernatural.

▶ **Car lights pulling into a driveway at night.** Make sure your lights are held in a safe and manageable way. Someone then stands in front of the window of a living room and swings the lights across the glass in one smooth motion, making sure they don't start and stop on the glass. When filming in the darkened room, it will appear as if car headlights have just gone through the room. Bear in mind, though, that, if you are filming towards the window, you need to keep the curtains closed, otherwise your car will be revealed for what it is – someone holding a light! The light in the room will also have to be at a suitable level for the 'car headlights' to be seen.

▶ **Daylight on someone indoors.** Shine as bright a light as possible 'hard' (no spun gel on the light) on to them. The bright white light will look as though sunshine is coming through a window somewhere.

Sunrise or sunset on to someone's face indoors. As above, but use an orange light.

USING REFLECTORS

Reflectors are another tool you probably need to know about. They are large pieces of reflective material that people hold as though they are about to catch an invisible pancake. They are used for boosting and redistributing light on a set without the need to move equipment about and are best employed when filming outdoors in the absence of artificial light, so that you can reflect sunlight wherever you want. You won't always need them – and you might not need them at all – but like other things in film making, they can be effectively and cheaply improvised.

To make a reflector you will need some lightweight material, such as cardboard, and then cover it with tin foil. The shiny side of the foil will make a hard reflector, and the duller side will act as a diffuse reflector.

Be mindful that reflectors can't bounce light over great distances and they have to be positioned rather close to the people or the things you are filming. Some of your shots may have to be framed (more later) rather tightly to avoid filming a hapless soul holding a reflector.

Key idea: 'Left a bit, right a bit, left a bit ...'

Since getting the lighting right for certain scenes on large productions can be a time-consuming affair, movies employ people known as stand-ins. As the name suggests, these people stand in instead of the stars so the lighting can be adjusted to the director of photography's or director's preference without the talent getting tired or annoyed. Usually, these people look rather similar to the actual star they are standing in for, to simulate how light and shadow will fall on the actual star's face. They are told to slightly adjust their position so the mark or marks can be established for the upcoming shot – where they will start from or walk to.

It is good to get into the habit of having a member of the crew double as stand-in so you can get an idea of the lighting and actors' positioning for certain shots and scenes.

Basic positioning

Changing the position of your lights can alter the mood of your scene in a variety of ways:

▶ **Placing a bright light under someone** so that it points upwards will make that person's face very sinister and evil-looking. You've probably seen this when someone has been outside at night shining a torch under their chin. It's just one way in which a tweak of the lights can give a powerful effect.

▶ The opposite of placing the light under the subject is, of course, **placing the light above the subject.** This has a completely different effect, as it makes the person look rather angelic, as if surrounded by an aura of spiritual light. Alternatively, it can make people appear surreal and disturbing. This effect has been used loads of times in sci-fi or horror films. It is also used in dream scenes where someone appears in the middle of a black empty space, producing that ghostly look.

▶ Staying with this unearthly side of lighting, another popular and easy method to give your film a certain level of weirdness is to **boost the light levels** up as much as you can. To see examples of this type of lighting, check out most films where aliens walk out of their spacecraft with bright lights behind them. The lighting is usually all the way up to reinforce the 'divine-like' entrance of the creature. *Close Encounters of the Third Kind* (dir. Stephen Spielberg, 1977) used this method to superb effect. It was also utilized in *Poltergeist* (dir. Tobe Hooper, 1982) in the scenes where ghosts started appearing. As the lady in that film says, 'Run into the light.'

However, when using the above method, you should be aware of the iris feature on your camera. If you are using a camcorder with an auto-iris feature, then you probably won't be able to get the last effect as the camera will automatically down-adjust the light level to what it thinks is an acceptable level. What you are essentially trying to do here is overexpose your footage. This is just one of many reasons why you need to take manual control of your camera at all times.

▶ **Side-lighting** is another basic way of altering the mood of a shot. As the name suggests, a light is placed to the side of an actor and lights up only one side of the face. This is used a lot, especially on baddies in the corner of a darkened room, to emphasize their 'shady' side, or some other criminal/deranged type sitting at a table about to describe how they are going to torture the hero.

▶ **Backlighting** comes next. Although it was mentioned as part of three-point lighting, it can be a powerful lighting set-up on its own. This is when a light is placed behind an actor and creates a silhouette effect. It is a classic method for filming someone without showing their face.

One important and obvious point to make here in regard to the above lighting methods, is the light itself. For example, if you are trying to side-light someone who is standing outside on a very bright sunny day, using a torch isn't going to work. The above lighting effects all rely on some amount of darkness existing to be effective. So, if you are filming in a room that has a lot of natural light coming into it, and you want to place a light under someone's face to make them look nasty, you will have to darken the room in some way – thick black sheets over the window would work.

Remember this

Don't approach your first day's filming without ever having switched on your lights. Experiment with them, see what effects you can achieve and generally find out the best way to use them.

These effects are all very well for the individuals in your film, but what about the set itself? For the set, a key light is placed in a position that will light up as much of the set as possible, and then 'fill lights' are used to fill in the gaps. This method gives a very standard well-lit look, but not everyone will want something like this. A little experimentation is all it takes to make your set more interesting. For example, imagine you are starting with a room that is pitch black. If you were to stick a light behind an open door then, depending on how bright it was, you would get a very dramatic shaft of light striking the room. Alternatively, you could position the lights so that one end of the room was in darkness and the other in light, so when someone walked from the far side of the room, they would emerge from the shadows. Very effective! Just experiment and you will soon find that your lights are an essential component to the film making montage. They may not be as cool-looking as your camera, but if you don't use any, your film will either be in complete darkness or dull. Try to keep the light levels and positions constant during a scene, or when you finish your film the light levels will look haywire as each shot changes in a scene.

Using a monitor

Using a monitor helps you to see whether what you are filming looks the way it should. For example: Is the light OK? Is the guy holding the microphone in shot? Is the colour good? Has the top of the actor's head been cut off?

Although video cameras have small colour or black-and-white viewfinders and flip-out screens, it is recommended that you use a colour monitor. Film and television productions use professional monitors all the time in order to check the quality of each shot. As an alternative, you can use a small portable television if you are using a camcorder. All you need to do is obtain a small colour television and connect your camera's AV leads to it. This way, you will have a large, full-colour view of what your camera is seeing, and you can make lighting adjustments or other changes accordingly.

Health and safety

Wires, cables and leads are probably the biggest potential source of accidents on your film. If they are not properly attended to, people can trip over them and cause the lights to which they are attached to fall and break. If you have a lot of cables and leads, try to bunch them all together and have them along the sidewall of the room where no one is going to trip over them. However, if they need to go across the floor, bunch them together and then cover them with a piece of heavy material (such as an old carpet piece) so it forms a 'bridge' people can walk over.

Focus points

✻ When filming indoors or at night, try to use some powerful lights.

✻ Don't rely on using domestic lights; they just aren't strong enough.

✻ Always critically assess each scene and shot for its individual lighting needs; don't assume one set-up will suit all.

✻ Practise three-point lighting whenever possible and use it as a template for other lighting set-ups by varying the number of lights and their positions.

✻ Don't overcomplicate your lighting – use what you've got.

✻ When possible, check the lighting in your monitor before taking a shot.

✻ Carry a reflector when outdoors – they are simple to use and can make a huge difference.

✻ Think about using coloured gels and scrims or different-coloured bulbs.

✻ Be very careful if you have lots of cables on the floor – secure them!

✻ If using lots of powerful lights indoors, open any windows whenever possible or switch the lights off to cool the location down.

Next step

Although crucial, sound is an aspect of film making that is sometimes neglected by budding directors or even by experienced ones who should know better. Therefore it is important for you to understand this area as thoroughly as you can and, ideally, it's best to have at least one person running sound on set, if possible. Sound, then, is the focus of Chapter 7.

7

Sound

In this chapter you will learn:

- ▶ *how vital sound is to your film and film making*
- ▶ *how to maximize the resources you have*
- ▶ *how sound can be used to enhance and improve your film*

Can you hear what they're saying?

When you are at the cinema, there are two basic things you take note of: the images and the sound. Just as the human eye is far superior to a camera at seeing things in different levels of light, the same can be said of the human ear in the context of sound gathering.

Stop for a moment and listen. Chances are that all is silent to your ear or, if there is some sound, your ears are filtering it into something manageable. If you had a camcorder and recorded the same 'silence' using its built-in microphone, then this 'silence' might be a hissing din. Therefore, when you are filming a scene it is important to ensure that you record only the sound you want. So how is this done? By paying attention to your sound recording.

The role of the sound department

As with other film making disciplines, sound is a subset with its own characteristics, skills and requirements. A bit like editing (see Chapter 12), the sound gathering and manipulation side of film making is a mysterious and often forgotten part of the moving image experience.

Although we may be familiar with the image of the lone man or woman holding the 'boom' pole with a microphone on the end, there is a lot more to sound recording than this might imply. That individual is just the tip of the proverbial iceberg; sending sound signals back to a mixer who ensures the levels are correct, and not too faint or overblown and distorted. On large productions, there may be several boom operators and mixers depending on the requirements of the production. Yet, sound production does not end on set. The recorded sound may be enhanced in the edit, cleaned up, generally altered in some way or even re-recorded altogether.

Then there is the work of Foley artists who create sound effects from scratch in various imaginative ways. A piece of paper being torn may be used as the sound of a huge canvas sail splitting in the middle of a storm, or pebbles thrown at a metal sheet could double as bullets bouncing off a tank driving through a war zone.

Working in the sound department can create challenges that pass most people by. Certain environments will mean certain audio difficulties have to be thought out, worked around and overcome. Reviewing a script from a sound recordist's perspective, you will be able to make recommendations or even advise why something needs changing otherwise the sound recording may suffer.

Like many elements of film making, sound recording is a huge subject with countless methods and tricks to ensure good quality. As with the visual side of things, you need to apply your imagination and resourcefulness to certain situations in order to get the best results.

Things to bear in mind

Your chosen camera equipment and where you decide to film will normally dictate what options are open to you. If, for example, you are using a camcorder, or any other video system with a built-in sound recording feature, then the sound from a person speaking in a quiet room may acceptable. If, however, you are outside on a busy street with strong winds blowing, then that person's voice will be just one feature of the recorded sound, which might seriously compromise things. With built-in microphones it is important to ensure the following:

▶ The person/people speaking are relatively close to the microphone.

▶ The environment you are in is quiet or sheltered from other 'audio distractions'.

▶ The person/people speaking project their voices if necessary.

▶ Any wind is blocked from blowing into the microphone (an umbrella, or filming around a street corner is good for this).

▶ You have some earphones plugged into the camera so you can gauge the quality of the sound – this is a must for all sound recordings!

Although many video camera systems have built-in microphones, some have an option that allows you to plug in a lead from an external microphone and point it at whoever is speaking. Therefore, your sound recording needn't be dictated by the distance of the camera from what you are filming. Thus, sound will be clearer and, because the sound is being recorded simultaneously with the images on the video, you won't have to worry about dubbing when editing.

Key idea: plants on set

Although boom operators provide the most obvious way of sound recording on set, it isn't the only one. Often you may discover you can rest the microphone somewhere so it is either out of frame or concealed by a prop. This practice is called 'using a plant'.

If you are using an external microphone in a windy environment, then you will have to gag it. You've all seen gags – they look like furry animals that have been skewered on the end of a microphone. This is a very effective, though not totally perfect method of insulating the microphone from the harsh effect of strong wind. External microphones, or plug-in microphones, are good for the simple fact that you can manoeuvre them to the best possible position for recording sound in relation to the actors who are speaking, instead of relying on the microphone in the camera.

With film cameras, you will need to record the sound separately. You will therefore need to think about how you are going to record your sound using an external and separate audio recording device.

How to improvise sound recording equipment

Fortunately, there is a lot of basic gadgetry, and accessories can help you out with sound recording. If, for some reason, you need to use an external sound recording device that is not connected to your camera, you are spoiled for choice.

Your mobile phone may have some kind of sound-recording facility. While its quality may be a little rough, it will be recorded in digital format and therefore be easy for you to upload into your editing and place alongside your images. Also, depending on its size, you may be able to conceal it on your actor to capture them speaking clearly.

The same could be done with an MP3 recorder. Its small size makes it ideal for putting on an actor or you could risk attaching it to some kind of boom to record all the dialogue for a particular scene. Nor should there be too much of a problem getting the sound data on to your edit computer.

A MiniDisc recorder boasts a bit more capability than the above and can have microphones plugged into it to maximize the quality of the recorded sound and dialogue.

Using a cheap computer microphone can sometimes work with consumer cameras. By simply plugging it into the microphone input jack you can get some decent results. If it has a long cable, you could even use it as a boom microphone. One disadvantage with some of these microphones is they can sometimes have a limited range, so be careful.

Key idea: Pistol grips

Unless you have worked around microphones a lot, it is sometimes hard to appreciate just how sensitive they can be. Much sound recording can be compromised by excessive handling noise as the sound recordist constantly fumbles with the microphone as they adjust their grip. Professional sound recordists will mount their microphones in a grip with rubber mounts and holders, allowing the microphone to be held without handling noise. When the grip and the microphone are put together, they resemble a pistol.

RADIO MICROPHONES

Radio microphones are handy things if you can get hold of them, or afford them. Just like other external microphones, they can be connected, via a receiver, to a camera and allow you a greater amount of flexibility regarding your filming options. You can, for example, move your camera around without having to worry about getting tangled up in the sound recordist's leads. You can also film a bit further away without having to think where to hide the external microphone and so on. You can hire these microphones relatively cheaply from a community camera hire outlet. They are best used in long shots, as they can eradicate the need for making a separate sound recording of the dialogue. However, a few words of warning: they can eat up batteries rapidly, so when not in use, switch them off and make sure they are disconnected.

When I worked for a shopping channel it wasn't unknown for an off-air presenter to be heard over the air going to the toilet as their colleagues were talking about Teflon cooking utensils. Radio mics have also been known to pick up the odd tummy rumble and stifled belch. When the microphones rub against clothes, they can create a very awkward and noticeable sound. Also, make sure they are concealed – otherwise they will ruin your scene.

Key idea: A microphone for all seasons

There isn't just one type of microphone used on all film productions. Some microphones have a relatively long range, some will record sound all around them over a certain distance, whereas others will record sound only from very close by. If you are able to get hold of some decent professional microphones, make sure you know what their capabilities are.

Continuity

As with lighting, you should pay special attention to the continuity of your sound. It is one of the things that can cause unpleasant problems when you are trying to piece your film together.

I think there is always an assumption in today's world, complete with the cameras that boast fully automatic features, that all is taken care of and all you have to do is hold the camera. This, alas, is not the case. I have often observed many first-time film makers just pointing their camera at things, not even thinking to listen to the quality of the sound by using headphones. I know of an access documentary that was made for a satellite channel about the police force in New York and the majority of the filming was done with MiniDV cams. Although the images were OK, considering they were filming in difficult conditions, the sound was horrendous. The MiniDV camera teams were more interested in getting the pictures and didn't bother to monitor the sound. The result was that it took some serious high-tech sound engineering to get the recorded sound to understandable levels – and all through want of putting on the headphones!

WILD TRACKS

A vital way to ensure that your sound continuity is taken care of is to record a wild track. Before I explain what a wild track is, I had better tell you why it is needed. As you know, a film is made up of scenes that consist of many different shots which have been filmed at different times instead of in one long run of the camera. This way of working can lead to lapses in continuity, not only with the basic visual elements of the scene, such as people's clothes changing, their positions in a shot or the lighting, but there can also be continuity problems with the soundtrack.

Imagine a scenario where you are filming a scene with two people talking. Now there is only one camera, so you will have to film the mastershot (the main referencing shot that covers both the actors), followed by the close-up, or medium close-up, on the individual actors. So you have at least three different runs with which to film your scene and three different chances to obtain three different background sounds that will severely mess up your work.

Somewhere outside there are some roadworks going on which the microphone is happily picking up. So, with the first run of the camera you have the mastershot, the corresponding dialogue and the rattling of power tools and dump trucks revving engines. Now it's time to film the close-up shots on Actor A. This is done and the roadworks have stopped but the microphone picks up a passing jet (this always happens to everyone!). Finally, it is time to film Actor B and the scene is filmed without any distracting noises. Now imagine it is some time later and it is time to put it all together in the edit. This is what would happen:

Shot	Dialogue	Background sound
Mastershot	Thank you for coming, Richard.	Power tools, revving engines
Actor B	No problem, glad to help.	Silence
Mastershot	OK, let's get to it.	Power tools, revving engines
Actor A	Like I said over the phone, this is big.	Passing jet
Actor B	Yeah, a lot of people want this money.	Silence
Actor A	Tell me about it.	Passing jet
Mastershot	So what's the plan?	Power tools, revving engines

… and so on.

If you were watching a scene like this in the edit, it would be dire and there would be nothing you could do about it short of filming the scene again or doing some ADR work. Now this is quite an extreme and overt example to illustrate a true sound disaster, but the rule here is to make sure that it's quiet when you start filming. 'Silence on set' is not just said to be cool, you know!

So, what do you do if you are filming outside on a busy street, where there's no escaping the noise? Although you may think that the sound will be fairly constant and uniform, you would be very wrong. If the same three-shot scene was being filmed on a street corner with the corresponding traffic sounds, then another problem would present itself in the edit. Allowing for not recording when a police car with sirens blazing goes past during the mastershot, or the beeping of the pedestrian crossing during the close-up shots on Actor B, you will end up with sound hiccups in the finished scene:

Shot	Dialogue	Sound
Mastershot	So let's go do this.	Background traffic rumble Jolt!
Actor B	OK, keep your eyes open.	Background traffic rumble Jolt!
Mastershot	You got the keys to this place?	Background traffic rumble Jolt!
Actor A	Sure.	Background traffic rumble Jolt!

… and so on.

What has happened here is that at the instant when one shot is linked up with another in the edit, the pitch and tone of the rumbling noises of the traffic jolts slightly, but enough to be noticed. Since the sound of the traffic changes in pitch and tone from second to second, it won't always link up nicely with the shot immediately after it. So, what do you do? You record a wild track.

This is essentially a guard against the above problem entering every scene you film. A wild track is a sound-only recording of the ambient sound around a scene. In the above example, it would be the noises of a busy street with all the traffic and so forth. So, if you were using your video camera, you would simply hit the record button and point the microphone (built-in or external) in a manner that allows it to best pick up the sounds you are after. This means that in the edit, the jolts and glitches will be masked and smoothed over – the finer technical points of editing such a manoeuvre will be discussed in Chapter 12.

Recording a wild track is a practice you should get into the habit of using just in case.

You may find yourself filming a scene where your characters are talking to each other and watching a television programme. One sound suggestion would be to film the scene without the television switched on, so as not to disturb the dialogue, and then record the sound of a television programme. However, owing to copyright problems (see 15), it may be better to record the sound of some people just mumbling to simulate the sound of a television programme playing in the background – although more commonly, in films and television dramas, the sound of gunshots and police sirens are used to serve this function which are later dubbed into the edit.

There are many fun things to record to add a bit more life and colour to your scenes. You may find yourself in a room with a grandfather clock. This is a lovely warm and atmospheric sound to include. So, as before, film the various shots of the scene without the sound of the thudding pendulum, and then record a wild track afterwards. Actually, a swinging pendulum going unnoticed when filming is very representative of the great 'terrorists' of film making. It is not a sound as noticeable as a pneumatic drill but, if ignored, the edited scene may have turned the gentle thud of the pendulum into something sounding like a disjointed disco beat. Another advantage of recording the sound of something is that you will be able to use it throughout your film, and future productions, as and when you need it.

Sound effects

I hope the above examples have piqued your mind into thinking about recording your own sound effects. Some of them are very easy to improvise. For example, once in an edit suite I suddenly realized that I needed the sound of feet running upstairs as I cut to an exterior of a castle. Since I did not have sound-effect files available, I simply got a microphone, put it on the ground and did some on-the-spot jogging. The result was brilliant and totally fooled everyone. To improvise a heartbeat, tap the microphone with your finger in a rhythmic, repetitive fashion. It is so easy.

Many professional sound recordists go out into the great outdoors and collect their own real sound effects. For example, they will go into the woods and record the sound of the wind blowing through the leaves on the trees, or the sound of a flowing brook, or maybe a busy street, a train in motion and a dog barking. The advantage of this is that the sounds are their copyright. Sound-effects CDs need special permission and payment before you are allowed to use them in a professional commercial film, as they are owned by someone else. So, get out there and record the sounds of the world!

Key idea: Free sound effects

There are lots of sound-effects websites all giving you access to free audio treats. In addition, some editing software already comes with an impressive array of sounds, ranging from birds singing to laser weapons firing.

The complexity of the edit method and the technology you use (see Chapter 12) will limit the amount of audio you can have in your edit. For example, the most basic edit method will allow you to include only the dialogue and maybe one sound effect (not at the same time) instead of dialogue and five sound effects (see Chapter 12 for sound in editing).

It is often said by sound recordists that sound is the element of filming that directors pay least attention to. They say that directors can sometimes think that the sound will 'follow on' and be OK in the overall finished product. However, films can be totally ruined by the director not having a basic awareness and consideration of the sound.

One common problem occurs if you are using a camcorder without a facility for a plug-in microphone and you wish to film two actors speaking far away from the camera. The trouble with that is you are not going to hear a thing anyone is saying due to the range of the on-board microphone. A cheat device commonly used in these situations is to record the actors' dialogue separately and then put it in when you get to the edit. You will then have your lovely shot of two people walking across the brow of a hill as the sun goes down, and still be able to hear clearly everything they say. Also, because they are far away from the camera it will be impossible to notice if their lips aren't in synch!

Remember this

Although this chapter deals with sound, you will notice that I'm starting to introduce techniques from the editing process. It helps a great deal when filming if you have an appreciation of the post-production process.

ADR and looping

As detailed previously in this chapter, often filming will have taken place in an environment with lots of sound pollution. There may be persistent traffic, aircraft and wind noise, which is not suitable to the setting of the film or plain distracting to the dialogue being recorded. In these situations, even the best efforts of skilled sound recordists and mixers are not enough. Despite their knowledge, skill and ability with their equipment, sometimes they just cannot get the clean sound they want. In these situations, a bit of ADR is called for.

ADR is an abbreviation that stands for Automated Dialogue Replacement. This is the process in which the actor will look at the playback of a certain scene, or scenes, that have been edited together and re-record their dialogue in a sound studio, attempting to get their words in synch with their lip movements on the film. The process is also called looping, after the practice of having a reel of film being played in a continuous loop over and over in order for the actors to practise the dialogue and ensure the synch is accurate. Nowadays, the existence of digital technology means looping a film reel is no longer necessary, although the name remains.

From an ice-cold technical point of view, ADR is perhaps the best way to ensure you get clear and clean sound for your film when in a challenging environment. However, from a dramatic stance, asking actors to re-record an emotional or demanding scene many weeks or months after the event may not produce the best results. It may also be impossible to get hold of some cast after the filming has been completed.

Again, with modern and commercially available consumer technology, ADR and looping capability is easily achieved. Turning a corner of your bedroom or home into an ADR studio is easier than you think.

Have a look for some ADR credits next time you watch a film.

Overcoming problems

Get into the habit of filming and recording with half a mind on what 'problems' a particular scene may present in the edit. For everyday examples of how the above problems have been remedied, take a look at news reports. Although you may feel that these are an unlikely source of film making knowledge, you would be very wrong.

Every day, news teams have to get stories out within a deadline and they are not usually in an environment where they can arrange re-shoots or ADR sessions. There is a general formula that news crews use when interviewing people, and it is the relation of techniques used in any film you see in the cinema. It generally goes like this:

person – cutaway – person – cutaway – person

Whenever you watch someone being interviewed in a news report, what you are generally seeing is maybe a 45-second edited version of something that may have taken several minutes to film. This is because, if the interviewee says something that is not required, this has to be left out of the report. So how is this done without causing a jolt in the sound and picture?

CUTAWAYS

Have a look at this imagined news feature:

Shot 1 – Person is answering third question.

Shot 2 – Cutaway of sheep in a field.

Shot 3 – Person is answering fifth question.

So, what the cutaway has done is mask two different discontinuous shots that would otherwise cause a jump cut (see Chapter 10) and it has taken your attention away from any jolt in the sound. It's very simple yet very effective.

This is a variation of the mastershot example earlier, but instead of filming and recording the sound from more than one set-up, it is only the shot that varies. Next time you watch a feature film or television film drama, look out for a scene where two people are having a conversation. There will usually be a cutaway taken from a distance – it's the more elegant relation of the news rush-job.

It is important to get a mental grasp of which shots and cuts you will be using in a film. This not only saves time in the edit process (as there is less to sift through), but it also means that things are filmed more quickly and efficiently as you know how you want it stuck together later and need only film what you have to.

I'm straying into the world of camera work and techniques here, but it illustrates how intricately connected the basic filming processes are – they are all part of the same whole. What happens with one process has repercussions for the rest, so get it right!

Microphone settings

Some of the digital video cameras that are available these days not only have a plug-in microphone socket fitted as standard but will have a facility that enables you to manipulate your recording levels. The two basic settings for recording levels are automatic and manual. No surprise there. But how does this translate into uses in your film?

AUTOMATIC SETTING

A camera that has its sound recording function switched over to automatic constantly monitors all the sounds it registers and finds a mid-level. This is a good system to have when you are in an environment with constant predictable sounds, for example, two people having a conversation in a room where there is a steady rumble of traffic outside. This is an ideal set-up, and the recorded sound will also be at a constant level with a good overall quality. Even if you were filming the crowd at a football match, a mid-point would be found and you'd have a decent sound level.

The only time when automatic recording levels are a drawback is when there is a sudden change in the sound level. So, imagine that the same two actors are talking while standing by a level-crossing and a train rushes by. What will happen here is that the sound record facility will think, 'Oh wow, that's loud! Let's turn things down.' So, when played back your shot will have the words from the dialogue, and then when the train rushes past the overall recorded sound level will steeply drop to a significantly lower level. Professional sound recordists call this phenomenon 'falling off the cliff' and it may help to imagine the sound level as a line (see Figure 7.1).

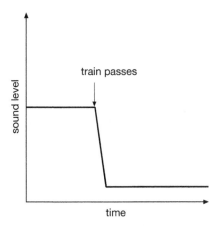

Figure 7.1

The most common situation where automatic sound levels cause problems is in scenes where there are gunshots. I've known a few occasions when people have filmed a great-looking gunfight scene, only to play it back on a monitor or in an edit suite and find that the sound of the first gunshot suddenly drops to almost nothing halfway through, and the rest of the shots sound about as loud as someone punching a pillow.

Again, these are extreme examples to illustrate a point. However, I hope it has highlighted a downside of the automatic function. By being aware of what your recording environment will be like, you can easily avoid this problem. Actually, automatic is the preferred way of doing things.

MANUAL SETTING

Having the option of a manual setting does have its own uses. Using the passing train example, Figure 7.2 shows what would happen if the camera was set to manual.

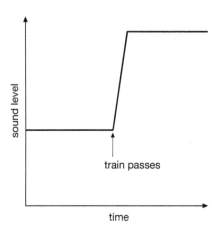

Figure 7.2

Since the camera's sound facility has been adjusted only for the relatively low-volume experience of two people's voices, the passing train will sound much louder and therefore it will turn the recorded sound into something that sounds like an atomic bomb blast. Manual sound is set at a certain level to record only sound from that level, for example, something softer will be hard to hear and something much louder will end up being a distorted din.

The gunshot example given earlier is a very good example of when to use manual sound. Using this, you could keep the levels high so that the bangs would sound like bangs. It can also be a good way of distorting things so that you can achieve the sort of effect you may want to go with your scene and film. For example, you may need to simulate a distorted radio message from a spaceship in distress.

Manual sound is a rather tricky thing to master overnight. It needs constant tweaking and monitoring to get it right, as the volume of someone's voice will be changing constantly depending on the emotional content of the scene, and also the ambient sounds of certain locations will present their own problems. Trying to adjust things manually throughout a camera run could end up with your soundtrack being alternately inaudible or too loud and distorted. Also, many camera menus may require that you stop recording to access the manual sound level control. So, this would be impractical.

However, the advantage comes from the fact that in excessively loud or soft audio situations you can adjust the levels better than you could ever achieve on automatic. Think of the manual level as a guard for the more extreme sound situations.

From a purely technical perspective, you should be putting your sound on manual at all times. However, for the low-budget film maker it can be difficult to adjust levels on a camera once it has started filming as it means getting in the way of, and possibly affecting, the camera operator.

Key idea

Many small film productions will use an SQN mixer for their sound recording and mixing. This device acts as an intermediate between the microphone and the camera, allowing the sound recordist/mixer to constantly monitor and adjust the levels of the recorded sound. It has inputs allowing several microphones to be used at a time.

A bad picture with good sound is easy on an audience. A good picture with bad sound is frustrating for an audience. A case in point is the documentary *Bowling for Columbine* (dir. Michael Moore, 2002) has some unlit footage filmed at dusk; the images are barely visible, but perfect sound saved the day.

Remember this: Sound recording tip

If filming next to a busy road you can reduce, but not eradicate, the sound of the traffic by using the bodies of the actors as 'sound blocks' by appropriate framing and positioning of the microphone. For example, if the microphone is close enough to the body, and away from the traffic, the body will shield the microphone from the sound of all the cars (see Figure 7.3). This technique is used by news reporters the world over.

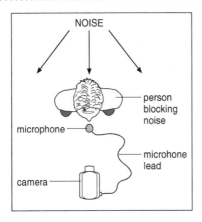

Figure 7.3

Focus points

* Always use headphones or earphones. If you don't, you won't know how good or bad your sound quality is.
* Try to ensure one dedicated person takes care of the sound recording.
* Have a think about the locations you are going to be filming in and make allowances for the noises that may creep into the film.
* Investigate what cheap microphones can work with your camera.
* If possible, always try to use some kind of external microphone when filming dialogue.
* If you are unable to get an external microphone, pay extra careful attention to getting the best out of your on-board microphone.
* If there is a sound disturbance during filming, stop and redo the shot.
* Never expect to get great sound from a filmed event; chances are you will need to do some Foley work.
* If you are unhappy with the recorded sound from some scenes, try to arrange some kind of ADR sessions.
* Sound is very important: if no one can make out what your actors are saying, no one will watch the film.

Next step

In Chapter 8 we look at locations. As we shall see, you should already have potential locations in mind while writing your script. Try to be realistic from the start and be prepared to improvise. Oddly, sometimes a stand-in for a location can be much more effective than the real thing.

8

Locations and obtaining support

In this chapter you will learn:

▶ *how to find or 'make' locations that will fit your film*

▶ *the importance of viewing locations prior to filming at them*

▶ *how locations can help get your film some official sponsorship*

Your equipment is all ready, but there's just one problem – you've got nowhere to film. Location is just one of the many things that you will have to sort out before those cameras start rolling. So how do you decide in what kinds of place you would like to film? The answer lies in the script.

There are probably a few broad bandings when it comes to the kinds of location your script will be calling for. Genre is the key element of your script and story and will influence the sorts of place you look out for. For example, a crime thriller would be well suited to city environments – secret meetings taking place under bridges, in downtown pubs and bars, streets and so forth. A sci-fi storyline would need industrial complexes, wide-open and desolate places such as a beach far from built-up areas, and an old open-cast mine is always a good substitute for an alien planet, especially when used in conjunction with a filter over the camera lens. An historic script would of course need period buildings – both exteriors and interiors.

Remember this

When you are filming, anything outside the frame doesn't exist. If you have a story set in a castle, and one doesn't exist in your country, then filming against a large wall with huge sections may suffice. Also, you needn't film in the midst of a forest; you could just go to a bunch of trees in your municipal park. Having your actors standing next to a small pond could double for the shore of a large ocean. The options are endless.

Be realistic

When you are writing the script, it is always wise to be mindful of the limitations that may be presented by an ambitious story. There is little point in writing numerous and marvellous scenes set in fantastic places if obtaining such locations proves impossible owing to the factors of expense, distance and the realization that such places do not exist (unless purpose-built). Try to think of locations as limiters to your story and script. Being aware of what is available and tenable to your production will allow you to set scenes and action in places that you know you will be able to get hold of. I know of individuals who have composed scripts without taking the above considerations on board and then moaned when they discovered they were not allowed to run riot through the local five-star hotel or some other important building.

That said, as with many things in the film making process, there is usually some way of improvising what you are trying to get hold of. Your ability to think laterally and be resourceful may save the day with regard to getting hold of your otherwise impossible and fantastic location.

Improvise your setting

Consider a script that opens up like this:

> **EXT: Aircraft Carrier. Landing deck — Day**
>
> The sea is extremely rough and the aircraft are preparing for take-off.

This might be a tricky one to arrange. You will therefore have to think of a substitute that conveys the same feeling. You could rig up a glass window and the area immediately behind it to look the part, with charts, aircraft diagrams, someone suitably attired looking out with a pair of binoculars, and so on. You could also move the camera back and forth rhythmically and occasionally spray water at the window. In the edit you could put in the appropriate sounds. Think laterally and approach a complicated location from another route. Now think about some more complicated locations mentioned in a script and see what you can come up with. For example:

> **EXT: Battlefield — Day**
>
> Explosions detonate and shots whistle near to a group of huddled troops.

Here you could have a trench in a field somewhere. The shot would help if it was quite close in. Shaking the camera once in a while would simulate a bomb exploding nearby and a bit of loose dirt chucked in time with the camera shake could represent debris which has been thrown up. The more ambitious of you might devise some way of creating smoke. You could also zoom in to the distance and go in and out of focus to simulate the soldiers desperately and frantically looking through their rifle sights at the unseen enemy. You could also do a few blurred whip pans to simulate bullets flying through the air.

> **EXT: Desert planet – Day**
>
> A lone figure walks across the expanse of the sand sea.

This is one of my favourites as it's so simple to achieve, but it does help to have a beach nearby – and preferably one where the tide goes out so far that it does actually resemble a desert. To trick the audience, use a red or orange filter which will instantly give your shots that 'off-world' look. Filming from a low angle towards the sun will further accentuate the heat of the place. Although having a beach where the tide goes out for a very long way is a luxurious way of filming such a trick, any rocky and sandy area will suffice – even a quarry, just so long as the picture is framed in a manner that excludes anything that will ruin the shot, such as a wall or a truck.

The smaller the location, the tighter the shot will have to be, but this will lend a strange sense of claustrophobia to the situation (more about framing later). Also, you will have to film things from as many different angles as possible due to the small size of the area. One trick of the trade is to light some fire lighters (the sort used for barbecues) and place them in front of the camera. Now zoom through the invisible flame and you've got instant heat shimmer – even if it is a midwinter's day. However, know where this flame is so that you don't burn your camera. The best example of using this heat effect is in the film *Dune* (dir. David Lynch, 1984). There is a scene where the Royal Family arrives on Dune and the entire clip is given an almost unbearable 'shot' of heat using this method – so effective you can almost feel it.

These examples are probably not what everyone will want to film, but they do reveal how settings can be effectively improvised by using different resources.

Inexpensive/free locations

So, your script includes many things: story, characters and settings. The settings are the places you will need to find or recreate. For many reasons, a lot of people choose to film low-budget films in their own or their friends' houses. The reason for this 'cottage industry' is that you have unlimited permission and access; you can do what you want (within reason); everyone you work with will probably know how to get there (ease of access) and it is free (biggest advantage). People's bedrooms, or rooms of a house in general, are great starting points for a low- or no-budget film.

By looking at a script you will see that there are probably a few scenes that take place in rooms. If it were the room of our private detective friend, Richard Vincent (see Chapter 2), then you could start off with just a desk, chair and window – maybe even just a desk and chair. The window could be blacked out and the room lit in a suitably 'crime-like' manner to emphasize the nether world that this fellow inhabits. Simple, sparse props can give a room great 'direction' and be very effective in illustrating a point in the film. For example, a room decked out to be somewhere in an embassy might need only a flag and a framed picture of a president or prime minister to tell the audience 'what's going on'. Start with the basics and then, if necessary, work your way up.

Remember this

Keep it simple. This goes for all aspects of the film making process.

You could even use the same room for a multitude of scenes by filming from another angle and altering the furniture and props. With such a set-up, many of the cutaways and single shot scenes can be put out of the way in relatively little time. Rooms are an amazing little-known-about resource, so make sure you can get hold of a few. Who knows, maybe your entire film could be shot in a series of rooms.

While on the subject of cheap and free resources, have a think of others that may be available to you. Public places such as parks, the countryside, the beach, a forest, etc. are all calling out for you to use them. They are all free, so see if you can fit them in somewhere.

Key idea: A battle of wills

Sometimes when filming in public spaces you can be surprised by an official appearing asking to see paperwork giving you permission to film. Often, these individuals can be over-zealous and misguided and with no right or power to tell you what to do. If you already have permission from the relevant authority to film, then stand your ground.

Once again, it is very important to know what category your intended production is going to fall into when trying to arrange permission to film in public places, as well as with many other aspects of making a film. This is because you will be asked if you are a professional/commercial company or an educational/community project. If you are a professional/commercial company, then you are more likely to be charged a fee for using the location than if you state that you are an educational/community-level organization.

Case study: Gothic horror

The best/worst example I know of was when I was doing some pre-production work on an experimental Gothic-type film based in London. I stumbled across a magnificent location that used to be a cathedral and was now used as a public forum for community arts 'happenings'. It was huge, cavernous and Gothic and looked perfect for the throne room for one of the characters in the script. Sadly, I approached the situation ham-fistedly. When I met up with the man who managed the site I introduced myself as being from a film company (I was just a private citizen), which made him think, 'Great – money!' When we got round to arranging filming, I thought it would just be a case of saying 'when' and then turning up since it was a free community resource. This was not the case. Since I had said I was from a film company (just to sound credible), he quoted me a huge figure. It was an impossible figure to work with and, by the time I explained it was really just a small-scale community production, it was too late and he wouldn't budge on the price. So, for the sake of wanting to sound like 'Mr Hollywood', I blew a unique location. I was never to make that mistake again. Remember: be realistic and be honest.

The size of your film is something to which you should always give serious thought. It may be hard, at first, to determine where things are going, but after finalizing the script, you may have a rough idea of what resources you intend to use. This consideration ties in very closely with the funding side of things, but don't go making your location arrangements on the proviso that there will be a big stash of money at your disposal somewhere down the line.

Film makers and those involved with television dramas and other programmes don't just flatly agree to a fee for filming somewhere. It seems that owners of huge palatial homes and country parks think television and film people have bags of money ready to throw at anyone who quotes them a high price. They often find out it's the other way around. If a price for a location is too high, the film/programme-makers will either go elsewhere or try to negotiate a lower fee. It's a practice you should employ. Look for what's free, and if it's not free see if you can get some kind of deal. If you still can't reach an agreement, look elsewhere.

Key idea: Production design

It is very rare that a location will suit the needs of the script or the vision of the director on its own. In such instances, the work of production designers can be invaluable. These people are charged with interpreting and applying the director's vision to various sets and locations. At its simplest, it may mean that a few choice props are placed in shot; at its most complicated, entire 'dummy' houses, rooms or even sections of towns are constructed. Although some may wonder why rooms and buildings have to be built instead of using real ones, it may be the case that an actual building is impossible to film in due to the limited space to fit film making equipment in, or that the real building is unavailable. Now, with the improvements in digital technology, entire films can be shot without any locations at all; instead they are added in post-production. For example, the film *300* (dir. Zack Snyder, 2006) did this – it was entirely filmed in a green-screen studio.

Visit your location

Once you have nailed down your location it is very important to take a recce. A recce is a look around the location to establish a few basic facts about it:

▶ How easy is it to get there (is it near a bus stop or will everyone need a ride there)?

▶ How large is it (will it accommodate everyone with the equipment)?

▶ Is it safe (floors, walls, electrics …)?

▶ What facilities does it have (electric outlets, toilets)?

▶ What permission is required?

▶ What is the layout like (so you can start thinking about your shots)?

▶ What are its opening times (if applicable)?

… And so on and so forth.

This is just another example of the preparation you should be aware of when making a film. There is nothing worse than turning up to film somewhere only to discover that there is nowhere to plug the lights in, or that it is closed on that particular day. All these things do happen! The most common and horrendous oversights usually occur with foreign locations. Stories abound of film crews being booked into hotels, flights arranged, cameras hired, film stock bought in, permissions granted, and so forth, only to discover on arrival that the country is having a major religious holiday and all the places that are required to be filmed are totally shut down. The biggest disasters are caused by the smallest oversights. Get to know your locations well – they are, after all, the silent actors in your film.

Consideration for others

Another consideration to bear in mind is any 'disturbances' you may cause. Some may be irresponsible on many levels. For starters, having the public walk by seeing people pointing guns at each other is not very smart. It may cause distress to some people, some may be seriously spooked and others driving past in cars may be distracted to the point where a crash may occur. Added to this, the police may not look too kindly on such things. Having your lead arrested due to a lack of planning and downright irresponsibility is not a great way to make films.

Always make sure that your actions do not inconvenience others. Depending on how large your film crew will be, you should plan accordingly. Just you with a camcorder filming someone walking on the other side of the street will probably go unnoticed. However, something involving lights, a larger camera and actors saying their lines will be very noticeable. Tell shop owners politely that you may be filming outside their shop next week, or whenever, and try not to get in people's way too much. It's just a case of simple planning and awareness on your part. If your script has a shootout scene in it, not only will you have to tell the local shop owners, residents and so forth, but you will have to notify the local police station well in advance. I don't have to explain what would happen if your actors went around with noisy blank-firing guns. Just have some courtesy and common sense!

Remember this

If it suits your script, think about filming on public transport. Although these locations may seem rather inconspicuous and dull, they are great as you can have a couple of people acting while out of the window things are going by which will give the scene a great deal of energy for a minimum amount of effort on your part.

From reading through the script it will be obvious what scenes require what type of location. However, you might not always be allowed to film somewhere you have your heart set on. The script excerpt given on page 15 was set first in a street and then in a bank. With that example in mind, you will realize it isn't as problematic to film something on a street – so long as it's not too busy – as it is to film in a bank. Turning up unannounced with your cameras and actors is a big no-no. The answer to the above location problem would be to:

1. ask permission from the bank, or

2. improvise elsewhere

Usually, the solution will be 2. (unless, of course, the bank manager is a frustrated actor and hopes for a part – that happens quite a bit, you know). Here are a few alternatives:

▶ a library

▶ a room with a table and 'Bank' written on the wall

▶ an office

▶ a university reception area

A bit of brainstorming, lateral thinking and imagination is all that is needed to come up with alternative venues.

Location lateral thinking in action

Once, while working on a film about the Roman Empire, the director suddenly realized that he needed to film a Judean general from the first century and in an appropriate location. Since this revelation was made in the latter stages of post-production, and we were doing our editing in the middle of a cold and rainy European city, there was no time or budget to arrange some filming over in the deserts of Israel.

The director's solution was to grab me, wrap a red curtain around my body, put a white cloth around my head and sit me down in a dark corner of an empty studio. By using a single light, a basic MiniDV camera, an historical-looking prop and having me pretend to write on a papyrus, he achieved a very convincing few minutes of footage that got fed directly into the edit.

Another film script needed to feature the crew of a German submarine during the Second World War. Since going to a real submarine at a museum was not an option, and hiring period military costumes too expensive, an alternative solution needed to be found.

The eventual location was the boiler room of a local high school with plenty of pipes, dials, metal and claustrophobic atmosphere. By using some eerie red and blue lights, simple props and military-looking shirts and hats, a convincing scene was filmed at minimal expense.

In another film about the life and death of an eighteenth-century gentleman criminal, I dressed an actor in some decent-looking pirate clothes from a fancy-dress shop and shot him walking around an area of countryside. For the scene in which he was hanged, I suspended a rope tied in a noose in front of an old high stone wall and pulled it tight off camera.

Remember this

Conjuring a location from nothing needs vision, commitment and persuasion. Don't see a location for what it is, but for what it can be!

Case study: Location, location

While making my first film, an important location requirement actually resulted in my getting some more financial support. I needed to get hold of a large, grandiose and impressive historical building somewhere, and somehow, that could be used as the headquarters of an espionage ring. A room in my house, or a friend's house, would not do, so I had to look at some alternatives. Eventually, I learned of a suitable location in a building owned and managed by the local government authority. After a series of phone calls, I was not only given permission to film there but allowed to use the building for free.

This was good news for financing my film, as I requested a letter confirming the agreement. I also asked for the letter to include a line about how normally the rental of the building would cost a certain sum of money, yet I was getting it free of charge. This was to show other potential backers that I was getting sponsorship in kind – in other words, goods or services for nothing which can otherwise be given a cash value. As a result, other people started to take me, and my project, a bit more seriously.

The reason for seeking support such as this is that, if you want to go down the route of applying for arts funding (see Chapter 9), the organizations which hand out this money insist that the arts practitioner (you) is making an effort to get support for the film under way, rather than just approaching them and asking for some cash! I cannot stress how important such letters and supporting documentation are in the process of getting your production moving.

The official budget for this film was tens of thousands. About three-quarters of that was sponsorship in kind – it existed only on paper.

Here are a few other suggestions of places you could contact for possible locations:

► the local health authority

► the school board

► community centres

► housing associations

The potential list is very, very long. They don't always have to be official buildings; you could ask the local restaurant, a farm and so on. Don't forget that letter stating that they are prepared to let you film there for free, whereas the normal cost of hiring out the place for the time you want it would be a certain price, cost or rate.

Remember this

Try to ensure that your letters of support are typed on headed paper from the organization or business you've approached; otherwise anyone could have written them.

The more places you can think of, the greater the potential for getting those lovely letters of support. It doesn't only have to relate to locations; you may get some free assistance from a lighting rental company, a caterer, a camera hire outlet and so on. Try to get as many goods and services for free as possible, but always get a letter stating how much this service would normally be valued at.

Focus points

✳ Be realistic when trying to get hold of locations.

✳ Don't always expect people to give you permission to film somewhere.

✳ Always have a critical look around a location before you decide to film there.

✳ When you get permission to film somewhere get some kind of official confirmation.

✳ If a location looks great, but is impractical to get to, or has some other problem, look somewhere else.

✳ Make sure everyone at the location knows who you are and what you are doing (some organizations are terrible at internal communications).

✳ Try to keep things tidy and clean up after you have finished for the day.

✳ Establish a room where you can keep things to charge or store when not in use.

✳ Try not to upset people who may use the location as their work place.

✳ Be safe with your filming: don't overload circuits, don't film while standing on wobbly chairs and don't set off any fire alarms!

Next step

Raising finance for your film can be an exhausting and soul-destroying process. There's lots of competition out there for the available funds, especially from conventional funding organizations, so getting funders' attention – let alone their money – is extremely tough. Newer forms of financing such as crowdfunding offer potential but have their own pitfalls.

Financing your film

In this chapter you will learn:

▶ *how to budget accurately for your film*
▶ *about some potential sources of funding for your film*
▶ *what to do if it doesn't go to plan*

Quick recap

Before we discuss finance, here is a short recap on what we have covered so far.

▶ Write the script or, at the very least, know what the film is to be about.

▶ Sort out your actors and make sure they are reliable and right for the part.

▶ Decide what camera system you want to use.

▶ Know how to use your chosen camera or find someone who does.

▶ Have an idea of what lights and lighting effects you want in the film.

▶ Figure out how you're going to record your sound.

▶ Decide where you are going to film.

▶ Obtain permission to film in the places you want (if relevant to your film).

▶ Make some kind of preliminary efforts to get official support for your film.

If you feel confident about the above, it's time to crank up another gear and think about how you are going to finance your film.

Key idea

Deciding whether or not you need to obtain funding for your film is a T-junction for many. One route may take you on an unpleasant journey with no guarantee of success, whereas the other will mean you get started more quickly, but without all the resources you want.

How much will all this cost?

Before you start thinking of the many ways you can get money to pay for aspects of your film (that's presuming you think you need any), you should first think about how much it is going to cost. It is very important to work out some kind of budget for your film, and your finance philosophy should always be, 'Don't pay for something unless there is no other option.'

As highlighted in the case study in Chapter 8, if I hadn't been careful I could have ended up paying for the hire of the lovely room in my local town hall at an expensive rate. As it was, I negotiated something. You, too, should try to see what's possible. Then, and only then, should you consider paying for things – but always try to wangle some kind of discount. You'll be surprised how prices can come down when you say you're making a film. When you come into contact with groups and organizations that help out film makers, they will be very aware of the problems you are experiencing, and you won't be the first person who has turned up with cap in hand asking for something for free.

Stop for a moment and consider this logic: to buy and rent things that you need to make your film (depending on its size, of course) calls for money. Obtaining money can be a stressful and tiresome exercise, as this chapter will highlight, so what many first-time and low-budget film makers do is to ignore this problematic issue in the first place.

I'll explain. When you are successful at getting money, you then spend it on renting a camera and kit, for example. Why not consider trying to get hold of the camera and kit for free? Directly target the resource you are after in the first place. As Chapter 1 stated, if you don't ask for something you don't get it. There is a whole world of potentially free and heavily discounted items out there just waiting for you to come along.

For some reason, there seems to be a consensus that in order for any kind of film to be made, vast quantities of money must be thrown at it.

Remember this

Making films is often about the art of improvising and making do with whatever resources are immediately available to you. Don't get hung up trying to get that 'magic cheque' that will suddenly green-light your film and allow things to start in the morning.

The reality of having the means to go ahead with making your project is rarely a glamorous thing – constantly assess what you have, what you need, and try to find out what the trade-off between the two is. All too often, people feel that they have to reach a certain equipment or finance threshold before they can go ahead with making their film. Remember, film making can be a 'cottage industry'.

Expenses

Let's now discuss the kinds of thing you will have to pay for.

ADMINISTRATION

Arranging all of the above, and everything else in this book, does cost money. Not great amounts, but buying printer paper, paying for photocopies, travelling to meetings, paying phone bills, faxes and general office-type things do add up. One thing likely to cause a 'cost spike' is phone calls. It takes a lot of phone calls to arrange, research and generally make a film, so beware and be prepared to expect a higher phone bill than normal. After camera hire, phone calls were the highest cost when I made my first film.

Obviously, costs can vary dramatically depending on how 'big' you see your film being.

CAMERA HIRE

This will depend on the system you have chosen to work with. You may be able to borrow camcorders and some other systems from relatives and friends or be lucky enough to afford your own. However, you may want to rent a prosumer or professional camera that is too expensive to buy. In this case you will have to hire it from somewhere for a few days.

CASSETTES, DISCS, FLASH DRIVES OR FILM STOCK FOR YOUR CAMERA

It's rather embarrassing turning up on set and realizing that you don't have any film, although I've been on shoots where this has happened. Borrowing or being given second-hand tapes may seem like a good financial move, but this is not the greatest way to achieve high-quality images or sound. However, one popular way of getting reduced-price, or sometimes free, film is to obtain surplus unused film from another production (although trying to find these productions and consequent surplus film is another matter).

LIGHTS

You will need to add these to your budget if you have decided on the more powerful and/or professional lighting systems that are usually hired out by certain companies, or if you need to buy some strong lights from a hardware store.

RENTAL OF LOCATIONS

In the event of a place not giving you permission to film somewhere for free (and no nice letter of support), and if it's absolutely vital for a particular scene, then you'll have to hire it.

FOOD AND DRINK

If you don't plan on paying your actors and crew, for the simple reason that you don't think you'll be able to, then you should at least do them the courtesy of feeding them. Having people stand around all day between takes isn't fun at the best of times; having them stand around all day with rumbling stomachs is worse. Don't forget that people can often feel faint under the hot lights, and this, together with an empty stomach, can spell disaster. No one is forcing them to attend, so keep them happy (cheap cafés and sandwich shops will do fine) and make an effort to get on with them – otherwise they may walk out on you.

TRAVEL EXPENSES

As with the above, it's a courtesy that will go a long way to showing the cast and crew that you care. However, make sure you stipulate public transport only, or some smart alec will turn up in a limo and hand you the bill.

ADDITIONAL COSTS

Depending on what your film is about, how ambitious it is and so on, here are a few other things you might want to consider when costing your film:

- ▶ make-up

- ▶ hairdressing

- ▶ special effects (see Chapter 13)

- ▶ costumes

- ▶ props

As with previous lists, this is not an exhaustive one and you will no doubt think up some of your own. For example, a period horror film will involve all of the above, whereas a documentary about a day in an office probably won't. Important note: Just because I have listed these things does not necessarily mean that you will have to pay for them. Your powers of negotiation will decide the day! But don't forget those letters of support.

Key idea

For those of you with modest film making plans, trying to get hold of money may, ironically, get in the way of your film making. Some films don't need any funding or money, and some film makers can, and have, wasted time and energy chasing funding and grandiose revenue streams when they had all their resources already to hand. Remember that successful productions have been made without any external backing.

Obtaining funding

Methods for obtaining money range from the simple to the sublime. I received only a few thousand in cash for my first film. You may think that this is peanuts, but what stranger is going to give you that amount of money? So, how and where can you obtain it? Let's take a look at some tried-and-tested methods.

1 PAYING FOR IT YOURSELF

Remember this

Did you know that George Lucas paid for *The Empire Strikes Back* himself?

Obviously, not many people will be capable of such expenditure, but if you have enough savings, and are prepared to spend them on a film, then that's great. If not, then you'll have to try …

2 ASKING FRIENDS AND RELATIVES

This is a straightforward and simple method: you approach them and ask. No doubt some of them, depending on how big your film project is, won't be able to afford to help. Some kindly uncle or aunt may hand out the occasional sum here and there but, on the whole, friends and relatives may, quite rightly, be extremely dubious about handing over their hard-earned money. If this method draws a blank, how about the next one?

3 APPROACHING SMALL- AND MEDIUM-SIZED BUSINESSES

This is another popular method of financing a film (and lots of other things). This avenue of funding is a form of sponsorship (see point 6) but on a much smaller scale. As such, it may take several 'bites' before you have enough interest and money to start things moving. I know a film that had all its catering taken care of, thanks to a local diner. While filming in Hungary once I got a 20 per cent discount off my hotel bills in return for mentioning the hotel in my film's credits. All it takes is imagination and persistence to get some results.

4 SELLING SHARES IN YOUR FILM

Unlike the above three examples, this has to be a very well-planned, well-thought-out and professionally tailored mode of getting money. What you are doing is selling interest in a business – that is, your film. The sale of the shares pays, or part pays, for the film. When the film makes money you pay back the shareholders at a previously agreed percentage. Like all business ventures there is a certain degree of risk involved – the shareholders are not guaranteed any returns. Also, some of them may get cold feet and suddenly decide that they want the value of their shares back. If the film isn't a money-spinner, the shareholders may get a tad irate with you.

If you want to pursue this line of fundraising, then it would be a good idea to consult a professional. Bits of paper with 'Film Share' written on them and sold at street corners will not do. Go to the local business centre, your bank manager, the local film office, and so on, and get some sound advice before you even think of getting things under way. Want something riskier? Then try ...

5 PAYING FOR IT ON CREDIT CARD

Those little oblong pieces of bright plastic have paid for more films than you might think. I've been at film makers' meetings and heard people talk about their experiences of this type of film financing. A member of a UK film agency suggested that I make my film like this, even though I was unemployed at the time. Obviously, it's very risky, but if a credit card is at hand then you can start paying for things right away, such as camera hire, transport or whatever. Now if anyone reading this has a credit card, then you will know how easy it is to spend money without realizing it. 'It's only plastic, there's no cash involved.' Such was the saying of many of my student chums while at university – before a huge credit card bill fell through the letter box with a resounding thud. It's easy to pay for things with a credit card when making a film but getting that money back to pay the eventual bill is another matter. The best examples I can think of where a film was financed by credit card was the low-budget satire *Hollywood Shuffle* (dir. Robert Townsend, 1987). Luckily for Mr Townsend the film was a big success and started his career. Also, Kevin Smith mostly financed the hit film *Clerks* by maxing out his credit cards.

An increasingly popular method of getting some funds for low-budget film productions is to sell acting roles, or some other kind of involvement, using the Internet bidding site eBay. Some producers and directors have bids for key roles such as lead male, or lead female actor, hoping for the bidding to heat up and generate substantial amounts to part finance the film. Other roles will be auctioned for lesser amounts.

While this is a clever and inventive idea it is important not to mislead people with this method.

Remember this

Don't promise a blockbuster production when you are filming a low-/no-budget film. Also, don't expect masses of revenue to be generated. Remember, too, that the people looking in on your eBay bid may think twice if things look amateurish, such as not having further links to other websites giving more details about the production.

6 PRIVATE SPONSORSHIP

Many large businesses and corporations are used to having complete strangers ring them up and ask them for money. In fact, they usually have their own private sponsorship departments.

Case study: Finding sponsors

While making one film, I received private sponsorship from two completely unrelated (and possibly unlikely) sources: Bass Beers International and Czech Airlines. Although they didn't actually give me any money, they did save me huge amounts by giving me things for free – thousands worth of beer, props and technical assistance, as mentioned before – while Czech Airlines gave me a 70 per cent discount on flights to Prague. The latter saved me a few thousand when I eventually took the cast and crew to the Czech Republic. Just because an organization won't give you money need not mean that all is lost – remember the logic about avoiding money and going directly for the resource.

Try to be strategic when you are contacting potential sponsors. Think of reasons why they should help you out. Is there any relation between your film and the nature of their business, for example? If your film is about a religious sect who shun alcohol, then it probably isn't a good idea to contact breweries for sponsorship.

7 ARTS ORGANIZATIONS AND FILM BOARDS

A great deal of focus is currently on arts organizations as potential sources of funding for low-budget films – and even some larger ones as well. There are numerous grants, loans and other financial packages operated by these organizations and they are usually very eager to help with advice and assistance in finding information about funding processes and so on. They are often the first port of call for people who have never done a creative project before.

One important thing they will tell you, and something you will see on application forms for money, is the importance of having other sponsors, or partners, that are interested in your film. This brings us back to those letters of support. These letters are the building blocks when it comes to obtaining money from national or regional arts organizations. Some grants state that you will need to have some money available, in addition to other support, before you can be considered for a grant payment.

They also won't always pay grants to individuals, which means you will need to have some kind of company profile with two or more members. This is to try to make sure people don't get paid grants and then run off with the money as both members are liable for the amount. Most banks will have some kind of club or business accounts that you can set up in the name of your company or film organization so that if you do manage to get a grant, or any other money, you can ask them to pay it to the name of the film company instead of your name. You may be required to open an account with at least two signatories.

Remember this

Having a company or organization name is a very good way of giving you and your film some credibility, especially when it comes to fundraising. Try to think of a relatively sensible name, as a silly arty name may not be an impressive calling card.

8 COMMUNITY FILM AND VIDEO COMPANIES

Once in a while, a community organization dealing with the hiring of professional film making equipment and services will run a bursary. This will be a relatively small amount of money that is occasionally given out to a local film maker whom they class as being a 'non-professional'. A drawback with these is that the subject matter and duration for the bursaries is often quite specific and it isn't a case of being handed some money and then filming what you want with it.

9 LOCAL FILM AGENCIES

These are grants and schemes aimed at encouraging local talent in film production. They can sometimes be quite non-specific with regard to duration and subject matter and thus tend to be very popular with local low-budget film makers.

10 NATIONAL FUNDING

This method of funding has overlaps with the arts organizations as well as with the grant making and charitable trusts, as details and information of their grants will be available from both. Although National Funding has grants comparable with the Regional Arts

Councils, they are not targeted at regions. Instead they are, as the name suggests, national.

National Funding gives money to lots of different causes but for arts practitioners, including budding film makers, there will be a fair number of grants that apply. The monetary value varies from hundreds to millions and, needless to say, the grant forms that deal with the larger figures are very detailed and complex – they require that you have money-giving partners and the form is a very official-looking document. The grants for smaller amounts are wonderfully simple. However, please realize that with all grant forms you will have to state exactly how much money you want, and why you need this much money – refer to the section on costing your film.

▶ **International Film Making Grants.**

While many countries operate their own moving image grants either as part of a national or regional arts funding organization, there exist other avenues for the cash-desperate film maker.

This is beyond the private or independent bursaries that likewise may be limited to the country it originates from.

At the international level, numerous grants and schemes have been set up to assist the fiction and documentary film maker. As you'd expect, it isn't a wild free-for-all where the prospective film maker merely need submit a basic request asking for cash. Many of the grants will have very specific requirements the film maker must adhere to. This can include stringent conditions on things such as the subject matter, a requirement for certain equipment to be used, the locations where most of the film will be shot, if substantial funding has already been secured by the producers and so on.

Many of these international grants may actually only be available to those residing, or producing the film, in certain regions of the globe. While this still casts a wide net, not all will be at the global level. In spite of all this, they do offer another level of funding for those who may have drawn a blank in other areas, or who quite simply have ticked many of the criteria boxes by virtue of their film's subject and location.

To list all relevant grants may be counterproductive as they can come and go, change criteria and so on. The www.filmdaily.tv website has a good handle on contemporary international grants. Although it's worth mentioning that many of the companies that supply and make film making technology regularly run grants and other schemes.

Plus of course, a regular Google search will reveal what is available in your neck of the woods at any one time.

Case study: Success story

One major aspect of the convergence of film making and Internet technology is the notion of making and uploading a short trailer in order to generate a bit of interest and backing for a film idea. Although this can be a very hit-and-miss thing to do, the potential for millions of people looking in on your idea is substantial.

In 2009 Uruguayan film maker Fede Álvarez uploaded the five-minute science-fiction short *Ataque de pánico* on to YouTube. The film was made for a budget of around $300 and is about giant robots attacking a city. To the amazement of Alvarez, a few days after being uploaded it was spotted by some major film studios and eventually a $30 million budget was agreed to make it as a feature-length film.

So it's worth a try perhaps ...?

11 CROWDFUNDING – PATREON AND KICKSTARTER

The current generation of film makers and film making technology has drastically altered the playing field in terms of allowing people to start shooting.

Gone are the days when cameras, edit gear and other film making paraphernalia were simply out of reach due to their availability and price. A low- or no-budget film maker dreaming of shooting a story back in the 1970s would have possibly been forced to use super 8 mm cameras and film, separate sound recording gear and 'flatbed' cutting and editing equipment. While many a film has been made this way, you can't compare the quality with a contemporary professional film – the grain of the film, the quality of the film, would all shout out amateur – yet this was the best you could get at the time depending on your circumstances. Even then, the price of the film and processing would add up to a possibly eye-watering amount.

Skip forward a decade to the 1980s and the world experienced a consumer boom in affordable camcorders using affordable tape cassettes. Many low-budget film makers picked up their VHS camcorder and shot high-energy films on abundant tapes. However, the quality still wasn't anywhere near what you would see on a major film release. The colours might be garish, bright lights would leave 'smear trails' across the frame and the definition could be rough-looking. Also, the editing could be clunky, with fast editing problematic due to the mechanical nature of tape-to-tape editing (this was long before digital editing, remember).

In the 1990s something very interesting happening with the 'digital revolution'. I'm not necessary talking about computers here, but rather camera formats were being produced at the consumer level where the images were processed digitally. The once ubiquitous MiniDV format was perhaps the most high-profile face of this digital movement and was used by amateurs, hobbyists and professionals alike. Fiction films like *The Blair Witch Project* and *28 Days Later* showed the world how very cheap formats could produce commercially and artistically successful films. Not to mention documentary film makers the world over were able to make compelling films without the need for huge camera crews. Now was the age when a single 'lone shooter' could produce an entire series! This was something almost unheard of before.

Overall, this demonstrated how the gap between amateur formats and professional ones was narrowing in terms of image quality, as gadgets and gizmos like depth of field adaptors gave MiniDV footage a rich glossy look. This is a theme mentioned in other chapters of this book, but here it demonstrates how contemporary film makers are no longer stymied by lack of access to professional formats, which had previously meant that they needed to acquire some kind of finance even to rent or buy cameras. Or, to put it another way, gone is the day when an impoverished aspiring film maker was shut out of achieving their ambition due to the general inaccessibility of movie-making kit.

Key idea

Nowadays the local photo or electronics store probably sells a camera that, if used properly, can produce results to rival a major release.

So surely this means the same funding or cash barriers have been removed?

Not quite.

While it's all very well a capable camera system may come your way after you save up for a while or as a Christmas or birthday present, it can still mean there are numerous other expenses you need to worry about. Plus, the effort required to make even simple vlogs on a regular basis can be considerable. Since giving up your job on the hope that your film making efforts will become profitable isn't an option for most people, luckily there are alternatives.

Yes, there are already ways to monetize your YouTube account which may work out for those receiving hundreds of thousands of views. For those just starting out or with smaller audiences, you may wish to pursue alternative funding streams.

Specifically, the websites Kickstarter and Patreon could be of assistance. (Of course, there are other funding sites out there such as Indiegogo, RocketHub and GoFundMe, plus many more).

Essentially, they are serving a need that all creative entrepreneurs desire – cash to get started! However, things are a bit more codified and better run compared to the old-fashioned method of perhaps posting a random video of someone speaking into a camera asking for money or calling up studios asking for funding. Also, it's less risky than getting several credit cards and them maxing them out. Instead, these services allow you – the creator – to legitimately ask for money in order to create something. If anyone is interested in your idea, they will contribute certain amounts of funding in return for some kind of reward such as a mention in the credits or an invite to the premiere. It's not just unknown first-timers using the service, but also established names such as Spike Lee who accurately says raising finance by asking around is nothing new. It's what many film makers have done over the years. In fact, Lee's appeal video in itself makes very good viewing as he describes the challenges of obtaining film funding and the pitfalls when it all goes wrong.

Kickstarter is best suited to a single film or project that has a definite beginning and end. Additionally, the funding window is set for a set amount of time. So, over this time you have to acquire the funding required (set out in the project details) in order to go ahead. Yet, this doesn't simply mean that you type in a few things and then sit back. You still need to raise the profile of your intended project via videos, copy, photographs and so on. All of which helps potential contributors get an understanding of your project and whether it's something they want to back.

Patreon is similar but different. This crowdfunding site tends to be favoured by vloggers, podcasters and generally people creating and delivering content on some kind of regular basis. The concept is that, if you like something and want more, then you will contribute to future productions. As such, it's open-ended and on-going with those funding your efforts essentially paying a subscription for your material. While some may think they can just watch the content anyway, seeing as it's being put out there, Patreon allows access to otherwise unavailable content just for subscribers or 'Patrons' as they site calls them.

This has allowed many content creators to 'ditch the day job' as the money received from Patreon has allowed them to turn professional and do things full-time. While such riches or lifestyle enhancement may not befall everyone who uses Patreon, it can at least mean that you are rewarded in some way for the often considerable effort required to film, edit and upload videos on a regular basis.

Remember this

One final word of caution about these sites: fundamentally things haven't changed from the days of ringing up people and asking for money. It's the same thing but different. Don't be misled into thinking just because you get a project listed on Kickstarter or Patreon all will be well and cash will start flowing. Rather, you are just one of many countless thousands chasing money for their project ... and, as such, you may get nowhere.

A long haul

There are many other sources of funding, from fiddly and complex multinational funding bodies to a simple small business grant or a local authority scheme. It's worth bearing in mind that a large organization may take a very long time to reach a decision. Don't expect a reply over the phone or within a week of making an application. These things are all reviewed, referred and considered for what seems like an eternity to an impatient film maker. Take this into account when planning things.

As I have highlighted a few times already, it is very important to know how big your production will eventually be. The reason why this has been drummed into you is so that it will not only influence your choice of equipment, but also how much money you may need. If, from having looked over your script and gauging your ambition, you feel that your film is a big production that can only be made successfully with the injection of serious amounts of cash then fine. But ...

Trying to obtain large amounts of money to start making your film is a thing that can turn your hair grey and ruin your life – I kid you not. This is why I have droned on about seriously thinking about what level your film will be at while trying to instil the importance of being a negotiator. If you realize that you are able to tell your tale effectively with the use of a camcorder, some friends and a small amount of cash, then that's great. A script will communicate to you what level it wants to be filmed at, and you may be mindful of this when you are sitting down writing it. Some of you may think your script will be best served by a bit of casting at the local drama society and by using some professional-grade cameras and equipment. Others will write the script with the solid intention of going the distance with 35 mm film of HDCAM. This varies from person to person as a lot of it is up to your ambition and spare time.

The bigger your intended budget, the more hassle involved in trying to achieve this goal. It is not a pleasant ride. It can be a frustrating catalogue of meetings with sympathetic individuals who smile at the right times but keep their purse strings closed. Everyone wants to get funding, you will not be the only one out there. It is a small network of industry professionals who once in a while attend networking events or will perhaps invite you for a meeting and give encouraging words. At the end of the day, no one is going to pour money into a project that is being undertaken by individuals with no track record. It is a really tough club to break into. You might go mad in the attempt.

If you pester people enough, a few doors may open. You may even just want to call up a big broadcaster and ask to speak to someone from the drama or comedy department – audacity and ingenuity remember – to see if you can come in for a chat or at least pick their brains in some way. They are usually quite eager to speak to new talent once they find out that you are not another desperate actor trying to get lucky. Although this may seem a very long-winded way of doing things (and it is), it's what a lot of people before you have done. Some have been lucky and others have not. But it's a vital first step into the realms of networking as this is the way in which you can enter a world that may allow your film to be made.

From this first meeting, or telephone conversation with someone who's in the industry, you may come away with a few names and numbers, which may in turn result in a few more names and meetings, which all help on the quest to get your film made. This is networking, and it is what I had to do a few times to get a few jobs as well as get things moving with my first film. Basically, if no one knows you exist and that you are carrying a film script around then there's no way you are going to get very far.

Many directors of dramas, documentaries and feature films got their foot on the ladder by just introducing themselves to some relevant people when they were all young guns. It is how the film and television industry works.

Getting the money together to make your film may be one of the most complicated and confusing odysseys you will ever experience. Have a serious think about whether you, and your family, are prepared for it.

Key idea

Film making is becoming more and more accessible and more democratized every year. Until the 1990s you would definitely have needed money to make a decent-quality film. Now it's the case that you probably won't need money to make a decent film. Think about it.

Assessing your resources

Congratulations! You've got some money. Now the question you must ask yourself is this: is it enough to make the film? If the answer is 'no', then you must either:

▶ re-budget your film, or

▶ try to get some more

To re-budget your film, you just have to make do with what you have, and this may not always be practical. However, remember that you may be chasing a dream when you think that you don't have enough money. Don't go killing yourself in an agonizing attempt to get more money. It may be that the resources and money you already have in your possession are more than enough to get your film made with a little ingenuity and improvisation. What you have may be all you need to make your film.

However, if this is not the case, then you have to take a long and critical look at what the proposed budget for your film is, break it down into individual costs – as per the section on costing – and see what things you can do without. If you truly, honestly, no-way-about-it feel that you need more, then you must try to get it. Now this probably has some of you groaning in anticipation at the thought of going through the rigmarole of fundraising again, but take note: when you have been given some money, people and organizations will take you quite seriously. The thinking behind this is: 'If they've been given money, then maybe we should.'

The process of accretion is quite fundamental to fundraising; the theory being similar to rolling a pebble down a snow-covered mountain and it turning into a huge ball of snow by the time it reaches the bottom (although sometimes the pebble gets stuck). With the money you've been given, it will definitely be worth contacting the aforementioned funding bodies again. They'll probably remember you, but this time you've got a sizeable sum of money that you want them to match.

Match funding is a tit-for-tat exercise in money raising. Someone gives you some money, then someone else gives you an equal amount, then with that money you go somewhere else and get some more, and so on. Do bear in mind, though, that it is not always as 'textbook' as it appears. It takes lots of telephone calls, letters, faxes, meetings, stress, anger and waiting. Even then you still might get nowhere.

Try to create and maintain a confidence in your project and yourself as a film maker. As mentioned in the first chapter, things will not always go your way. Be prepared for disappointing outcomes and let-downs and then think of a way around these obstacles. Making a film is not something that everyone can cope with mentally. It's not just a hobby or a pastime, it's an obsession, and unless you adopt this obsessive way of thinking you may not get very far.

Focus points

✻ Critically assess your financial needs; just because you are making a film doesn't always mean you need lots of money.

✻ Keep reviewing your resources; you may discover you can go ahead with things ahead of schedule.

✻ See if local stores can assist with providing things like tape stock or food.

✻ If appropriate, give thought to raising finances through Internet bidding sites. At worst, it may provide some income to cover basic costs.

✻ Research what funding in your country and area is available to you.

✻ Realize that there are thousands of film makers trying to get at the same funds of money as you.

✻ Although films can be addictive things to make, don't ruin your financial health by spending all your savings or maxing out on your credit cards.

✻ Network and try to make friends with arts bodies and professionals; they may give you a heads up on some available funding.

✻ As technology advances, it is getting cheaper to make a decent film.

✻ Lots of money doesn't mean you will make a great film.

Next step

In Chapter 10, I look at how you can fine-tune your film making. As in many areas of life, attention to detail is crucial. If your film is to be successful as a piece of film making, you will need to keep track of a wide number of issues, from framing to continuity. It can feel like you're juggling with too many balls, but there are lots of techniques to help you pull it off.

10

Fine-tuning your vision

In this chapter you will learn:

▶ *the importance of planning and/or storyboarding your film*

▶ *the basic rules of filming and presenting your actors*

▶ *how to translate script into moving images*

How on earth am I going to film this?

Imagine for a moment that you are very knowledgeable, qualified and competent in all aspects of operating any camera system under the sun. You also have all the related pieces of equipment and kit that will allow you to achieve any camera effect. Now here's a task for you. There is a large, lush oak tree in the middle of a field and it's a calm, bright, sunny day. Your task is to film the tree for 30 seconds.

Look over the situation again and then really think hard about what you will do. Some of you may feel a bit mystified by this; others might already be erupting with vivid and fantastic ways to make filming the tree look very interesting and 'art house'. The important point is that, when you're a film maker, it's your role to tell a story in a primarily visual way. You've got to make things interesting to look at. If your solution to the above situation was to film it straight on for 30 seconds, then you seriously need to rethink your visual approach.

Storyboards

One of the elements that fine-tunes the latter stages of pre-production is the storyboard. You probably all know what a storyboard is and what its function is. It's the visual instructions for the camera work of the film; it's how the shots of the various scenes will be framed – that is, visually presented. It's a very important function of large-scale feature-length films. Imagine a top Hollywood director making his or her way through the hordes of crew, extras, actors, equipment, props and so on, and saying, 'Oh dear, I haven't really thought about how to film this scene.'

In the context of low-budget, small-scale films, the role of storyboards is very subjective – some need it, some don't. I would have liked to have had a storyboard for my first feature film, but I didn't know anyone who was prepared to draw thousands of comic-style pictures for free, so I had to give it a miss. Instead, I took a close look at every part of my script, divided it up and marked out what the camera moves, framing and so forth were to be with a red pen next to the relevant text. Very simple indeed. If I had attempted to draw a storyboard myself, it would have been a confusing mess of stick people in one-dimensional rooms.

If you are a bit perturbed about how your film should look in relation to formulating some kind of provisional mental storyboard, then simply rent a collection of films by your favourite directors and take a look at how they do it. Another good method for generating ideas is to read comics or graphic novels. They contain a wealth of statically framed pictures, and I personally reckon they're the best method to pick up ideas about how to present a scene as it's easier to 'pause' a comic book than a video.

Remember this

To practise framing, look through the eyepiece of a photographic camera to see what looks hot and what doesn't. We will come back to framing later, as it is a gigantic subject.

Continuity

Continuity is the basic insurance that elements of a scene remain consistent throughout. For example, making sure that people are wearing the same clothes in a scene, that their hair is styled the same way, or that the decorations on the walls don't move around. Lapses in continuity can have varying effects on a film.

In a very serious, no-laughs-allowed kind of film, continuity errors are gravely embarrassing. Imagine in *Schindler's List* (dir. Stephen Spielberg, 1993) if Schindler had entered a room wearing his trilby and then exited wearing a baseball cap? Ouch! The balance, tone and mood of a very serious and intense film could be ruined. In zany comedy films continuity errors can have the opposite effect – they can enhance the film and make things funnier.

In general, you'll probably find that the only people who spot continuity errors are the film's director and over-zealous, geekish film critics. I'll cite an example. How many of you have ever spotted the fellow in the green T-shirt suddenly standing behind Chewbacca and Han Solo in the cockpit of the *Millennium Falcon* as they escape from Tatooine in *Star Wars*?

Continuity errors are usually the result of a set that is very busy with lots of people bumping into and unwittingly moving props, light angles, and so forth. Also, when a scene isn't filmed in one session, or over consecutive days, the original set-up might not be fresh in people's minds. It is particularly in the latter case that actors may turn up wearing different clothes, or decorations on a desk may be rearranged or partially missing. The best way to combat this is to use a photographic camera – preferably a Polaroid. By doing this you can visually document your set/actors' clothes for the purposes of smooth continuity, so that when you return to film the scene, you can point to the photo and say, 'This is how it was last week.'

Make sure you use a marker to write on the back of the Polaroid picture referencing date and scene, otherwise you could end up with a collection of photos that don't make any sense to you. Continuity just needs some basic planning and awareness to keep it in check.

Key idea: Guerrilla film making

This is an expression used to describe certain aspects of low-budget film making. It gets its name from the practice of turning up somewhere in a car unannounced, filming, and then going away again. As a low-budget film maker you may not always have the time, money or inclination to plan your filming in a certain location and sometimes you just have to go for it like a film making special forces commando.

Jump cuts

These gremlins usually go unnoticed when filming but raise their ugly heads during the editing process. They will be re-examined in the chapter on editing, but for now it's important to know how to guard against them while actually filming. Imagine a scene where a man is walking down a street and in mid-step he's suddenly and awkwardly indoors in the middle of a telephone conversation. This is a jump cut.

Jump cuts can be two shots from two different locations, or one shot that has the 'middle' missing. In the latter case, an example would be someone opening a door and then suddenly the door would be closed and they would be out of shot. These instances can seriously confuse the viewer. The best example of a jump cut I can think of is in the film *Poltergeist* (yes, it can happen in big films!). There is the scene when the husband and wife are talking in the kitchen just after their daughter has been supernaturally propelled across the floor, and then suddenly they're at a neighbour's door. The viewer is left wondering what has happened.

When filming, the best way to protect against jump cuts is to film cutaways (see Chapter 7). These are shots that can be stuck between takes to link them together seamlessly. One cutaway for the above example of the man walking down the street would be to film a static of a house, which could then be placed between the two other shots. This would mean that the man doesn't appear 'magically' in conversation on the phone. The viewer will assume he was walking to the house in the cutaway. Simple.

Cutaways are a very good and essential practice to get in the habit of when you are filming. It is another example of filming with an eye for, and appreciation of, what you will do when you get to the edit stage of your film. You can be filming two shots and then 'cover' yourself by filming a cutaway so that you don't get caught out when editing. You can never have enough cutaways.

It should be said, however, that jump cuts can be used successfully to compress time in the film's narrative and make things a bit weird and disorienting. Take a look at some of the frantic and energetic sequences from *Natural Born Killers* (dir. Oliver Stone, 1994) to see what I mean.

Key idea: Just the one camera?

When looking at any film, it is only natural to think the scenes were all filmed from varying angles simultaneously. This isn't the case at all. Usually, there is just one camera on set that changes position and films the same action over again from different angles. This is called Single Camera Directing. More than one camera may make it awkward to film the set without seeing crew, lights and so on, and also there is the expense of hiring more than one camera plus the crew to go with it. However, for difficult-to-repeat shots, such as complicated stunts, several cameras may be used.

Good and bad framing

Framing is a truly enormous subject. It is essentially a subjective thing because no two people will be inclined to film the same piece of dialogue, or the same scene, or the same shot in the same way. That said, there are a few basic technical rules to take into consideration. In no particular order these are:

FILMING PEOPLE

In your film, there will no doubt be dialogue. This obviously needs to be filmed but, before you film a two-minute conversation using a single mastershot, think about what you are trying to do here. You are illustrating how two people are interacting. That's no big revelation. However, within that simple statement is the driving force of your framing: you have two people, who will, perhaps, be sitting opposite each other, so one will be on the left and one will be on the right. It's very important to remember that last bit: one will be on the left and one will be on the right. If you get this simple equation mixed up your scene will look terrible.

So, with the basic mastershot there is Actor A on the left and Actor B on the right (see Figure 10.1).

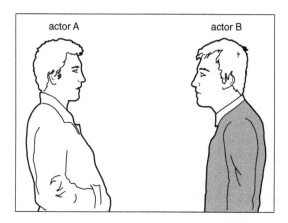

Figure 10.1

Figure 10.2

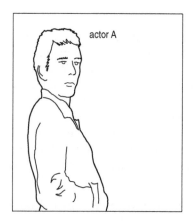

Figure 10.3

In the cutaway of Actor B, the face is looking to the left (see Figure 10.2). In the cutaway of Actor A, the face is looking right (see Figure 10.3). Thus, in the edited scene the actors will be facing their respective directions all the way through the scene. What I'm saying here is: don't cross the line. This expression is a basic framing rule. If you can imagine the above filming set-up from overhead, and if you were to draw a line between the two actors, then the camera will always stay on one side of the line; otherwise people will start to look as if they keep spontaneously changing direction (see Figure 10.4).

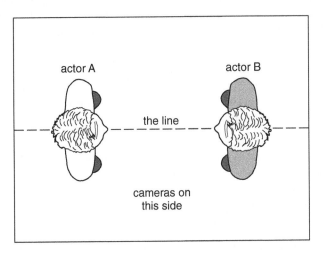

Figure 10.4

The best example of this rule is television coverage of a football match. Team A has the goal on the left and Team B has the goal on the right. The cameras are always on one side of the pitch. Imagine if a camera was filming a footballer running with the ball and then it made a reverse cut to a different camera view from the other side of the pitch. It would appear as though the footballer had instantly started running in the opposite direction. This is why, during football matches, the cameras will usually only ever cross the line if they have got better coverage of a goal or corner kick and then there is normally a sign or note made that they are using a view from the other side of the pitch.

Even if you are filming a few people it is very important to ascertain where the line is. It may be between two points in a room, for example. Ignore this line at your peril, unless, of course, you wish to make the situation look manic and surreal. Crossing the line is often used during interrogation scenes to illustrate confusion and put a 'twist' on the passing of time.

With these pointers in mind, it is important not to lose track of the basic need to present your subject in an agreeable way. This basic framing (as opposed to sequences, which we will look at later) is the way your subject – a building, person or object – is presented. The way it is done can have very strong effects on the film's narrative and visual style. Imagine you are filming a woman speaking into the camera lens. If she was in the centre of the frame, then the viewer's attention would be totally on her (see Figure 10.5). If only her head, from the eyes up, were visible in the bottom left corner of the frame, then she would look very inferior, insignificant and ridiculous (see Figure 10.6).

Also, when an actor is speaking to someone in a scene you must frame accordingly. For example, if you have a side view of someone speaking to someone out of shot to the left, a good way to frame it would be to have the actor on the right of the frame, facing the space to their left (see Figure 10.7).

If you did this shot with the actor 'crushed' against the left of the frame with a large gap behind him, then the effect would be very odd. It might also suggest to the audience that something will jump on the actor from the space behind him (see Figure 10.8). Don't believe me? Then read on ...

Have you ever seen a film, usually a horror or thriller, when the hero has just run away from some monster or baddie and they've come to rest in a long corridor or alleyway? Ever noticed how the panting hero is usually in the left or right foreground while the entire length of the corridor/alleyway is visible behind them (see Figure 10.9)? It makes the audience think that something's going to come down and get them, doesn't it? However, just as with continuity, unorthodox framing could be the way to present your film in the way you want.

Rules aside, framing can give your film a certain style. By carefully considering what shots to use you can add a bit of weight and power that will complement the script and help tell the story. For example, consider the old gem in Chapter 10:

Figure 10.5

Figure 10.6

Figure 10.7

Figure 10.8

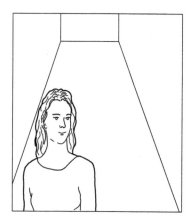

Figure 10.9

EXT. Desert town. Empty street — Day

A cowboy walks down the deserted main road. He
stops and lights a cigarette.

Nine times out of ten what the director will do here is film a low-angle shot from the ground that shows the entire length of the road with all the shops, saloons and buildings and then one black boot will appear at the edge of the frame. So, if the road goes off and to the right of the frame, the foot will appear in the bottom left of the frame (see Figure 10.10).

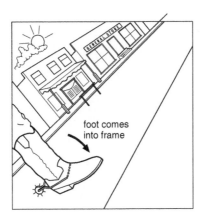

foot comes into frame

Figure 10.10

You must have seen a film like this. What a shot like this does is tell the audience that the foot (that is, the cowboy) means business. He is a powerful individual and he has just arrived – really arrived!

Now imagine if the framing had been different. For example, the shot has been the town from a distance and walking towards it, in the middle ground, is a black-clad figure. It just wouldn't have the same gravity to it. The latter shot would just say to an audience that someone is going towards the town – it is a completely different shot, which implies a certain feeling to the audience and puts a different mood in their minds.

Not stopping here, how would you continue the scene using interesting framing? There are quite a few possibilities. Since we are trying to establish the fact that this cowboy character is rather mean, how about placing the camera in front of him, low to the ground, facing upwards and walking in front of him (see Figure 10.11)? The effect of this would be that the cowboy would look like a giant, so reiterating the power he is supposed to have. However, one drawback with this framed shot is that any suspense you might be trying to build up would instantly disappear, because the man's face (depending on the detail included in the shot) and entire form would have been revealed. So, how could we continue with the mystery/enigmatic figure idea? How about, again, putting the camera low down, in front and walking ahead *but* only looking at the boots (see Figure 10.12)? This shot would create a bit more suspense and keep the mystery side of things going a bit longer, because once again the audience will be thinking, 'Who is this guy?'

Figure 10.11

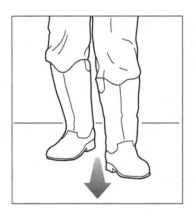

Figure 10.12

Figure 10.13

There is so much you can do here. Next would normally come a shot taken from inside a building looking out of the window towards the road as the cowboy passes (see Figure 10.13). This would suggest that the cowboy is being watched by someone as he saunters through the town. Then, to finish things off, there may be a long shot (see Figure 10.14), before the cowboy stops and the film cuts to a close-up of his hand striking a match (see Figure 10.15). The camera follows the lit match as it is raised to the end of the unlit cigarette. Then, as the cigarette is lit, the head raises up and from under the wide brim of the hat the cowboy's face is revealed as he exhales smoke.

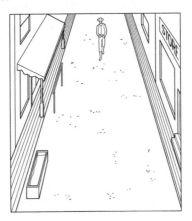

Figure 10.14

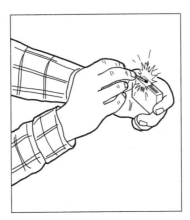

Figure 10.15

This probably describes most cowboy films where Clint Eastwood makes his entrance. The amazing thing is that all this comes from a part of the script with no dialogue. You will need to pay attention to these 'gaps' just as much as the speaking parts. It's the simple, silent interludes that string together the scenes with dialogue in a film. Very special care has to be taken with them, otherwise your film could turn out to be very flat and dull.

Think of some more examples to help you generate other ideas. At first, keep things to just four shots, for example:

EXT. Inner City. Busy street — Day

A tough-looking man walks down
the street.

This character is probably a bit mean, inhabits a murky underworld and probably frightens people around him. So how would we go about this framing set-up?

Shot 1: Filming through the window of a bar with a smoking ashtray and half-full beer glasses on the table as gangster walks by.

Shot 2: Camera in front of gangster as he walks; close-up on cigarette coming out of mouth and then slight zoom out as he exhales.

Shot 3: Long shot looking up the pavement as he walks away from the camera. People he passes timidly get out of the way and look at him as he walks by.

Shot 4: Low-angle long shot on floor of alleyway with overturned bins and garbage on the ground. Gangster walks into alley and then walks past camera.

So, without using any dialogue – and assuming the character is suitably tough-looking – we have established that this gangster inhabits a world of seedy pubs, he smokes, people are scared of him and he goes for meetings in seedy alleyways. A dangerous character has been established, all achieved by using the camera.

The cowboy and gangster examples are quite enigmatic and mean character illustrations, but not all films are like this. Not all of you will be making a cowboy or gangster movie. What about if you are making something romantic? Try this one, still keeping to just four shots:

Shot 1: Medium long shot of woman's face through crowded room. There is no one next to her.

Shot 2: Medium close-up of man's face; he smiles as he notices something or someone.

Shot 3: Camera moves towards the woman; she looks into the camera. She is slightly startled.

Shot 4: Two shot: the man approaches the woman; he offers her a glass of champagne.

So, from this lovely little example we can see that: the woman is on her own at a busy party; a man notices her (we presume); he moves towards her through the throng of people (simulated by the camera); he comes up to her and gives her a glass of champagne.

Again, there are other things to consider when talking about framing. So far I have just been talking about people, but what about objects and scenery? Remember in Chapter 8 when I said that your locations (and, by default, props) are your silent actors? You have got to give them some camera time, as it all adds to the colour of your film. Basically, there is no point having a great location, indoor or outdoor, if you are not going to film it. Consider this example set in an English boarding school in the 1930s between a headmaster and a mischievous young pupil:

INT: Main corridor of Saint Cuthbert's
Boarding School — Day

Headmaster Davies hurries up to Jenkins,
a young schoolboy.

Headmaster Davies

(shouting)Get in my office Jenkins. And
wait.

Jenkins

Yes, sir.

Jenkins walks into the room.

> ### INT: Headmaster Davies's office — Day
>
> Jenkins enters the room, closes the door behind him and sits down on a chair in front of the desk. He looks at the army photo of the headmaster, the stuffed moose head on the wall and the cane resting against a chair.

Right, I reckon this pupil is about to get beaten. Let's skip the dialogue and concentrate on the part from when Jenkins is sitting down. How can we put a sense of doom and fear into things using only the inanimate objects in the room and the location itself?

Shot 1: Film a close-up cutaway of a photo showing Mr Davies in army attire (disciplinarian).

Shot 2: Film a wide shot of the boy sitting on his own in the middle of the large room (vulnerable).

Shot 3: Film a close-up cutaway of a stuffed moose's head hanging on the wall (scary).

Shot 4: Film a close-up cutaway of a cane resting against the chair (the child is going to get it).

It is hoped that a certain sense of dread and overall foreboding will have been established by the framing here. Furthermore, the close-ups on those selected objects will make things a bit more intense.

All these simple details give your scenes, and overall film, the colour and life that it needs to sustain pace and, importantly, the audience's interest. The combination of the context of the scene in the script and what location and props/decorations are available, will tell you what details you need to film. Listen to your silent helpers.

This, as you may be starting to see, is a HUGE subject, and one that really does not have an end. It is extremely subjective yet, at the same time, is dictated by the nature of the script and overall story. Remember that your camera is not just a box of a certain size that records images. It is a storytelling tool. It has the power to capture moving images in imaginative and delicate ways. Use it well, don't just point and shoot.

Remember this

As a rule of thumb, think of what the scene's mastershot will be and then add detail. Soon you may have forgotten about the mastershot and dreamed up dozens of effective, well-framed shots for your scene.

Your observations of other films will no doubt make you aware of the various effects that can be created with imaginative framing.

Knowing when to stop filming a shot

When you film two people talking, the end of the conversation, and usually one of them exiting the area, will be the cue to stop filming. But what do you do when there is no dialogue and it's a shot of someone walking around a city, for example? Easy! If you are filming a long shot (a shot of something from far away) looking up a street, then when the actor walks towards the camera and simply goes past it, that's your cue.

Many people tend to make the mistake of following their subject – most commonly a person – way longer than necessary. If a person walks off, a common 'fault' is to swing the camera around to follow them and then zoom in as they walk away. This can be very awkward to watch as you can tell that things have gone on for longer than they should have.

Key idea

If you are filming people walking through a location, be it a building or city, have them move across the frame instead of towards or away. This way it will be easier to establish the edit points instead of having them go off endlessly into the distance.

If you are following someone with the camera, then you've got more choices of when to stop. You could follow them for a while, then stop until they walk out of shot, with the camera 'stopping' on an interesting building or billboard sign. Alternatively, you could stop just before a corner and wait for them to walk round it. The choices are limited only by your vision. Again, this is another enormous subject!

Knowing when to stop filming largely ties in with being aware of editing when you are filming. Don't just go filming things without an overall plan. Remember framing sequences a few pages ago? This is a great method of planning your film as a series of well-thought-out visual stories with considered framing, lengths of shots and so on, instead of a jumble of shots that are crudely stuck together.

Key idea: Shot length

How long should your shots be? They should at least be long enough to cover the point of the shot at hand; long enough to capture the intended lines of dialogue or a piece of action, etc. If you are filming something a bit more uncertain, then try to think of, or set up, a convenient end for the shot. If you have someone walking down a long street, don't follow them the whole way. Also, ensure that you don't stop filming until a few seconds after the action or dialogue stops. If you stop recording the instant something ends, you may find that a few vital moments have been left out, giving you various problems in the edit.

Keeping track of what you have filmed

In the process of making your film, you may possibly produce hours of material for a production that is only several minutes long. Although the editing process is something that comes later, and will be discussed in another chapter, it is always worth thinking about it during your filming.

Although on the day of filming things are fresh in your mind and you think you will know how things will be pieced together in the edit, often this is not the case. When the day of reckoning comes in the edit suite, you may be horrified to realize you haven't got a clue what the footage you are looking at means. Shots that may have seemed perfectly clear on the day may appear as bizarre oddities with no explanation.

Therefore, it can be important to keep track of things during the filming process. A great, simple way to do this is by using a clapperboard or some other simple marker. One of the main purposes of a clapperboard is as a reference point for the editor so they can know what shot it is and what part of the script it relates to. This is very vital on some productions as often the editor starts putting things together with no input from the director and they may not be familiar with the script or story.

If you want to use this method, you need to have a standard system to make it effective. It can be a good and simple idea to just mark your script into shots (called slates on movies), so that your clapperboard can be marked as 'Slate 10 – Take 3' and so on. This way you will know what part of the script it is from.

An overlooked but important aspect of using the clapperboard is to make sure it is held in front of the camera for long enough so that the editor can clearly make out the information written on it. If not, it defeats the point of using it.

Another method is for someone on the crew to keep tabs on things by creating a log sheet. Due to the frenetic nature of film making, and the particular nature of some low-budget films, this isn't always possible. However, if you can manage this, it means you have a ready-made log of all your shots. The best way to reference a log sheet is to have the tape number (if using tapes), the time code count from the viewfinder or flip-out screen, the description of the shot and the page of script it comes from in a tabulated form. If using an HDD or flash drive camera, you could reference the shot (or file) number with its description. Log sheets will be re-examined in the chapter on editing.

Key idea: The many sides of film making

On large productions, keeping track of what is being filmed is an important job role. In these cases, a script supervisor is charged with keeping track of things so the editor's job is made a little easier. This person will have pages of the script called sides, and each time a shot has been taken they will mark on the sides which bit has been filmed, with the slate number and other pertinent information. So, when it ends up in the edit suite, the editor can look at the script pages and reference them with the information on the clapperboard.

WHERE'S THAT FILE GONE? ON-SET DATA WRANGLING

With the steady migration of cameras towards tapeless workflows, a certain simplicity has afforded itself to film makers. Gone are the days of juggling tapes, getting a tape jammed inside a camera, wondering if you've got enough stock to shoot on or whether things have been labelled up appropriately.

In many ways, however, things are just the same. It's just that the same concerns manifest themselves in slightly different manners. You can still run out of storage media; it's entirely possible that, at the end of a day's shoot, you haven't a clue what any of the files are or which is the drive with the material you need. It's just that the age-old problem has manifested itself in the latest incarnation of storage.

Also, the ease with which files can be transferred from their recording media on to something else compounds the problem. All those digital files that can reproduce like rabbits seep on to different drives to the extent that no one knows which is the original. This can create immense confusion and, amid the high-octane pressure of a film set, can be a real spanner in the works as everyone stops to make sure that the files on the camera's only available drive have indeed been transferred instead of being permanently deleted by mistake. Believe it or not, this kind of on-set data accident is more common than you think. It's not a facet of film making that gets much exposure, yet it's one of those small details that can have a huge effect on your film making efforts.

So, what simple procedures can you put in place? The first is a basic point that many, surprisingly, don't practise – when your drive (if you only have one) is full, transfer it to some kind of intermediate or editing storage. This sounds basic, but some get in the habit of deleting, on the fly, the takes and files they reckon are not needed. However, if all you have got are a load of files with alphanumeric titles, it will soon be nigh-on impossible to remember which is which as you try to free up some memory. An erstwhile simple 'delete and carry on filming' routine becomes a frenzied panic as you struggle to remember which was the great take you wanted to use in the edit, while all the while time slips away in the venue you have hired or it starts raining, cutting your shooting day short. Before long, everyone starts screaming at each other and the whole process can descend into chaos. Again, I've seen this happen.

Another method you can choose – rather dull and unglamorous as it sounds – would be to have a member of the crew keep track of each shot. In the business, this person is known as the logger. In close liaison with the camera operator and director the logger notes down what's being filmed, its file name and whether it's a keeper or something to be discarded. In this way, if push comes to shove your camera's drive can have select files deleted while leaving the takes bound for the edit. Again, this is, or should be, a basic practice.

This method has the advantage of feeding into your editing further down the line as you can easily see which files you want to bring into your edit or which you can do without.

Key idea

Some of the memory cards designed for use with 4K and other high-end cameras can be very expensive, meaning that some film makers may only be able to afford a couple. For this reason, being able to free-up memory on these cards is essential to the filming process.

Of course, on larger productions this is all a streamlined process with data wrangling, note taking and metadata considerations (more on this later) being key job roles. Owing to the important requirement of ensuring the camera is freed up to film, which is after all *the* reason it's there, managing file-based work flows is an entire branch of film making. Also, for many film makers the flexibility of file-based film making means that the director can have the takes edited as soon as the shots are finished and therefore have a near-real-time rough editing process underway so they can see how a sequence works when put together and, if necessary, reshoot.

In fact, the complexities of some shoots go beyond the 'take out the memory card and connect it to the laptop' routine, but rather involve servers, networked editing, secure storage, access rights and some rather complex IT infrastructures to manage the masses of memory heavy files being produced. Then, of course, in today's 'leak it to social media' culture, some files can be made accessible only to a few key members of the post-production team just in case any star-struck member of the crew decides to grab something for his or her Facebook page.

Yet, going back to the smaller scale, this latter point could be a source of annoyance to the director. Given the informal nature of some low-/no-budget productions, it may be hard to demarcate who should have rightful access to the material filmed before it's edited into the completed film. It's entirely possible that the camera's owner or the film's editor may – without asking first – upload material it to their social media pages, much to the annoyance of the director. While it's unfeasible to implement the kind of IT network mentioned above to avoid such leaks, it is something to think about and discuss with your crew beforehand. After all, there's not much point making a film if the whole world can see it piece by piece as it's being made.

A benefit of the way in which these files are created is the important metadata given to each one. Not only is the format, date and time printed on to the file but, depending on your camera system, other key film making information such as exposure, f-stop and frames per second can be available to view. This data can be extremely useful should you need to reshoot any shots from a particular scene, as you can go some way to recreating the conditions as per the original shoot.

Whatever method you choose to employ, ensure that it's simple and doesn't snarl up your filming.

Other points to consider

POWER SOURCES

If you are filming indoors, then all you have to worry about is where the nearest plug socket is in case your batteries run out. If it's far away from the camera, then get an extension lead. However, if you are filming outside there will be no plug sockets available to you, so you will have to utilize the camera's battery. Always make sure it is fully charged, or your camera might suddenly die in the middle of a shot. If you have acquired a camera without its battery, then make sure you obtain a battery that has the appropriate power rating for your camera, otherwise your camera could drain it in a matter of minutes, or it might be too weak to power the camera.

Be aware of the fact that, owing to the increased conductivity of metal in low temperatures, batteries don't last as long in cold and freezing weather. When in a cold environment, keep them warm by wrapping them up in an old sweater or blanket – seriously!

SET CONTROLS TO MANUAL

Although the use of, and reason for, manual controls have been covered in a previous chapter, this is something you must keep remembering and practising.

It is very easy to forget all about the white balance, exposure and focus in the heat of filming. Do this at your peril. If you are lax with this side of things, your footage could be a write-off or at least give you totally the wrong mood compared with what you were trying to achieve.

It would be tragic to take care setting up your location and getting the actors in place with their lines rehearsed only for the camera work to ruin what could have been a great shot or scene.

Remember this

Forget the marketing that may accompany your camera telling you about its 'full automatic capability'; such an expression is tantamount to swearing to the diligent camera operator. Never trust your camera to film anything with its settings set to automatic. Always use manual.

TRIPODS

Sometimes tripods have a purpose; sometimes they don't. If you want a steady shot, then you will need a tripod – no one has a hand or shoulder steadier than a tripod. Most of the shots you watch in a film or television production will have been filmed on a tripod. Steady shots tell the audience they are watching a film – basic but true. Steady shots can make things look very professional and make your production a bit special – because most home movies look as if they were filmed during an earthquake.

Shaky shots make a film look amateur. However, if you want your film to look like the classic television series *NYPD Blue* (1993–2005), then your tripod should be locked away for most of the filming. If you admire the shaky camera style of these productions, then you must give careful consideration to why you want to use it and how you are going to achieve it.

This camera technique is most often used to confer a sense of documentary on what you are watching. It looks like it is real and not a drama. However, although the movement of the camera may appear rather chaotic, it is actually highly choreographed. It is never a case of camera operators just turning up and filming what they want to – if this were to happen, the results would probably be difficult to watch. During dialogue, camera operators know exactly where to point the camera, they don't just swing around blindly looking through their viewfinders every time they hear someone speak.

I know a few people who have tried to imitate this style without giving any thought to how to achieve it, and the results were painful to watch.

Holding cameras by hand, having them on shoulders, stuck on skateboards or generally moving about, can kick a bucket load of energy into your film and make it very 'real'. A famous example of a hand-held camera being thrown about the place to create a 'real situation' is in *Dr. Strangelove* (dir. Staley Kubrick, 1964), when the army is storming the air force base. The hand-held camera footage looks as though it is actual archive from the Second World War. It's brilliant and incredibly lifelike. Also, more recently, the beach storming scenes during the opening sequence of *Saving Private Ryan* demonstrate how effective hand-held camera work can be.

LOOKING AFTER YOUR CAMERAS AND EQUIPMENT

It goes without saying, really: treat your equipment with respect and keep it close at all times. It's also worth mentioning that, if you are renting a camera, give it a thorough check-up before you take it away; otherwise, the tiny scratch on the lens that was already there might translate into an extra-large invoice for you when you return it.

Also, when you are filming a scene outside and you stop to take a break in the local café, take everything with you. If you don't, it won't be waiting there for you when you return! Theft of equipment is probably one of the biggest problems productions face when filming on location.

GET THE BEST YOU CAN AFFORD

If you intend to work on video formats, then buy the best recording media you can afford. The better the make, the better the visual quality will be. You all know the big names, so buy them. They didn't become big names for nothing.

FILM AS MUCH AS POSSIBLE

Again, this is a consideration for video users. Since video stock can be cheap and reusable, it will pay to film as much as possible so that you have a good choice of camera angles, cutaways, reaction shots, and so forth when you come to editing.

If you are using film, then try to get it right first time; otherwise you could soon run out of film and money.

MORE ON FRAMING

Although framing has been discussed previously, there is one more aspect of this behemoth to think about: guarding against invaders. Be careful when you have framed up your shot, check it again to make sure that when you play it back at a later date you don't discover that the lead actor has a tree branch sprouting from his left ear, or that a chimney is sticking out from the top of someone's head. Pay very close attention to these saboteurs that slip into your shots and remain hidden and silent in your viewfinder. The best/worst example of this was a news report from the steps of the Museo Nazionale in Rome, Italy. In the hectic bustle to obtain a shot of the reporter amid the chaos of what was going on, only the 'Nazi' part of the museum's title was visible next to the reporter's head. See the section on using a monitor in Chapter 7.

DOWNRIGHT ERRORS

These are things that generally compromise the look of your film. Imagine a period drama set in the seventeenth-century French countryside, with two young lovers walking down a narrow lane, when suddenly a fluorescent-clad mountain biker speeds past them. Not good! Actually, while on this subject, I am sure that a modern fibreglass sailing dinghy merrily sails past Ben Affleck as he jumps into his car at the quayside in *Pearl Harbor* (dir. Michael Bay, 2001). Sad of me to notice …

Focus points

* Framing is everything.
* If it helps you, try to work out a rough storyboard before you start filming.
* Think about your shot composition all the time, otherwise your film may suffer and be unwatchable.
* Try to use some kind of system that enables you to keep track of what you have filmed.
* Think about how your location and props can be used to give a shot and scene more mood.
* Your camera is an important storytelling tool, so use it to its fullest potential.
* Always try to think about what cutaways you can use to cover any problems you may encounter in the edit.
* Pay attention to things that may change throughout a scene; lapses in continuity can utterly destroy an otherwise great sequence.
* Take care of your film making equipment; without it you have no film.
* Always be creative in your approach to filming your script.

Next step

We've already seen the importance of attention to detail in earlier chapters, but in the following chapter we will look at some of the nitty-gritty things that have the potential to trip up even an experienced director from time to time. Think clocks, candles and cigarettes, and you'll get the picture.

11

Silence on set ...
and action!

In this chapter you will learn:

- ▶ *how to arrange the day's shooting*
- ▶ *what on-set occurrences to be aware of*
- ▶ *how to manipulate time and space by using your camera and imagination*

Time to get ready

Your actors have learned their lines; the camera system has been chosen and rental terms agreed (if you have to pay for it); someone (preferably you) knows how to use the camera and has stock to go with it; you know where you are going to film; you've sorted out some lights; you've told everyone that you'll cover their transport and food expenses (if you've got enough cash); the costumes (if needed) have been chosen and acquired; the props have been obtained; and the money has cleared into the 'company' account (if you've won any funding). Now there's only one more thing to do – draw up the schedule or call sheet. It's all very well having everything ready to go, but does everyone know the who, where and when of it? The schedule is the timetable of filming for the entire production and will contain the following for each day of filming:

▶ Who is involved – actors, actresses, camera operators, sound people, crew in general.

▶ Where it will take place – the specific address of the location with perhaps a photocopy from the local A–Z map book (if no one knows how to get there).

▶ When it will be – the exact date, along with the time it will start, and perhaps a rough stopping time.

▶ A basic template of a call sheet for a production may look something like the one overleaf.

It is a simple document that lets everyone know what is happening, although you could include additional information such as:

▶ Who is bringing the lights (if any are needed)?

▶ Who is bringing the props and costumes (if any are needed)?

▶ Who is bringing the sound equipment (if any separate equipment to the camera is needed)?

▶ Who is bringing the extension leads? (Very helpful on set.)

The type of film you are making will dictate what else is needed. With my first film a friend and I brought all of the above stuffed in the back of her old, beaten-up Citroën car, along with a few crushed actors clutching their crumpled costumes. It was all very exciting. There are few feelings as intoxicating as the anticipation of the first day's filming.

Key idea

Communicating with your cast and crew is a huge part of film making. It doesn't take much for people to forget things over the course of a few days or to realize that you haven't told everyone what is going on. Always make sure you have a list of your cast and crew in your production office and ensure they all know what the filming days and locations are.

Call sheet
Production name: Date:
Director Mobile phone number: Home phone number: Address:
Camera operator Mobile phone number: Home phone number: Address:
Sound recordist Mobile phone number: Home phone number: Address:
Actor 1 Mobile phone number: Home phone number: Address:
Actor 2 Mobile phone number: Home phone number: Address:
Actor 3 Mobile phone number: Home phone number: Address:
Meet 08:30 Supermarket Car Park, High Street, City.
Drive/Walk to location: empty shop, number 100 High Street, City.

09:00—09:30	Set up equipment
09:30—13:00	Film Scene 2
13:00—14:00	Lunch
14:00—17:00	Film Scene 5
17:00	Pack away equipment, return to Supermarket Car Park, High Street, City.

Film it right

As I have often reiterated, film with an eye to easy editing. Although the editing process occurs in the latter stages of making a film, it is very important that you are aware of the post-production side of things as this will help you film in a way that will make life easier when you come to edit.

It is a very chilling feeling to sit down in an edit suite to work on your masterpiece and suddenly to realize that one (or more) of your scenes just don't 'add up' the way you thought they would. The most common mistakes that reveal themselves in post-production are:

- ▶ lack of continuity
- ▶ lack of cutaways
- ▶ awkward cuts

A film littered with the above mistakes will look as though it was made by five different directors who have never met each other. It will appear a very disjointed mishmash of images that will be hard to watch no matter how much you like it. Continuity errors can be subtle or incredibly overt. Someone who changes their clothes and hairstyle with each shot has been the victim of a very careless director (or whoever's task it is to keep an eye on the continuity). However, there are many things on a set that, while being hard to notice, are conspiring to make your film look terrible when you get to the edit stage.

Key idea: Lights, camera, action – not!

Those first three words are one of the myths of film making. Although it may have been the case in earlier days, the protocol now is a bit less glamorous. When a shot is ready to be taken, 'turnover' will be called out, giving everyone warning that the cameras are about to roll; after that the camera operator will say 'speed', meaning that the camera is rolling, then finally the director can call 'action'.

Although you don't need to get into this exact habit, it's very important that everyone on set knows what is about to happen. All too often the camera operator of a low-budget production will humbly shout 'Go' and then a few people will look at him or her and say, 'Eh? Are we ready to film?' Whatever you figure out, make sure you all know what the procedure is.

Continuity issues

CLOCKS

The most common culprit is the wall clock. With all the chaos and bustle on your set, everyone will ignore the clock until it is time to edit and you notice that the time changes by 15 minutes in each shot. This is especially bad if the scene is only supposed to last one minute. Even major films fall prey to this 'enemy'. So, what safeguards can you use to ensure a clock doesn't ruin the continuity of an otherwise perfect scene?

▶ Don't have a clock on the set unless it is essential to the scene.

▶ Don't have the clock in focus – it then won't matter if the time changes by 15 minutes with each shot.

▶ Switch the clock off after each shot. If you have a scene where a visible clock is an essential part of the scene, then simply take the batteries out or unplug it every time you say 'cut'. Obviously, with an LCD clock you will have to reset it each time.

CANDLES

Candles are other objects that cause headaches and need special consideration on set. Like a clock, they will change over time: get shorter, or get shorter and produce huge arrested flows of dripped wax. So, if you are filming a romantic set-up with two diners facing each other over a table with a candle, the candle will reduce in height over time. No surprise, but it is one of those things that is forgotten and can ruin your scene. Just like the clock, the candle can alter in height to the point where it can make your scene look ridiculous. Imagine if the candle dropped by a couple of centimetres in one shot, then grew by four in another. So, what safeguard can you employ here?

▶ Use slow-burning candles.

▶ Extinguish the candle after each camera run. This keeps the candle height consistent but may fill up the set with visible candlewick smoke.

CIGARETTES

Cigarettes are another pest to watch out for. Things can go totally haywire due to the fact that cigarettes change their state more quickly than clocks and candles combined. It is quite possible to see a one-minute piece of film where in the first shot the actor lights the cigarette, the next shot shows him stubbing out the cigarette and the third shot shows him smoking a full-length cigarette again – all in the space of one minute.

The advice with cigarettes is not to have your actors smoking a full one in a scene, otherwise the above will probably happen – especially if the actor is a smoker anyway and will carry on smoking between takes.

FRINGES

Watch out for fringes and other manifestations of hair. With all the heat from the lights and the general troublesome work of being on set, it is only natural that an actor with a fringe, for example, will brush their hair off their brow from time to time. This will translate into radically different hair arrangements from shot to shot.

CHANGING SCENERY

Changing scenery can also cause nightmares. I don't mean chairs, curtains, furniture and other props being moved and knocked about (although that too), but other things that you will not have much control over. Imagine the following scenario:

Our pals Actor A and Actor B are filming a scene in a street with numerous parked cars. The continuity hazard here is that one of the parked cars may move off and be replaced by something else. Thus, owing to camera cuts, repositioning and so on, one shot may have a lime-green Harley-Davidson parked next to the actors, and another a dirty great truck. This is an extreme example, but you will be surprised how many things your prospective audience will notice. Even if a car moves off further down our imaginary road, someone will notice it if it is a feature of the shot.

It is amazing what gets overlooked amid all the frantic work of filming. While you are trying to make sure that everyone is in their positions for the next take, and that the camera is in the right position and so on, it is only natural that some apparently minor detail of the location you are filming in is ignored. But, it doesn't stop with cars.

THE WEATHER

There is also the weather to think about. Starting a scene with bright sunshine and ending with thunder and lightning may be great for a horror film, but for other scenes it could be a bit of a disaster. Even filming by some trees that get blown suddenly by gusts of wind could spoil things, especially when you remember that some scenes will be filmed in non-chronological order. So, as you go from shot to shot you will have still trees – moving trees – still trees – moving trees and so on – not forgetting the associated sound problems I told you about.

When you get to the post-production stage of your film and you discover scenes with problems like these, the only way to fix things is to film the scene again. This may not always be possible due to resources, actors being unavailable and so on.

The other option is to edit from what you've got regardless.

Remember this

Get it right on the day. Think ahead. Plan for everything.

Cutaways

Although cutaways were mentioned in Chapter 10, they are also brilliant safeguards for a multitude of potential problems in your films – not just for covering over jump cuts. Think of cutaways as not only an invisible yet very strong glue that will bind together the many shots that make up your film, but also points of visual detail within your story. A cutaway is a shot that reveals some detail that is not covered by the mastershot. Essentially, it is a method of bringing attention to something by changing shot or simply by adding a bit of relevant detail to a scene. Cutaways serve some basic functions:

▶ they link up two awkward shots

▶ they bring attention to something pertinent to the scene

▶ they add a bit of depth and detail to the scene

Imagine this scenario in a script:

> INT. Richard Vincent's office — Night
> Richard Vincent is seated behind his desk.
> He is sipping a small glass of whiskey and
> reading the sports pages of the newspaper.
> As he reads he raises his eyebrows.

It could be filmed as follows:

Shot 1 – Wide shot. Richard behind his desk.

Shot 2 – Cutaway, close-up: line from newspaper '… golf player spontaneously combusts …'

Shot 3 – Close-up. Richard raises his eyebrows.

So, through this shot sequence and cutaway method, we can see what is causing Richard to raise his eyebrows. If there was no Shot 2, then this scene wouldn't make any sense as the audience wouldn't know what was going on, that is, why he raised his eyebrows.

Now have a look at this example.

INT. Richard Vincent's office — Night
Richard Vincent is sitting behind his desk.
He is sipping a small glass of water and reading the sports pages of the newspaper. Somewhere in the building some glass smashes. He goes to investigate.

The following is how not to film this scene:

Shot 1 – Richard seated behind his desk.

Shot 2 – Richard walks into the corridor; he is holding a pistol.

Although the above may not read badly, in the context of moving images it would be a rather awkward edit. It would appear as though Richard has suddenly 'teleported' himself from Shot 1 to Shot 2, especially since in Shot 1 he is sitting still and in Shot 2 he is moving. Shots that go from stationary to movement, or movement to stationary, need special care otherwise they will look uncomfortable when edited together. It would be better to do it like this:

Shot 1 – Richard behind his desk.

Shot 2 – Shot of exterior of building. Sound of breaking glass. Shot stays on building.

Shot 3 – Richard emerges from a door in the front corridor, holding a pistol.

By using Shots 2 and 3 we have a more flowing narrative, the audience will have an idea of what is going on and the shots will link together better. Also, the cutaway will compress the time of the scene – during Shot 2, it will be assumed that Richard has heard the noise, got his gun and gone to open one of the doors into the main corridor. Such is the power of a good and precise cutaway. Since films do not take place in real time, cutaways are one method of shortening the length of time it would take to shoot it as real. To shoot the above in real time, you would not only have to film the shots as listed, but also Richard hearing the noise, getting out his gun, getting up from his desk, exiting his office and making his way to the main corridor door.

Remember this

Approach each shot critically. Think about how it links in with the rest of the scene and the film. Don't just think of it as a functional item to display your actors' movements.

How about the following for a quick and easy way to compress space and time via a cutaway?

> **EXT. Motorway near London — Morning**
> A car drives away from London.
> It arrives in Edinburgh.

To do this in real time and real space would be ridiculous – you would have a shot that lasted hours. One way around this is:

Shot 1 – Car drives on motorway heading in the direction of sign that says, 'To Scotland'.

Shot 2 – Wide side shot. Car drives into frame past camera and out of shot.

Shot 3 – Car drives on motorway heading in direction of sign that says, 'Welcome to Edinburgh'.

Depending on the framing used with these shots, you would have a very effective mini-sequence about travelling from London to Edinburgh. If such a sequence was filmed without Shot 2, it would give the audience a bit of a jolt as the shots would not link up very well. It could be given a bit more flavour by having a few shots of the car filmed from bridges over the motorway, or of the hands on the steering wheel, the foot on the accelerator, spinning wheels, and so on – all of which would reiterate the fact that the car is travelling and moving.

The subject of cutaways is a massive one and could easily fill a book on its own. I therefore cannot go into too much detail here for fear of never ending. However, take a look at your script and each page will have the potential for possibly several cutaways to be employed. Pay attention to parts of the script where it calls for a change of location or even movement within the same location (such as a character moving from one side of a house to the other). Your cutaway can act as a screen to conceal the fact that change has taken place. It can be used to link shot with shot or scene with scene.

Key idea

Always film plenty of cutaways in each location even if it isn't part of your plan. You may find they save your life in the edit.

For daily examples of cutaways, I again recommend that you watch news reports. Whenever there is a news story, look out for the cutaways and consider why they were used. The most common reason for using a cutaway in this environment is to join up seamlessly two different parts of an interview with a politician, member of the public or whomever. In the middle of an interview with a farmer, for example, there may suddenly be a cutaway of the farm land. What this cutaway does is mask the fact that two different and awkward shots have just been 'nailed' together. Most commonly, the camera operator has zoomed in or out rather quickly, reframed dramatically or perhaps a long section of the interview has been removed (see Figure 11.1).

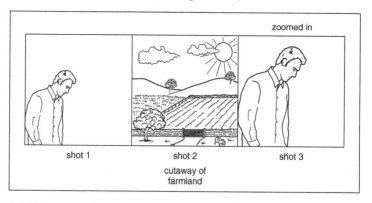

zoomed in

shot 1   shot 2   shot 3

cutaway of farmland

Figure 11.1

Study news reports; they use cutaways day in, day out, and because of this the level of finesse is not as high, and therefore more noticeable, than on your favourite film.

Cutaways are a great way of linking up shots that would otherwise result in a 'jump cut' and can help you out enormously in the editing process. However, you will not always want to link up your shots and scenes using this method. There are some great ways in which you can not only change shot, but also change location and time by using some slick camera work.

Key idea: ATTENTION! The 1st AD, aka the sergeant major

As highlighted in a previous chapter, a set full of people can soon turn into a confused crowd of distracted people. It doesn't take much for people to not pay attention, to creep away to smoke a cigarette or to disappear altogether. Likewise, technical crew can look bewildered as they wonder what they are supposed to be doing and where they are supposed to be. In these circumstances, you need a 1st AD – a first assistant director.

These are the disciplinarians who bark commands and pass on orders about what is happening, what the next shot is, who needs to be on set, where the equipment has to be placed, and generally keeps order on set. Above all they shield the director from the hassles of shepherding a crowd of people so that they can concentrate on directing the film.

Cuts

Straightforward cuts are the most popular way of changing shot, scene time and location in films. In fact, they are the most popular way of changing scenes in films. So how can this be done without the use of cutaways? Let us take the example of a picnic under a clear, cloudless blue sky. Look at this:

Shot 1 – Group of people eating their picnic. Then tilt up to clear, cloudless blue sky.

Shot 2 – Tilt down from clear, cloudless blue sky to people packing up their picnic.

When a shot cut like this is viewed, it will appear as though time has magically passed in a few seconds. Because the end of Shot 1 and the start of Shot 2 are both of exactly the same thing, it appears that there has been no shot change. The audience, therefore, has been very brilliantly fooled into thinking that nothing (i.e. the time) has changed, when in fact it has. If you can get around to thinking in shots and cuts, then you will find it easy to visualize your film.

The huge advantage of this method of compressing time and space is that it relies only on you having a camera. There are many opportunities in a film to transport people through time using this camera trickery. Say, for example, you have a scene where someone is waking up, taking a shower, getting dressed and then leaving their home and you want to compress all this into a few seconds. Here is a very basic method:

Shot 1 – Shot of wall in apartment that shows bedroom door, bathroom door and front door. There is a briefcase on the floor by the front door. A man who has obviously just got out of bed, walks out of his bedroom, closes the door and goes into the bathroom, closing the door behind him.

Shot 2 – Bathroom door opens. The man is wrapped in a towel. He opens the bedroom door, closing it behind him.

Shot 3 – Bedroom door opens. The man is fully dressed. He walks to the front door, picks up the briefcase, opens the door, exits the flat and closes the door behind him.

This is a very basic and very efficient way of doing things – albeit possibly comedic – and it can be quite effective, depending on the overall mood of the film, and what look you are trying to achieve. However, it is very important to get the shots perfect with this sort of cut. If, from shot to shot, the camera position is moved in any way, then the whole point of the exercise will be lost – the audience will know there are cuts, and very awkward ones at that. Also, if the doors are closed in one shot and open in another shot, or props are moved around, then the effect you are trying to achieve will be ruined.

Let's try the same scenario again but make things a bit more interesting.

Shot 1 – Close-up of alarm clock going off. A hand switches it off.

Shot 2 – Close-up of slippers. Man's feet go into them and walk out of shot.

Shot 3 – Close-up of bathroom door handle. Man's hand turns handle and he opens the door and enters.

Shot 4 – Wide shot of bathroom showing bathroom mirror. Man walks past camera, his reflection is also visible in mirror, then walks out of shot. Sound of shower running.

Shot 5 – Medium close-up of steamed mirror. Sound of shower dies. Man's hand wipes mirror and he begins to shave.

Shot 6 – Medium close-up of bedroom door. It opens and the man enters. He is wearing a bathrobe and towelling his hair dry. He walks out of shot.

Shot 7 – Close-up of wall. Man enters frame from below as he straightens his tie.

Shot 8 – Medium close-up of briefcase. Man's hand picks it up.

Shot 9 – Long shot of front door from outside. Man opens door, exits house, closes door and walks into camera blacking out the picture.

Not only will this make for interesting viewing, but also it will mean that 15 or 20 minutes in real time have just been compressed into a sequence lasting a few seconds – all using cuts that work and flow with one another in a logical manner.

Remember this

Think visually and use your imagination.

Once again, although some of the examples in this chapter are editing issues and can only be fully viewed in the edit stages, it is very important to have a strong grasp of edit concepts when you are filming. Without an awareness of post-production, you may end up filming various lovely individual shots that do not work when edited together. The relationship between filming and editing cannot be overemphasized.

Another important thing to consider is to know how much you are able to do in a day. I remember my very first day directing, thinking I could get two scenes out of the way – I managed to get only about half a side of a page completed before I had to flee the building I had hired. Don't assume that a complicated scene with several characters can be completed before lunch; otherwise half the cast might sit around twiddling their thumbs and then hear you apologetically say, 'We've run out of time.' So, learn to understand what your filming pace is.

Finally, silly as it may seem, keep tabs on what you have filmed, as sometimes, with all the confusion, doing things over several days and so forth, you may forget that you have already filmed a scene or certain shots. Conversely, you may think that you have filmed certain shots and scenes when in fact you haven't. Get into the habit of putting a line through the relevant parts of the script to indicate that they have been filmed or refer to your log sheets if you have been keeping any.

Focus points

* Make sure everyone involved knows when and where filming is to take place.
* Ensure everyone on set knows the process for when filming is about to start.
* Avoid situations where your cast and crew wander off without your knowledge.
* Try to keep order on your set as fooling around can eat into your time.
* Although film making can be a very tiring process, correct any mistakes and redo takes when necessary.
* Think about how your shots can be used in the edit.
* Be creative when thinking about how to film the passing of time or changes in location.
* Think in terms of shots and cuts.
* Be prepared for some stress.
* Try to remain calm at all times.

Next step

Editing is a part of the film making process that is often neglected, and yet it's in the editing suite that a film really gets 'made'. It is a craft all of its own and could easily be the subject of a whole book, let alone a single chapter. In Chapter 12, I will introduce you to some of the key aspects of this intricate, painstaking yet ultimately engrossing process.

12

Completing the moving 'jigsaw'

In this chapter you will learn:

▶ *the basic points of editing*
▶ *how household technology can help you put your film together*
▶ *how to spice up your film with some music and sound effects*

If there is one thing many first-time film makers don't take into consideration, it is the editing. Editing is a facet unique to film making. Even though the process of making films shares lots of elements with photography, drama and other visual arts, editing is found only in film making.

Sadly, editing is an invisible component to the film making experience. When done well, editing is completely unnoticeable; it's only when the process is clumsy that an audience will sit up and detect its presence.

Understandably, after the glamour, excitement and fun of filming and being around cool-looking cameras, the task of editing is something that is all too often ignored, unappreciated, frowned upon or simply misunderstood. Without editing, your films will be a random collection of shots with terrible sound, littered with mistakes, questionable camera angles, muttering from behind the lens and generally the kinds of thing that will make it painful to watch. Editing is the antidote to these situations.

For many, the editing process is a bit of a mystery. There is an assumption that the footage goes into some room to be tinkered with and a few days later a finished film is automatically and effortlessly created. This couldn't be further from the truth.

One of the great misconceptions of editing is that it is a simple, logical process in which the footage produced during filming is pieced together in a predetermined order. This is not the case at all. Editing is where small editorial inflections and other factors can be imparted to the film so that performances are heightened, the sublime made overt, reality reconstructed to new forms and drama and suspense conjured from otherwise ordinary material.

Editing is an entire creative process and film making discipline in itself. So, it is essential that the basics are understood before you even film your first shot. Believe it or not, a few hours' worth of filming can take you days, or even weeks, to edit. Also, when writing and filming your idea you usually think that you know how things will be put together. However, when the editing process is up and running, unplanned alternative choices can present themselves and add unexpected dimensions to your film.

It's only when you are seated in front of your edit system that the realization of this power can hit you. Make no mistake, the choice available to you can make your head spin, as there are countless ways to do each step of the edit process.

Key idea

Editing is a powerful discipline. When you edit you are quite literally controlling and shaping reality.

So, what is editing? Editing is the process in which your shots are arranged, where some shots may be deleted or discarded, the volume adjusted, simple effects put on, music and text added and generally things put in a presentable manner. Or in even simpler terms, editing is the process in which you refine and enhance your film.

The role of the editor

As consumers of films and television, we all know who actors are, we often know who the directors are, and we even sometimes know who the writer is. However, what about the editor? Who is this mysterious figure? Why don't we know more about these individuals and what they get up to?

Considering just how important an editor is to the moving image industry, it's almost a crime that the public has only a vague, at best, awareness of the role. When watching the opening credits of a film, the editor is one of the few names that crops up – that tells you just how important they are! In fact, along with a camera operator it would be quite impossible to make a film without an editor.

So, who is an editor? The simple answer to this question is that it is the individual who gets all the footage after the cameras have stopped rolling and then puts it together according to the script. Things are a lot more involved than this, because not only is the editor a technical expert like a camera operator or director of photography, but they are also an artist. They are charged with creating something entertaining, interesting, moving, emotional, and the list goes on.

An editor is the person who guides an audience through a story. An editor must have empathy with the story and decide what things are unnecessary and what is essential to a story. The decision to focus on one thing instead of another in order to give a scene a greater impact is the editor's decision. Just like the director of photography and director, they are one of the few people on a film crew who can have a strong artistic and emotional effect on a film. They truly are lords of the industry while at the same time being almost entirely unknown.

On many productions, an editor will begin their job while the cameras are still rolling. They will start piecing together scenes, or bits of them, with the available footage to give the director an idea of how the film looks and is coming along. The practice of editing concurrently with the filming process saves a lot of time; if things were to be left until after the last day of filming, this would have a negative effect on a film schedule. As such, it's more time-efficient to start cutting the film while the filming unit is still active as pick-ups may be required.

In such instances, the editor will cut the film into something called an assembly edit. As the name suggests, the available footage has been pieced together according to the script. However, this is always just a rough copy that will undoubtedly be altered several times over. When this assembly has been completed, the editor will then really start to weave the magic of their craft. Scenes can be radically rearranged, shots from other places in the film added and innocuous details sprinkled into the narrative. Basically, the script is transformed into an exciting and engaging piece whose potential can never truly be realised until the edit process is in full swing.

On big productions, the editor may be head of a larger department. There may even be two or more main editors working on separate storylines that will be interwoven as the editing progresses. Underneath such lofty people are assistant editors, loggers, telecine operatives, secretaries, managers, accountants and various technicians responsible for managing the images once they come out of the camera. Together, they fall under the general title of 'Post-Production Department'.

Editing is an entire industry of its own. Depending on the format the film was shot in, the moving images will either have to be processed (in the instance of film stock), put on to hard drive (in the case of solid state and disc-based cameras) or simply taken out of the camera (in the case of tape-based cameras). Once the media, whatever it may have been filmed on, has been extracted, it usually finds its way to a process where it is transferred into a format for editing and viewing. This may mean it is put on tapes for uploading to an edit system, but also it can mean putting on to viewing copies. A viewing copy could be a VHS tape, DVD or MiniDV format in which the film's rushes/dailies are stored. They will have imprinted information on the actual picture that relates to reel number and time code (see the section on logging in Chapter 12).

As you might imagine, on a big production a lone editor could be overwhelmed by the amount of information he or she has to deal with. In turn, this could impede their work as a creative artist. Next time you watch the credits of a film look how many names follow the editor's.

A brief history of editing

Until the early to mid-1990s, before the advent of widespread computerized editing, things were done using the actual film, or rather a copy of it, called a work print or cutting copy. The machinery used probably would have been a 'flatbed' machine called a 'Steenbeck', which looked a bit like a motor engine. These were mechanical devices in which film reels were run through, viewed, cued up into the right place, spliced, cut, taped together over and over. Bear in mind that the films would have been in lots and lots of strips or reels, so the physical workload would be massive – the required shots were located and then run through the machine to be cut together in order with other shots. Music, dialogue, sound effects and titles would all have to be added at some point, too. Eventually, when the film had been cut into a final version, it was then used to produce something called an EDL, or Edit Decision List, in which the shots used while working with the print, or cutting copy, were matched using the negative. This negative assembly was then used to produce the final print.

Even when tape-based systems grew in popularity from the 1970s onwards, in television news reports or some television programmes, things were not much better. The master tapes came out of the cameras, or studio recorders, and were placed into a player that matched the format of the tape. This player was connected to an edit controller, which in turn was connected to a recorder with a blank tape inside. All three were connected to a monitor, or monitors, and the idea was that the required bits of the master tapes were recorded on the blank tape. Just like its celluloid cousin, this could mean hunting around for all the different tapes and then later having to put on sound effects, titles, music and so on. Likewise, if something needed changing, everything back up to the point of change would effectively be lost. This style and technology of editing was known as linear editing (still used today in dark corners of some news-based organizations or as a cheap way of editing your film by hooking up two VCRs to your television).

These two phases of editing were very fiddly and thankless tasks.

Luckily for today's film maker there has never been such an abundance of editing techniques. However, at the fundamental level, not much has changed – only the technology.

Today's computerized editing is often called non-linear editing (or NLE). This essentially means that you can edit in any order or in any chronology. Back in the 'old days' a film was edited in a linear manner. The problem was, if you were at the end of the film and wanted to make a change to the start of the film, you would have to undo many elements such as sounds and, of course, the film at a certain point. This took lots of time. Nowadays the editor can make changes anywhere in the film without affecting the other parts. They can effortlessly access any single frame in an instant, instead of looking through the reels of film hanging around the edit room. The best way to compare this old method of editing with today's is to look at writing with a typewriter versus writing with a word processor; they both do the same job, but the latter is much more flexible.

Be thankful this age is no more. Nowadays your average PC or Mac can come with some simple editing software already on it that allows you to start 'cutting' your film from the outset.

For the more ambitious, there are software packages available from most high-street retailers that needn't break the bank and are very similar to what the professionals in Hollywood are using.

Some of the more popular consumer systems are listed below:

▶ **iMovie** (usually comes installed with Mac computers)

▶ **Windows Movie Maker** (usually comes installed with PCs)

▶ **Adobe Premiere Pro** (a consumer-level version of a professional system)

▶ **Pinnacle** (a popular edit software owned by the AVID edit corporation)

▶ **Sony Vegas** (a fun and groovy-named edit system that's been a hit with some low-budget film makers and students)

▶ **Final Cut Pro X** (a highly capable Mac-based consumer version of a popular professional system)

Also, don't forget that some new cameras will come with their own individual basic edit software on disk.

Getting started

To begin editing your film you will need the following things:

▶ A computer with some installed editing software

▶ Your footage in editable format

▶ Your digital video camera if using tape

▶ A FireWire to connect the camera to the computer if using tape

You may also want to think about using the following:

▶ Some headphones and/or speakers so you can accurately hear what is going on in your film such as dialogue, interviews, music and so on.

▶ An external hard drive for storing all that extra information (video footage takes up a lot of disk space!).

▶ A comfortable chair – editing can be extremely addictive, so it's important to make your stay in front of the computer as pleasant as possible.

▶ Your script, or story outline, to help remind you of what your film is about and how to order the shots (there's more on this later in the chapter).

Although you will have used your camera for filming your project, it also serves a dual purpose as being a 'deck' in the case of MiniDV-based cameras. In film making terms, a deck is a machine used to play tapes for the purposes of edit upload or viewing. In this context, you will be using it to upload to the computer. For uploading (or capturing or digitizing, as it's properly called), the camera needs to be in playback mode and connected to the computer using the FireWire cable. This special cable allows the video to go from camera to computer. If you are using a tape-based format, then the tapes need to be 'cued up'; in edit-speak, this means the tapes have to be in the correct position. For example, if your tape is at the end, you will have to rewind it. Some software allows you to control the camera via the edit interface (see below). For HDD and flash drive cameras it can simply be a case of selecting the files you want to use and selecting them for import.

Key idea: What the pros do

Essentially, the only difference between editing something on a home computer and in an edit suite is the expense and amount of technology. In the edit suite of a feature film, the tapes will more likely be called the digital intermediate – where the film stock has been transferred on to tape. Instead of using a camera to play in these tapes, a dedicated tape deck is used. Also, don't forget that some digital intermediates may be direct to hard drive and bypass tapes altogether, such as was done for *The Curious Case of Benjamin Button* (dir. David Fincher, 2008).

Although there are numerous widely available consumer-level editing packages, their interfaces are generally the same. This is what some tend to look like:

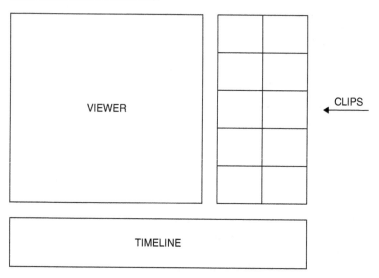

Figure 12.1

The squares arranged vertically on the side go by a variety of names but are sometimes called the panes or clips. This is where your video footage goes after it has been captured. When you click on each of these 'clips', it will appear in the large square.

The large square is often known as the viewer or the preview monitor. This is where your clips can be viewed when they are clicked on individually, and where your film is shown when clips have been placed on the timeline.

The large rectangular panel at the bottom is called the timeline or the storyboard. This is a graphical representation of your film. It is made up of your clips that you drag into it, plus any added sounds, effects and so on. When you play your film, the playhead moves across the timeline. Many edit systems allow you to toggle between a basic display and a more accurate one, depending on your edit needs.

Seeing as there is just the one area to view your individual clips and film, you have to be mindful of clicking on either the timeline or clips; it depends on what you want to watch.

Other consumer-level edit systems vary from this example as they have two viewing windows and may look like this:

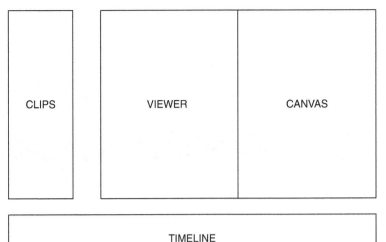

Figure 12.2

The big benefit of this layout is that the editor can see what is being edited and the source clips at the same time without having to toggle back and forth. Also, the timeline can be more sophisticated and allow for multiple elements such as extra audio, graphics and so on.

Key idea: 'But my camera's not digital!'

For some of you out there, it may be the case that you are stuck with using an older camera format. This may be because it's all that is available to you or perhaps there is some important footage filmed some time ago that exists only on an older system. The problem with these analogue formats is they are incompatible with modern digital editing software. However, fear not. Some of these cameras have newer digital versions that take the same tapes and work with editing software. Also, there are DV Converters which act as 'adaptors', changing analogue signals into digital.

Logging, sub-clips, bins and media management

As previously highlighted, the filming process can generate a mass of footage that is not commensurate with the duration of the final product. To capture and keep every single frame of this, and then edit with it, can be very arduous and sometimes counterproductive.

LOGGING

It is much better to review and figure out exactly what you have filmed, what is good for your film and what exact pieces you want to use. In edit-speak, this is called logging. Logging is the simple, but often long, process of reviewing your footage and making a note of it using timings and a brief description. Log sheets are used and can look something like this:

Tape or reel	Time code start	Description	Comments	Page of script
001	00:00:00:15	Car pulling up outside house	Take 1 – out of focus	2
001	00:00:00:56	Car pulling up outside house	Take 2 – good, use this one!	2
001	00:00:01:11	Actor gets out of car, walks towards door & presses buzzer	Take 1 – good, use this	3
001	00:00:01:29	Close up of buzzer being pushed	Take 1 – too much camera shake!	3

and so on …

As a result, when you get to the capturing process you can be very selective. This is a great help if your computer has limited memory capacity as you can digitize only what you require. However, as mentioned in the chapter on filming, you need continuous time code for logging to be effective. If you have constantly reviewed your footage as you have been filming, then the chances are that time code breaks have crept on to your tapes (if you used tapes). For the purposes of logging, this means that your time code effectively recycles after each break. Therefore, you may end up with multiple occurrences of the same time code, which will render your log sheet (and selective capturing) useless.

With cameras that do not use tapes, the logging process is a bit different. A flash drive or HDD camera will separate the clips according to each time something was recorded. Therefore, it will make viewing things a bit simpler as you won't need to play through an entire tape.

The logging process can have further benefits – you can take the information from the log sheets and create something called a paper edit. A paper edit is when you make a paper-based plan of your film. In many ways it's exactly like the edit itself but done with text information. A paper edit may look like this:

Tape or reel number (if using tapes)	Time code start	Time code end	Description and dialogue
2	00:33:13:14	00:33:17:00	Wide exterior shot of apartment building at night
4	00:12:01:11	00:12:30:11	Masked Man climbs up apartment fire escape at night
5	00:55:01:21	00:55:02:10	Shot of apartment window from inside getting smashed by someone on fire escape
5	00:10:45:05	00:10:48:14	Close-up of feet walking across glass littered carpet
5	00:10:54:08	00:10:57:10	Close-up of gloved hand trying the handle of a safe

and so on ...

This can be a very good method of getting the outline of a story to work in your head before you commit to the edit process itself. Also, for psychological and stress considerations, this is a very calm introduction into editing as a whole without jumping in at the deep end and drowning in countless clips of video.

Key idea

On some film productions, the logging is done at the same time as the filming. The person responsible will liaise with the camera operator for the time code count and then write what the corresponding action was, and also with the director to see if they reckon it is worth using in the edit.

SUB-CLIPS

Another way to enhance your knowledge of exactly what you have filmed is to create sub-clips. As the name suggests, a sub-clip is a smaller part of a larger clip. Usually, editors will capture a large chunk of footage in order to be time-efficient, such as one tape at a time. They then look through it and isolate takes, shots and so on into small pieces called sub-clips. Next, these sub-clips will be labelled with a short description, some of them deleted, and then the remainder filed away into things called bins.

BINS AND MEDIA MANAGEMENT

A bin, in edit-speak, is a place to put similar shots together. It comes from the 'old days' when film was actually stored in large containers, called bins, in the edit room. With computerized editing, a bin is a folder in your clip storage area that contains certain types of clip. You can have as many as you want to suit your needs. If you are making a music video, you could have one bin for all the shots of the guitarists and another for the singer; or if your film is a news report, you could have one bin for each interview. Bin labelling can be a personal thing, but the main point of labels is to help you manage your media and make your editing more efficient. Without such practices, your editing will be a tortuous ordeal of constantly having to look through numerous unlabelled clips for the shots you need.

On major films bins tend to be arranged according to scene, and then the clips labelled according to slates and takes.

Please be aware bins are a feature found only in the more capable edit systems. However, even the simplest editing software allows you to label your clips.

Key idea: No computer?

So you don't have any editing software? That's no problem ... almost.

It is not unknown for people to edit their films as they are going along shooting them. This 'in-camera editing' means that the story is shot in chronological order according to the script on the one tape. If something has to be redone, then the unusable take is deleted and recorded over. Obviously, this is a very complicated way to make a film and if anything needs changing retrospectively, then you will either have to go back and change everything or try to film over something in such a way that the subsequent scenes are not affected.

This was a relatively common way of doing things at the amateur level years ago, when even basic linear edit systems were expensive. Some cameras still have throwback features from this era with fades, dissolves or audio dubbing facilities where sound effects, music or narrative can be added to the images on the tape. In fact, there are sometimes film competitions where entrants have to make a coherent film using one super 8 mm cartridge (see Chapter 4 on cameras).

EDITING IS LEGO

The easiest way to think of editing is to compare it to building something with Lego bricks. When you capture your footage and it goes into your edit program, the footage is graphically represented as coloured rectangular shapes, or blocks, with a relevant video frame in the middle. All you are doing is building a linear shape with those rectangles or blocks by dragging and dropping using your mouse. Just like Lego, if you don't like the way it is, you can remove some pieces and replace them with others or completely change the order.

The mechanics of editing

Modern computerized editing is frame-accurate. You can access any single bit of your footage in an instant. The footage you need can be called up, put on to the timeline, cut a bit and even got rid of altogether. That is the basic concept, but how do you actually edit?

Edit systems at the simpler end of the spectrum, such as iMovie and Movie Maker, can operate solely on the 'drag and drop' principle. You look for the required footage in the clip storage area, click on it and then drag and drop it on to the timeline. This is editing at its most simple. However, on slightly longer projects, or ones with lots of different shots, this method of editing can be counterproductive. You may end up with a very busy timeline and sometimes it is easy to drop your clips in the wrong place and knock things out of order. In some cases, they disappear as they get 'absorbed' by the sheer mass of clips on the timeline. Also, you must consider that the clip you have just dropped on to the timeline may need significant altering to make it the correct length or to just extract or isolate the bit you need. These might be superficial gripes, but they serve to illustrate that your editing needs to be as accurate as it can be otherwise you risk it looking like raw unedited footage.

Another unpleasant aspect of these simple edit systems is that they are destructive. Every time you put something on the timeline and hack off a bit, it is gone, there is no original master you can go to if things go wrong (unless you laboriously make copies of each clip). Therefore, the further you go with your editing, the further you are from having all your footage intact.

More capable edit systems like Adobe Premiere Pro and Final Cut Pro X do not suffer from this inconvenience. No matter how much you put down on the timeline, no matter how much you hack off, no matter how big a mess you make of things, your original clips will remain unaffected. Believe it or not, even if you drag and drop entire clips on to the timeline they will remain intact. Essentially, the material you edit on to the timeline is being referenced from your imported clips.

Mark in, mark out, overwrite, insert

These are probably the four most important concepts and manoeuvres of editing. Yet they are only features of the more able edit systems. This is when the frame-accurate concept comes into its own as you can highlight exact pieces of your footage to be placed on the timeline.

So, how is this done? Each time you call up a clip in the viewer, not only can you play it, but you can also set things known as mark in and mark out points. As the terminology suggests, sections of a clip can be given selective points and when you place the footage from the clip on the timeline, only the footage between the in and out points will appear. Then, if you want to use a bit more of the same clip, you can reset the in and out points. Therefore, you can edit using only the parts you want.

However, that's only half the story. Once these mark in and mark out points have been set, you can place the footage on the timeline by either performing an overwrite edit or an insert edit. An overwrite edit (usually denoted by a red symbol on your edit interface) puts footage down over on the timeline (whether there is something there or not) and insert edit (usually denoted by a yellow symbol) puts footage down between clips already sitting on the timeline.

The real strength of this method of editing is that you can 'tell' the computer exactly where you want the footage to go on the timeline, either by parking the playhead somewhere on the timeline, which will be where the selected footage starts from, or by giving the timeline itself a mark in point which, again, will be the point the incoming footage starts from.

If you decide upon one of the more able consumer-level edit systems, then this is really the way in which you should be editing. If not, then you are wasting the capabilities of that software and ultimately making more work for yourself.

Basic principles and getting started

You should consider editing as an essentially solitary job, so try to avoid situations where you are editing 'by committee'. This is usually a fatal mistake as people will rarely agree on how something as subjective as an edit should look. Avoid these situations whenever possible. By all means have people look in on things now and again to give you their opinions, but also feel that you can ignore them if need be. On large productions, an editor will largely work on their own and then the director will come in at a later date to look over things and suggest changes.

Another important pointer is not to feel compelled to include everything you filmed. Just because you shot something (or a friend or colleague did), it doesn't mean it will be right for the edit. There are two reasons why footage and/or scenes are dropped from a film: they make the film too long, or simply don't work out as expected when edited together.

Even in productions where the script and story have been planned well in advance, leaving things out or having things end up on the 'cutting room floor' are a key feature of editing. Bear in mind that even the biggest films have to be trimmed down to size. In many cases this has meant that scenes that took weeks to film, cost millions to produce, were difficult to achieve and starred some of the biggest names have been cut from a film. Just take a look at any DVD extras disc for proof of this.

It is never easy chopping things out, nor is it popular with other people who may have worked with you, but it is essential to creating the best final product.

Remember this

'You have got to be BRUTAL!' – *Lord of the Rings* and *King Kong* director, Peter Jackson, talking about cutting scenes from an edit.

SO WHERE TO START?

If there is one thing that can challenge the novice editor and professional alike, it is the conundrum, 'Where shall I start?'

Sometimes hours, or even days, can be lost as an editor deliberates about starting with shot A or shot B or shot C. This illustrates a basic principle of editing – there is no right or wrong, there aren't even that many rules. It's a case of what looks right and good!

Key idea

For every shot order you decide upon there are probably three equally appealing and valid alternatives. Stay focused, don't hesitate, and trust your instincts.

The best way to start anything is to cut together some shots that will have some relevance to the first scene and possibly have some relation to the rest of the film. OK, that's a basic assumption but it is a great starting point. Edit together shots that build up towards establishing and telling the audience where the place is and what is going on. In many mainstream feature films, the first few minutes are usually given over to this alone (see below).

You may discover that editing is an organic process and, once you have edited together the first few shots, things tend to follow on of their own accord. Although that sounds a bit weird, you will be amazed how editing can have a life of its own. The thing to avoid in the early stages of your edit is ruining it with an abundance of transition effects. These will be described later on in the chapter, but for the initial stages of your film's edit, keep the visual elements quite simple. Just cut from shot to shot without any fancy edit effects, otherwise your pacing will become confused and the visual feel could get lost under unnecessary edits.

Key idea: Make it flow

Once you have cut through all the theories, essays, psychology and concepts involved with editing, there is one basic consideration to have in mind: editing is mostly involved with ensuring that movements, emotions and actions connect into a smooth flow. Or, at an even more basic level, your cuts act to ensure shots have a continuing action. A scene showing someone getting a saw out of a tool shed and sawing a piece of wood in half would show the components edited together so as to create the illusion that the entire process had been filmed from various angles simultaneously. This grammar of editing supposes that, when a cut takes place, the last frame of the outgoing shot will match up with the first frame of the incoming shot – for example, a shot of a hand placed on the tool shed door handle will cut to a shot of the door opening.

Remember this

Although this flow of editing is something easy and logical to start off with, be warned: it's easy to sleepwalk into editing your entire film in this manner as you effectively try to show a real-time story taking place. At some point, you will have to change time and/or location (see below).

Styles of editing

When editing, it is important to realize that your audience is actually quite sophisticated. Many editors make the mistake of thinking they must spoon-feed the viewer at each stage of the story, and all too often there is an over-abundance of explanatory shots that should not have been included.

This is related to the important fact that when watching a film you are not processing events in the way you are normally used to. Put another way, if you were to do something in real life, you would experience and see every single step of that process. When this human psychology gets carried over to film making it is sometimes incompatible with the grammar of the medium.

Therefore, when editing you have to forget the normal thought process slightly and think in terms of the edit. Don't feel compelled to show every single step of a process or journey. If someone is making a cup of coffee, then a shot of a kettle boiling and then a shot of a person sipping the drink will be enough for the audience to realize what has happened. If someone is going on a car journey, a shot of the key turning in the ignition and a shot of the car pulling up somewhere may suffice. It is very easy to fall into the trap of having to explain every single stage of your film to an audience who you think won't understand. Avoid this trap and it will streamline your editing and the thought processes behind it.

To extend this concept, also recognize that your film itself is a selective look at something. Whether it is a factual or fiction piece, every so often your editing should be leaping from time-and-place to time-and-place. As an editor, you don't need to worry about the bits in between as they are irrelevant to the story and serve no purpose. Stick to only what you need to get your story across to the viewer. Although the story may be big, the film and edit should only reveal/select important pieces, otherwise it will be too long. This, alas, is why the book is often better than the film.

The theoretical side of editing is something that could be expanded upon and discussed until the end of time. However, the type of script you are working from, and in turn the style of shots you are working with, will often be key indicators as to what style you should adopt.

Take, for example, the style in which many of today's historical dramas are edited. Films like *Pride & Prejudice* (dir. Joe Wright, 2005) starring Keira Knightly and *Becoming Jane* (dir. Julian Jarrold, 2007) starring Anne Hathaway have what could be called a measured pace, where the detail and richness of the footage is lingered over for relatively long periods. It is as though each shot is being held up on a plate for the viewer to examine and appreciate. Also, due to the nature of the dialogue, individual lines in this kind of film tend to have more resonance than they might in an action movie. Here the lines are a considerable part, if not the focus, of the shot or scene, instead of just a rushed detail as may be the case in a film with a faster pace. Films like this do not adopt this lingering pace without reason – this style of editing resonates with the subject matter and enhances the overall presentation. It's almost as if you are walking through an art gallery and absorbing each painting (or shot) at your leisure.

At the opposite end of the spectrum are films where the editing is very fast and rough, verging on disjointed and dizzying. This style of editing relies upon abstract details and wide shots just as much as any other does, but here the shots are seen for only moments. The audience is given just enough time to recognize what they are seeing, and then shown something else. This kind of editing can also be used to induce a sense of claustrophobia – details can be rapidly linked together in order to give the audience information about the scene without giving them the relief of any expansive shots. This is a very contemporary style of editing, and movies like *Man on Fire* (dir. Ton Scott, 2004) typify its bold and dangerous approach.

Case study: Fast and furious

Man on Fire revolves around the efforts of private security operative, Creasy (played by Denzel Washington), to trace some child kidnappers through the urban sprawl of Mexico City. The film is edited so as to present a series of very small vignettes of life in the city's underbelly – rarely is there a moment when the audience is given time to comfortably absorb what is going on. Shots are held together just long enough to give a sense of atmosphere, location and danger. They are edited at speed and without mercy. Often jump cuts have been thrown in for good measure. It is interesting to note the emergence of this style of editing in modern film. A film edited in such a fast and traumatic style in the 1980s or earlier would probably not have been released; the implication is that audiences are becoming more sophisticated in terms of the kinds of film – or the kind of editing – they can tolerate.

Edit concepts – movement, time and space

When editing, you are shaping a certain kind of reality. As hinted at before, your take on the world is different from how it is when you live and experience it on a daily basis. As such, there are some factors you need to be very wary of when you are editing:

- space

- time

- movement

These features need to be reconciled with each other very carefully otherwise your edit could be a painful thing to view. Shots need to be able to flow into each other almost as if dovetailing from the start to the finish of the film. Otherwise they need to be cut boldly to prove a point, bring extra attention to a situation or move the action elsewhere. Space is one of the more obvious factors to notice as an editor. Imagine a situation with two shots:

Shot 1 – A man turning a corner and coming into view walking down a corridor towards and past the camera.

Shot 2 – The same man walking along a road.

There is a right way and a wrong way to edit this.

The wrong way would be to cut from the first shot when he was still walking towards the camera and then cut to him walking along the road. This may be very awkward to watch as the viewer would see the man go from one location to another without anything to indicate how this was achieved. Better would be to have the man walk past the camera and out of shot and then cut to him walking along the road. This would suggest to the viewer that after he exited the shot he made his way to the road. In edit-speak, the moment the man leaves the shot is called an edit point. It is a place where you can 'step in' and make an edit. In general terms, having the subject leave a shot is usually a great edit point. The reverse of this situation could also work. If you were to change the order of the shots you could have the man walking along the road, and then you could cut to the corridor shot before he turns the corner and comes into view.

When an audience sees an edit like this they will assume the person has logically got from one place to the other even if the intervening time gap is short. Remember, you don't have to spell everything out for your audience as they are cognitive beings and will understand what is going on. However, when something is put together badly they will be confused. To go one step further, your audience is also very quick at noticing movement. Even subtle differences can be easily picked up and noted as flaws. Some shots edited together of someone sitting in a chair can be compromised if one of them contains a slight movement that is at odds with the others.

However, movement can also be a key ally in editing. Often two or more shots will work well together if they share a feature of movement. For example, a shot of a basketball being thrown could cut well with someone catching a football. Here the motion of one shot links into the next. In the film *Me, Myself & Irene* (dir. the Farrelly brothers, 2000) this is done to comic effect when the main character played by Jim Carrey pulls down his trousers to defecate on his neighbour's lawn and then the shot cuts to some chocolate ice cream being poured into a cone.

Next comes time. This is another feature that you need to handle with a modicum of care lest your film be some bizarre collection of random events. Like movement, there has to be the inference that there is a time gap between certain shots. This can be done as in a sequence (see Chapter 11 on filming) or by some simple editing that has many overlaps with movement. Just as in the movement examples above, by having shots that suggest time has elapsed you don't actually need to see that time elapsing. Still using the same shots as before when the man walks past the camera and we cut to him walking along the road, the cut itself hints that some time has elapsed. Also, as before, because the subject of the shot leaves the frame, it is easier for the audience to assume there has been a passage of time from one shot to the next. In other circumstances, simple cuts like this can be used to imply a large distance or large amount of time has elapsed.

Key idea

A device sometimes used in editing to transport the action to different location or time is to use an object. This object will then become the thread that links up different shots. For example, imagine a wide shot where a detective is handed a photo of a missing person while in a police station. Next, we see the photo in close-up being handed over and then a wide shot where the detective is showing it to someone on the street. This is a very subtle yet clever way of 'moving around' in your edit and one your audience will be impressed by.

Overall, with editing you need to be able to suggest how the film has leapt from one location to another, or how time has passed, or how certain movements work with each other. Again, this is all down to simple cutting most of the time. Indeed, sometimes all three concepts can be conveyed with one cut.

Key idea

Have an action-packed set of events you need to cram into a really short space of time? Then you need a montage sequence! It's simple and it's fun. Condense months of an athlete's training into a few minutes with inspiring music and lots of running past waving onlookers (*Rocky*).

Need to get your action hero equipped for his next mission? Then get him down to the local gun store and have him attaching holsters, weapons, ammunition, bandanas and camouflage paint before he takes on the baddies (Sylvester Stallone in *Rambo* or Arnold Schwarzenegger in *Predator*). This edit practice was satirized in the film *Team America: World Police* (dir. Trey Parker, 2004).

Although these are some guidelines and rules, film making is a creative art and therefore should not be bound by the things you read here or elsewhere. It is your prerogative as a creative individual to corrupt, ignore and change these guidelines as you see fit. If you want your film to be experimental and abstract, then anything goes. Bear in mind that one of the most popular mediums for short film making today is the music video. Most of them are abstract presentations that don't make sense to anyone but the director. (Have a look at Beck's 1993 'Loser' video (dir. Steve Hanft) for a good example of this.)

Basic grammar of the edit

If you think of editing as a language, then like any other language extra meaning can be imparted on things by subtle inflection, emphasis, precision and sequencing. An edit can be a minefield of confusing opportunities. However, you can think of all the choices open to you as a way of shaping your story into something that appeals to you and will ultimately make the film more individual.

A common pitfall for new editors is to merely edit what is in the script or story outline. To simply bolt together your footage and sound verbatim as per the words on the page will probably produce a very dull edit. One of the truly exciting things about the edit is that it's where the footage can be electrified and take on a life of its own. Editing according to rigid instructions can sometimes sap the energy out of this.

OK, this can produce a bit of a dilemma: edit the film or edit *my* film? Well, that is the perennial question in edit suites the world over. It can cause editors, directors and executive producers to fall out and even sue each other. Hopefully, at your level of film making, such litigious proceedings will be avoided.

Back to the matter. Within the editing of a simple scene you will have the ammunition to change emphasis and story all the time. By choosing certain kinds of shots over others, you can produce something radically different from what the story outline is. Shots that are close-ups can increase intensity in situations that are anything but. Emphasizing objects over people can calm things down or up the threat. Totally unrelated shots may suggest passages of time or that a great story is about to be told. Put simply, the possibilities are bound by what shots are available to you.

Let's have a look at an edit scenario in which two people are in a police interrogation room. One is a police detective and one is a known criminal accused of a jewel robbery. The scene revolves around the accused being grilled about his connection to a robbery. The script reads as follows:

INT. DAY. Maple Street Police Station. Interrogation Room Number 3.
Detective Smith is walking around the small room. Jones, a known petty criminal, is seated at the table in the centre.

Detective Smith

We have witnesses that say you were seen in the house at the approximate time of the robbery.

Jones sits at the table and does not respond.

Detective Smith

Glass dust and fragments on the clothes you were arrested in match the glass of the smashed window at the house.

Jones sits at the table and does not respond.

Detective Smith

A search of your apartment revealed the jewellery that was reported missing.

Jones sits at the table and does notrespond.

```
                    Detective Smith
    We know you did it. Even if you don't talk
    this evidence will put you away for a
    long time.
```

The shots available are as follows:

Shot of a masked man smashing a house window at night

Shot of a masked man emptying a safe full of jewellery

Shots of the accused sitting in the interrogation room denying
   the crime

Shots of the accused looking impassively at the detective

Shots of the detective making accusations

The literal way to edit this would simply be cutting from Detective
Smith to Jones depending on whose turn it is in the script. Essentially
this would be an edit of exactly what is on the script. It is a very
traditional way of editing, but what else can be done? One option
would be to see Detective Smith only at the start and then use the
shots of Jones sitting at the desk. All the while Detective Smith's
words could be heard, but the shot would always be of Jones sitting
impassively. This way of editing would impart a kind of intensity
and a feeling of claustrophobia to Jones. Also, it would emphasize
the trouble he is in. Furthermore, it would take the focus off the
detective and give Jones an increased importance in the scene. Such a
consideration may be important depending on the script.

Another way of editing this would be to intercut Detective Smith's
questions with the shots of the crime being committed and then at the
very end have a shot of Jones. This would give the scene a powerful
dynamic and even reach a kind of crescendo at the end with the shot
of Jones. The important thing to bear in mind about this option is that
the shots of the crime taking place are not in this part of the script.
However, there is nothing that says they couldn't be used. It's good to
always be mindful of the script and footage you have in its entirety.

To extrapolate the principle, if there had been close-up shots of
Detective Smith's side-holstered pistol, then including such shots
could have made things more threatening. Likewise, close-ups on the
eyes of either character can exaggerate stress and threat. Also, close-
ups on hands moving could imply that Detective Smith is getting
increasingly annoyed or Jones is under more pressure to answer the

questions and confess. Another typical shot would be a close-up of the second hand moving round a clock face to heighten the tension. Just having these simple and almost innocuous shots can make a huge difference to the character of a scene. As with filming, the possibilities here can be endless (as long as the shots are available).

Key idea: Need a pick-up?

Something that happens often during editing is when you realize you don't have enough footage to either tell your story or edit together some of the scenes. The extra shots required are called pick-ups. As an edit becomes more fully formed, it's quite natural for pick-ups to be needed.

Remember this

A script has the words on it, but the editing has the pictures. As a film maker, and as an editor, it will be important for you to think very laterally at times. Not only will you be shaping the film into an order or narrative that does not concur with reality, but you will at times be bringing people's attention to the microscopic level with the editing in of innocent details – these have an impact on the way your audience will interpret a scene and film.

Over the years there have been various psychological insights and essays written about how editing plays on our mind. Many have cited famous examples of shots being played with in order to create false senses of mood or location. For example, a shot of a smiling man intercut with a cute baby in a pram may indicate the man thinks the child is sweet. Whereas you could take the same shot of the man but intercut it with a plate of food, then the implication would be that the man is looking at, or thinking about, the food. These are basic examples but serve to show how the edit can corrupt story and reality to its maximum effect.

Key idea: Moving statues and a pram?

Perhaps the most famous example of using the editing process to create and fabricate mood, as well as focus on the subtle, is in the Soviet film *Battleship Potemkin* (dir. Sergei Eisenstein, 1925). During a scene in which troops open fire on a crowd, a baby in a pram becomes the focus of the action as it trundles down some steps amid the chaos and panic. In addition, shots of lion statues in different poses are cut together to suggest they have become agitated and dismayed by the massacre.

A popular method in many feature films is when a medium close-up, or close-up, of someone is held for a bit longer than normal. This usually implies that the character is bad or suspects something. Again, this illustrates how much power a single shot choice can have in the edit.

Hopefully, you can now visualize how having some shots instead of others, or having a non-conventional arrangement, can alter the dramatic impact of a scene.

The power of cutaways

We looked at cutaways in previous chapters, but it is not until you get to the edit that you can really appreciate what they have to offer.

The interrogation room example above also shows the importance and power of cutaway shots. The shots of the glass being smashed and the jewellery being stolen were cutaway shots that had relevance to the scene and added another layer of narrative. At a simpler level they looked good and interesting, and this is always a decent thing to aim for.

If you are making a factual piece that relies on interviews, or people talking to camera, then things will be a bit easier for you. It will be a case of selecting which bits of certain answers you want to use and putting them in your preferred order on the timeline or storyboard. However, when you edit an interview, or interviews, in this manner there will be jump cuts that represent the missing pieces. Again, jump cuts are things we looked at in previous parts of the book, but in editing you will learn how to physically manage them. For example, if an interview lasts for five minutes and you use only the first 30 seconds and last 45 seconds, those two bits will cut together very awkwardly – in edit-speak, a jump cut.

In these situations, editors rely on cutaways (see Chapter 11). In terms of editing, a cutaway serves a dual purpose:

▶ It shows something relevant to the scene or the interview.

▶ It covers jump cuts and smoothes over the edit.

When editing this is how it would look on the timeline.

Without cutaway:		
Outgoing shot	Incoming shot	
With cutaway:		
Outgoing shot	Factory cutaway	Incoming shot

In the first instance, you can see the two shots next to each other. When these clips play, the person talking will suddenly change their pose. In the second instance, after the first interview shot there is a cutaway shot, and then it goes back to the person talking. The cutaway shot of the factory hides the fact that some of the original interview has been cut and in turn hides the jump cut.

That's movie magic for you!

Although that example was using a factual situation, you can use the same principle for editing a conversation in a fiction piece. For example, you can shorten a story-based dialogue by using cutaways or simply add a bit more visual vibrancy to things.

Cutaway shots are something you can't have enough of as they can get you out of trouble in an edit and they add extra dimensions to your film. Without them, a film can be very dull and lifeless.

Remember this

Don't be afraid to experiment when editing and try things that are totally different from your expectations. You may surprise yourself and discover something that really works.

This aspect of editing holds true whether you are making a short film or something on a bigger scale. When editing the final film of *The Lord of the Rings* trilogy, there was a struggle trying to decide on how to edit the start of the film. In the end, and totally without forward planning, an abandoned scene from the second film featuring Sméagol/Gollum (played by Andy Serkis) fishing with Déagol was placed at the start.

In a fiction piece, your main source of how to start and continue your edit will come from your script or story outline. However, that doesn't mean there aren't going to be some difficulties in deciding where to begin. A film that features dialogue (and most do) rarely jumps into things or immediately starts with people talking. Most of the time there is some preamble known as a sequence (see Chapter 11) in which various relevant images are cut together to create an introductory buffer zone before the first conversation or the speaking occurs.

For example, imagine a short film about two people talking on a bridge spanning a small river. Instead of suddenly starting with the first line of dialogue, there could be a few shots of the river, swans paddling about, reflections of buildings in the water, riverside trees swaying in the breeze, a few details of the bridge itself and so forth, and then it could move into the dialogue.

Such an approach to editing makes things richer and more appealing to view. You may even find you impress yourself with subtle edits like this. Also, in real terms, you will find your film making is much better than some other films out there if you just take a bit of time to think about what's going on behind and around your story.

Key idea: The proof is in the pudding

You will only know if something looks good or works after it has been edited. If not, try arranging the shots another way.

Using jump cuts deliberately

Although jump cuts can be the hallmark of bad editing or a lack of appropriate shots, sometimes consciously using them can give a scene a special edge. By playing on the fact that they create a strong, and sometimes unpleasant, jolt in the film's narrative, they can make the passage of time confusing or seem disturbed. On a few occasions, this can be very apt for your edit.

Imagine a situation where someone is trying to defuse a bomb. Having jump cuts and generally cutting together shots that clash will create a certain intensity that 'standard' editing may not be able to achieve. Deliberate jump cutting is often used for scenes where there is stress, danger, violence, a sense of urgency or lack of time. Also, they will tend to work best when the shots themselves are very energetic, as this will heighten the intensity of each jump cut.

However, they are also a way of progressing through time in a staccato manner. In the 2005 version of *King Kong*, Naomi Watts' character is seen putting on a succession of dresses while looking in a mirror. The shot remains static, but she is seen in a variety of poses and dresses that have been jump cut together. The effect of the scene shows her stress and confusion at trying to impress someone by being unsure of what to wear.

Remember this

Be warned – jump cuts are risky. Use sparingly and with extreme caution.

Key idea: From edit suite to audience?

An overlooked aspect of editing is how to get the film off the computer and on to something more practical. It can be an utterly forgotten consideration after you emerge from the imaginative labyrinth of your edit. Some people choose to do a play out in which the film is recorded on to a digital tape. This has the advantage of happening in real time. Others prefer to export the film as a file. A drawback to this is the disproportionate amount of time needed to export the film. Whatever method you choose, or have available, make sure your film is on a transportable medium as soon as possible after completion.

Dealing with continuity while editing

We looked at continuity before, and while it is something that is supposedly the job of certain individuals on set, it is the editor who normally has to deal with errors of continuity. As previously discussed, a busy film set with various shots and scenes being filmed out of order, and usually with only the one camera, will often produce situations where the continuity is completely scrambled. It's sometimes only when the footage is reviewed prior to, or during, the editing that these disastrous mistakes are noticed.

If there is one cruel lot of being an editor, it is the blame they will get for editing something that has mistakes in it. However, when you are an editor these continuity problems are not your fault and you can only use the footage available. Continuity concerns are usually the last thing on an editor's mind. Often, a continuity of emotion or narrative will take precedence over physical continuity. Put another way, getting the story and action flowing is sometimes more important than anything else.

Picture a fight scene between two men. The filming for the scene has been hand-held and energetic so as to match the energy of the fight. Likewise, the editor has been instructed to cut as fast as possible to further up the ante. However, in the post-production process the editor notices a problem; as the fight scene is being edited there are shots where one of the men is brandishing a knife and in others he is fighting with his fists. Owing to the way the shots have been filmed, it is impossible to correct this in the edit.

From a purely technical point of view, you would either need to re-film this scene or abandon it. On the other hand, from an emotional and narrative perspective things may work out just fine. When edited together the fact that the knife appears then disappears may not matter as the action is so frenetic, plus the overall thrust of the scene isn't compromised.

Key idea: Continuity – what's that?

Although continuity is a major aspect to manage in fiction films, there is one genre of short film making where it is often ignored: the music video. These films that appear all over the world and are viewed by millions, possibly billions, sometimes throw the concept of continuity out of the window. Rap artists can appear in a video yet change environment and clothes constantly. Singers and rock groups can change instruments, stages and back stage areas with every change in beat. Singers can be driving a car and then walking down a street and then be somewhere else completely different. Yet, do we care? No. Because the important thing is the music and individual images, not the physical continuity.

In the film *Top Gun* (dir. Tony Scott, 1986) the final dogfight at the end of the film is full of errors – the wrong jet fighters fly past, sometimes their wings are configured differently from the preceding shot, and so on. However, it was the emotion and action of the fighting that most cinemagoers were watching, not the technical lapses in aviation accuracy.

Your scene doesn't even need to be as action-packed as this to have continuity errors. Imagine an emotional, tearful scene in a bar where a couple is breaking up. Everything could be perfect except for the fact that one of the drinks on the bar has varying levels of wine in it: full – empty – full and so on with no explanation as to how this is happening. Now if you are using the wine glass as the main reason for thinking the scene is uneditable, then you are slightly missing the point of editing (and of the scene) because it's the people with their emotions and acting that are the focus of this scene, not the drinks glasses.

These two examples go to show that sometimes in an edit you have to make difficult decisions to get things moving. In these situations, it's important to know whether or not technicalities should outweigh emotions from the director's perspective.

Now this isn't an invitation to become a lazy or sloppy editor, but it goes to show that sometimes the emotion of what is happening on screen can supersede, and effectively blot out, any technical continuity errors. Without being too cruel to your prospective audience, you will be amazed how much you can get away with as editor with regard to covering up errors such as this. Sometimes it is only geeks writing on web forums that bother to make note of such details.

Keeping it simple

There is another important consideration that can overwhelm an editor. It is trying to juggle editing video, sound, music, titles and effects all at once. The best advice here is to only do one thing at a time. After all, in professional edit situations these elements are usually done by teams of different people in different departments. If you try and edit all the components simultaneously, you will end up getting seriously confused and lose sight of what you are supposed to be doing.

In real terms, this would mean just editing the basic visual components first. So just edit your shots until they are in a manner of your choosing and only then put in your cutaways. When you are finished with that, move on to applying music. When that's done, move on to simple effects and then after that, titles.

Many editors come up with their own way of doing things; some work with dialogue sound first and then add the shots later, for example. However, the point is to not try and put everything down at once, otherwise your edit will get bogged down by information overload and you may end up getting seriously and horribly confused.

Key idea

Editing can sometimes be a tortuous, frustrating and maddening experience owing to the creative and technical stumbling blocks that sometimes appear. It doesn't take much to turn your editing room into a 'padded cell'!

Manipulating sound with vision

One of the great things about editing is that you don't have to use your shots in the way you filmed them. So far only the basic placing of shots on a timeline has been examined. The whole point of editing is to manipulate the image and the sound to maximize the look and impact of your film.

If we look back to the examples of Detective Smith with Jones, or the two people talking on a bridge, a popular technique would be to introduce the dialogue sound while other shots are being viewed. For example, shots of the crime being committed while Detective Smith talks or hearing the conversation of the men on the bridge while seeing shots of the river and swans.

How is this done? Depending on the kind of edit software you have you can extract, or remove, the audio from a video clip and treat it as a separate element. In other words, you can move a clip's video and sound around independently of each other.

Using the bridge example, if we play the edit we can see the clips of the river, the swans, the reflections, and then while the reflection shot is playing the start of the dialogue is introduced and finally the two people are seen along with their dialogue.

It is important to realize that not all consumer edit software can do this. Some software only allows you to edit the clips as a whole – you can't go taking them apart and using the different bits. After all, some of these packages are just made for extremely simple video projects and therefore do have limitations.

Not only can you create little tricks like this, but also other basic sound edits. In Chapter 7 we looked at filming different shots when the ambient sound was varied. When shots like this get edited together there can be jumps in the sound which can be just as noticeable as a jump cut. Most of the time, the sound is removed altogether and some sound effects or music added. The truly ambitious among you can extract, or cut out, the sounds from a clip and then use it elsewhere it under a relevant clip or clips. For example, going back to the conversation on a bridge, the sounds of running water could be played under all the shots.

Not only can sound make a scene a bit more pleasant to watch and add realism to things, it can also be a great device to assist in editing changes of time and location. Imagine this script situation:

> INT. DAY. A busy office. James Novak is
> working at his desk. He occasionally looks
> at a fishing magazine next to his computer.
> A colleague approaches his booth. James
> looks up.

> **Colleague**
> Thank God it's Friday. I can't wait to get out of here.
>
> **James**
> Yeah, me too.
>
> **Colleague**
> You got anything planned for the weekend?
>
> **James**
> Maybe take in a little fishing down at the river. I dunno, though.
>
> **Colleague**
> Sounds good. Catch you later.
>
> The colleague walks off and James goes back to casually flicking through this magazine as the office throngs around him.
>
> **EXT. DAY. Banks of the river. It is a bright sunny day and the sunlight is sparkling off the fast-flowing river. James is setting up his fishing rod and is preparing to make his first cast of the day.**

One way to transport the story from the office to the shores of the river would be to introduce the sound of the river flowing while James is still in his booth. After James finishes his brief conversation with his colleague, the audio from the river could be gently introduced as he goes back to flicking through his magazine until it gets louder and finally the picture cuts to the river.

This is a common device and is regularly used in films when someone is dreaming. Usually the sound of an alarm going off, or the voice of someone trying to wake them, will be introduced into their dream sequence. Furthermore, this device goes to prove just how laterally you have to think, because nine times out of ten we will be looking at a visual approach and solution to our editing. Also, it reiterates just how important sound is to film making.

Basic effects

Once your shots, cutaways and ambient (or spoken) sound have been reconciled with each other, a whole new aspect of editing awaits you – effects.

Now 'effects' doesn't necessarily mean blockbuster special effects that you see in your local multiplex (although more on those later), but more simple and subtle things that can further refine your film.

The two most popular effects are fades and dissolves. In edit-speak, they are known as transitions.

A **fade** is the edit term for when the picture fades to, or fades from, black. For example, at the start of your film it is usually handy to fade the picture in from black as it implies that the film is being introduced. Likewise, at the end of a film, it is common to see a fade to black as this implies that it is the end and the film is kind of saying 'goodbye'. However, you don't always have to keep these fades to start and end a film. Sometimes having a fade in the middle of a film would imply a passage of time, for example:

```
Shot of house at night (FADE TO BLACK)
(FADE FROM BLACK) Shot of house in day
```

By using the fades creatively, you will make the audience automatically realize that those two fades back to back represent night coming and going. More movie magic! Also, it once again demonstrates how powerful editing is as you are shaping the reality of an environment or a situation.

The cousin of the fade is the dissolve, and it is another popular effect many film makers use. So, what is it? This is the effect where one shot fades away and another one fades in. It is also sometimes known as a cross-fade or cross-dissolve as it goes across two shots. The dissolve is an effect that needs to be used with some care and consideration as, in most cases, the novice editor will use it on every shot. The result will mean a decent film gets reduced to visual farce.

A dissolve works best on two shots that will complement each other. In other words, two adjoining shots that display some similar characteristics such as a shot of a wheel spinning and a shot of a washing machine going around. When a dissolve is placed between these two shots, the transition from one to the other will be subtle and smooth. Likewise, a shot of an open area of countryside may work well if it dissolves into a medium close-up of someone's head as there will be space for that person to 'appear' from.

Conversely, if you were to put a dissolve between a shot of a wheel spinning and someone sitting down and talking the result would be near surrealism. In fact, it may just look plain awkward and have your viewers scratching their heads wondering what is going on. That said, depending on what kind of film you are making, this may be the effect you are after. As mentioned earlier in this chapter, it's all about experimenting and it is your choice whether you want to alter the reference points of editing.

Dissolves can be used to transport your audience from scene to scene. Take a look at the following script situation:

> INT. Newspaper printing works — Day
> The round paper rollers on the printers
> are spinning at high speed.
> EXT. Road somewhere in a large town — Day
> A car is travelling along the road.

Here is how the two shots could be placed next to each other with a dissolve.

Shot 1 – Side shot of spinning cylinder. Zoom in.

Dissolve.

Shot 2 – Side shot of moving car wheel. Zoom out.

We have two shots of spinning/revolving objects and, when they are linked by a dissolve, the changeover will be very, very smooth. If you are using this method, it helps a lot if you have objects that look similar (spinning/revolving things in this case) and if the framing is also the same – that is, the objects being filmed fill the same amount of the frame. If this is not the case, then things will look awkward despite the best efforts of your dissolve. A shot of the spinning machinery from an oblique angle and from far away would not go well with a spinning car wheel that fills the frame in a close-up.

Consider this other dissolve opportunity:

> EXT. Forest — Day
> A group of people are having a picnic and
> enjoying the summer's day.
> They finish and leave.

Shot 1 – Group of people eating their picnic, then tilt up to moving leaves of the trees.

Dissolve.

Shot 2 – Moving leaves of the trees, then tilt down to the people packing up their picnic.

Although this example would mean filming the same set of moving and swaying tree branches and leaves, not having a dissolve would cause a jump cut, as there would be a jolt from the leaves and branches suddenly moving differently between the two shots. The dissolve would effortlessly aid the shot transition. For me, the dissolve was created for shot changes such as the ones I have just highlighted. However, remember the two shots will look smoothest if they are:

▶ related – if they are of similar moving or shaped things

▶ if they both fill the frame in the same way

As an example of point 2, there is a dissolve in the film *Vanilla Sky* (dir. Cameron Crowe, 2001) that goes from a back street to a hospital corridor. The framing is so precise it looks more like morphing than a dissolve.

Other simple effects that many of these editing packages come with include things such as wipes, clock wipes, star wipes, ripple edits and things which, to be honest, are rather tacky and will immediately make your film resemble a cheap and badly made wedding video.

However, it should be said that many of *Star Wars* creator George Lucas' films make use of wipes and clock wipes. These are the effects when one side of the shot horizontally slides, or is wiped away, and another shots slides, or wipes, in its place. With a clock wipe, the change mimics a fast-moving clock hand going round.

Remember this

The best thing to remember about these effects is that, although they are there to assist your editing, use them only if you need them, instead of using them because they are there.

Music and sound effects

Earlier in this chapter it was highlighted that many first-time film makers sometimes get stuck when it comes down to the editing. Most of the time they have not properly assessed exactly what their edit needs are, or even realized what editing entails. Carrying on from this situation is the consideration of sound.

In Chapter 7 we looked at how important sound recording is to your film and how to record and create your own sound effects. Also, a few pages ago we looked at how sound can be used to help your editing move across locations and timeframes. Your recorded speech and the ambient sound you obtain are vital elements of your film. In many ways, this is half the experience for someone watching your film. Therefore, you should bear in mind how you can use audio to enhance your production.

Earlier we examined the example of the conversation on the bridge. In the edit, the sound of the running water was put under the shots to create a pleasing soundscape instead of using the sound from the individual shots, which in turn avoided sound jump cuts. This is something you can expand upon and is only limited by your imagination.

Still using the example of the bridge conversation, the volume level of the running water could be high to start with and then lowered when the conversation starts. Also, other things could be put into the mix: maybe a couple of seconds of the swans calling, or wind through the trees. Many elements can be added to create a rich audio experience that will immediately propel the film on to another level. Just imagine this scene without sound – the audience would immediately realize something was wrong, plus it would be very, very boring. It's amazing what sound can bring to a film.

However, it is very important to mention that some of the more basic consumer-level edit systems won't be able to perform edits like this. All they can handle is the video clips and nothing else, because their timelines are very basic. More sophisticated edit packages like Final Cut X Pro and Adobe Premiere Pro, or even the basic iMovie and Windows Movie Maker, allow you to have more than one audio channel. This means you can have more than one sound at a time. Not only can different audio be placed on different channels, but the volume of those individual clips can all be different, allowing you to get the best effect from them.

Of course, it is not only sound effects that add drama and depth to a film. Music has a very important role to play. Music can intensify a scene, whether you are making a factual or fiction piece. It is an essential part of the film making puzzle, and, just as with sound effects, without it your film will be a bit on the dull side.

Titles

The text, writing or titles on films are perceived as being perhaps the least exciting, or known about, bit of editing. Ignore them at your peril. Without them no one will know what your film is called, who is in it, or who directed, filmed and edited it. If only to acknowledge those who may have helped you make it, and to prevent them lynching you, pay attention to your titles.

In 'ye olde' days of editing it was common for the titles to be designed, made and filmed by specialist technicians completely separate from the editor and editing department. This is still true where there is a need for titles that are full of wildly animated graphic images and so on. However, if all you want to do is add some text to your film, then your edit package (no matter how basic) will be able to do this for you.

Just like the transition effects mentioned earlier, the titles are an aspect of editing where you can get seriously carried away. There are usually myriad options for writing your titles – from basics such as font, size and colour, you can also play around with background shadows, transparency, design colourful boxes to put your titles over and so on.

The type of film you are making will tell you what kind of style you should be using. For example, an interview with a priest probably won't benefit from a lurid Day-Glo orange set of titles. Just like the effects, remember to use the various title options only when you need them, not simply because they are there.

One other danger when creating titles is to patronize the viewer and label everything with titles. One of the weird things that happens when you edit something is that often you assume your audience won't be able to follow anything without you helping them along every five seconds. Although it's usually a good idea to put some text of someone's name and job, or role, if you are editing an interview, avoid the temptation to go overboard and title other tiny 'footnotes' that the audience will probably figure out anyway.

Even in the occasional feature film there is often the case of some over-zealous titling. In the film *Unbreakable* (dir. M. Night Shyamalan, 2000) the opening moments had some lengthy titles devoted to describing some statistics about comic books, even though it was of little relevance to the film apart from one of the characters having a comic book shop. Likewise, the science-fiction action film *Paycheck* (dir. John Woo, 2003) starts in a similar way in its description of the plot and role of the main character, all of which are revealed as the story progresses anyway. This highlights what was mentioned earlier in the chapter about spoon-feeding your audience information. Don't worry. They will be able to figure out what is going on without the need for a chunk of explanatory text.

Perhaps the most famous example of 'over-titling' is in the film *Blade Runner*. Upon seeing an early edit of the film, the studio bosses panicked and were worried that moviegoers would need a lot of help understanding things. As a result, a rather long descriptive series of titles starts off the film (as well as narration throughout).

Now what?

When you have finished editing your film it needs to be put on to some kind of portable storage medium. There is no point editing your film if it stays on your edit suite without ever seeing the light of day.

Many choose to export their film as a file and use this to make a DVD. Others may simply use this file to upload to a video sharing site. Some editing software programs have simple options asking if you want to export your film specifically for Internet, CD-ROM or DVD use.

There is also the option of playing out your film to tape. This is like digitizing your film, but in reverse; the images go from the computer to your camera. However, you need to have a camera with a record function when in playback mode to do this.

Remember this

'A movie is never finished, only abandoned.' George Lucas

Those words ring very true. When you get absorbed into the editing of your film, it is sometimes impossible to know when to stop. There are endless tweaks, amendments, nips, tucks and tinkering opportunities that could keep you going until the end of time. With every edit there will come a time when you must realize that enough has been done and then walk away. If not, you may go too far and end up ruining a perfectly decent edit in the quest for unobtainable brilliance.

Keeper of the histories: archiving your material

This is a problem faced by many film makers after a certain period of time – keeping track of things from completed projects, abandoned shoots or just the stuff filmed for your own amusement. In other words, maintaining an effective archive of your material.

Following on from data wrangling, archiving is the next step in managing the often huge mass of material generated over time. There are many similarities with wrangling, although archiving is a way in which shots can be kept – ideally in perpetuity – so you can easily keep hold of them and use again should you need to. Also, like data wrangling, archiving is a whole industry in itself, complete with departments, specialists, hardware, software applications and a whole raft of protocols and procedures.

It's a fact that many people can be rather lax with the storage of their material. Let's face it, filming things is the fun part of the business for many and keeping tabs on things many weeks, months or years after the fact can be regarded as a trivial nuance. The notion that film images and raw clips are 'on a drive somewhere' can lull us into a false sense of security that our material will sit pretty until we need it. In all likelihood, it's possible that things will simply get lost or be put on storage media not fit for purpose.

Remember this

Archiving is an aspect of your film making that needs attention and care if you are not to lose everything, either through faulty storage media or simply not knowing where anything is.

Over the years masses of film and video material have been transferred from their source material, such as film, to contemporary formats on a regular basis. This work is either done by dedicated archive houses or by the studios themselves. The formats these materials have been transferred to includes VHS, SVHS, BetaSP, DVCam, DVD, hard drives and so on. While these may seem like ancient historical curios to some, at the time they were the newest and best storage media and thus used extensively until the next supposedly better format came along. This has meant that every few years archive houses – the ones that can afford it – have had to move their images to a new format. Unfortunately, the only way to know if a format is any good as a legacy format (that is, one that's good to store images on for a very long time) is to observe it over time. Some formats have shown themselves to be less than great and have degraded and failed over time. Coupled with the fact that the machinery to play older formats is often no longer made, this means that much audio-visual material is at perpetual risk of permanent loss. Not to mention the fact that the original format holding the images may itself be in bad shape.

Many people have been caught out by using supposedly capable formats that have since proven to be very unreliable. Not too long ago everyone started backing up their material using external hard drives. A sure thing, right? Wrong, after some years this storage media showed itself to be anything but reliable, with data loss after around three to five years being a common issue.

For several high-profile film makers this has meant that some seminal movies have only been saved at the last minute.

Case study: Just in time

During the 1990s ahead of the reissues of the original *Star Wars* trilogy, George Lucas discovered that the original film negatives were in danger of imminent and irreparable degradation. Thus, each frame was painstakingly restored ahead of the film series' re-release. Skip forward to 2016 when several shots of original unused material for the first *Star Wars Episode IV* film were included in *Rogue One*. This just goes to show how useful it is to maintain your material and know where it is. You never know when you'll need it again!

Getting back to your film making, your archiving can be as simple as an area of your edit computer's drive with a simple 'Archive' folder in it. Then arrange things via project name and date, with each clip in turn clearly labelled. Again, these are all simple pointers, but they make things very easy and manageable if you are to easily know where things are. There is many a film maker who has drives full of alphanumeric audio-visual files that make sense to no one. After a while the amount of unlabelled unclassified material on a computer can effectively mean that it's too much effort to look for something so it effectively gets lost.

Remember this

Don't simply use an available external hard drive as a kind of slush mechanism to dump your material. As many a film maker is finding out the hard way, these devices are proving to have a relatively short life.

However, depending on how active you are, after a while you will start running out of memory no matter how much capacity your computer has. This is why many film makers have used cloud storage or Dropbox-type methods to ease their archive storage. Since film and video material is rather memory heavy, some of these services do charge depending on how much you want to keep. Yet, some avoid this method as they are worried by hacking and data access breaches.

If your archive contains tapes, once more, label them so that you know what's on them and store them somewhere handy. Ideally, you should have some kind of tape log that describes in detail exactly what is on each tape together with a list of shots and time code. Even better would be to digitize them – if you haven't already – and store them in the one of the methods described above. For the truly detail-oriented, any shot logs you have for the tapes would likewise be converted into digital format by scanning to pdf, or tabulated and word-processed, so each digital record is tracked in a database given the content and location. For example:

File Name	Description	Comments	Location
KungFuZombie Film Clip001	Dave Jumping Through Window	Take 1 (trips on the cat by accident)	Main Edit Computer/D Drive/Film Archive/ KungFuZombie folder

Obviously, this is a lot of work, needs constant updating every time something is moved or brought into the archive environment, and requires great accuracy. Not all film makers have time for this, as their focus is understandably on actually making a film. However, further down the line, having such clearly kept records could save an immense headache when you are looking for things. And, let's face it, there's no point filming something if you have a ready-available clip to use instead.

For some of the older analogue formats like VHS or something from a discontinued domestic camcorder you have to find a device that is still capable of playing the format and use an analogue to digital converter.

If you still have the original camera that you can play out the tape with, then that's the hard part out of the way, as there are numerous, and budget, analogue to digital converters widely available. Failing that, many companies specialize in this kind of work.

At the time of writing, server-based storage is the preferred method of storing material for those who can afford it. It does away with concerns about physical tape or film formats degrading, getting damaged, misplaced or no longer being supported by manufacturers. Also, depending on how things are networked and integrated into a film company's editing infrastructure, clips can be instantly called up and placed in an edit, thereby doing away with the lengthy and expensive transfer and digitization process. However, it does mean that the record keeping demands can be very extensive, with highly detailed content management systems (such as Hewlett Packard Records Manager) required to keep track of it all. In addition, getting a system in place that's fit for purpose in terms of tracking and calling up the actual clips can be expensive and, thus, only within reach of big business or major studios only.

Yet, if there's one lesson archiving has taught us, it is that no one format has the answer to keeping material safe for ever. That's just impossible. Current popular server-based storage solutions are not infallible. Data can be lost, things can be wrongly labelled, viruses can affect files and hackers may gain access. There's just no absolute guarantee.

Key idea

The best you can do is keep track, know where stuff is and regularly check that your video (regardless of format) is still playable.

Glossary of basic 'edit-speak'

an edit	The incomplete or completed film.
capture (or digitize)	The process of uploading your images to a computer.
cued-up	Having the tapes in the right position.
cutting	A common slang term for editing.
(the) cutting room floor	Common edit slang for when some footage has been removed from an edit.
deck	The name of a digital tape player for editing from or viewing.
digital intermediate	Name given to the digital format of the rushes/dailies used for editing.
dissolve, cross fade or cross dissolve	A simple effect in which one shot fades away and another fades into view.
fade	A simple effect where the image darkens or lightens.
FireWire	A popular name for the cable used to capture or digitize the footage.
jump cut	A shot that has a sudden jolt in it.
linear editing	Editing a film in chronology with its script.
log	Paper list description of the shots generated while filming.
non-linear editing	Editing on a computer.
paper edit	An edit plan drawn up on paper using information from the log.
titles	Computer-generated writing that you can include in an edit.
transitions	Effects used to move between shots (see dissolve and fade).

Focus points

* Decide as early as possible what edit system you will use or will be able to obtain.
* Be fully aware of its memory capacity and what external drives you may need.
* Know what it can and can't do.
* Be as organized as possible with your footage – log and label your images whenever possible.
* Try to keep your editing simple, don't overcomplicate it with superfluous transition effects.
* If your edit system has the capability, think about putting different types of footage on different video tracks – dialogue shots on one, cutaways on another, and titles on the next and so on.
* Don't try and cover up mistakes with tacky effects; critically assess whether you need to film any pick-ups.
* Save your work every couple of minutes.
* Don't overdo things; editing can be highly addictive so take breaks and pace yourself.
* Know when it's time to stop editing. It doesn't take much to turn a perfect film into a mess.

Next step

In Chapter 13 we look at the special effects. In recent decades, digital technology has made the creation of special effects ever more sophisticated but also more expensive and time-consuming, as film makers' ambitions and audience expectations rise. However, for the debut film maker less is often more and the oldest (and cheapest) tricks sometimes the best.

13
Special effects filming and editing

In this chapter you will learn:

- ▶ *what special effects are*
- ▶ *how to plan special effects*
- ▶ *how to achieve simple and cheap special effects*

In today's technology-intense world, a new film release is rarely considered a proper event unless it can boast of impressive and countless special effects. It almost seems as if, in order to justify itself, a movie needs to be teeming with head-spinning and eye-watering visual elements that will hypnotize and enthral the audience.

Certainly, it is true that the modern moviegoer has been spoiled by the progressive improvements in the realism and sophistication of special visual effects over the last couple of decades. Indeed, nowadays a person sitting in the cinema is expecting something special, something never before seen or simply something designed to impress. While this is the popular impression of special effects, what often goes unnoticed is that most films these days, regardless of genre, will incorporate some kind of visual enhancement.

In fact, the origins of 'playing around' with filmed and artificial elements is as old as cinema itself. All the way from films such as *Le Voyage dans la lune* (*A Trip to the Moon*) (dir. George Méliès) back in 1902, to the epic sweep of *Gone with the Wind* (dir. Victor Fleming, 1939) right up to *Star Wars* and beyond, special effects have been an integral part of the film making experience.

Why are special effects so important to film making and why does the industry lay claim to them? The answer is simple. Special effects (like film itself) are a way of showing the impossible to an audience. Or at the very least, showing things that would be very difficult or expensive to achieve in reality.

Some special effects can be bombastic sequences that are the focal points of a film, whereas others are so subtle they are ignored. One important point to mention when talking about this subject is that the special effects you see at your local multiplex, or on extended DVDs, are produced by film making at its highest level: expensive cameras, controlled studio conditions and expert, painstaking work on sophisticated software packages.

So, there is no point kidding yourself into believing you will be able to achieve all these things with your small camcorder and basic editing software. However, you will be surprised just how much you can achieve with limited resources.

A brief history of special effects

As mentioned, special effects are nothing new. The only thing that has really changed over the years is the methods by which we can achieve them, and their sheer realism.

Prior to the digital revolution, special effects were achieved by using a combination of models and paintings. Sometimes these were filmed separately or they were used in conjunction with each other. The reasons these special effects were used are the same reasons we use them today – they were needed to achieve something that was either impossible, too expensive or too dangerous.

Without computers to help them, film makers turned to artists and model builders to help them achieve their visions. A filmed shot of some dusty ground on the back lot of studio may be transformed into the depths of a desert by editing in the work of an artist showing huge rocky outcrops and sand dunes.

Sometimes visual effects were even simpler and used something called a glass shot. Until relatively recently, some artists would paint a landscape, or scene, on a wide sheet of glass. Some parts of the glass would be left clear. It would then be placed in front of the camera so that parts of the picture would show whatever was painted on the glass and the clear parts would allow the actors and any props to be seen. Believe it or not, even such special effects-heavy films as *Return of the Jedi* used this technique.

Glass was also used for other techniques called mirror shots. In this method, a clear piece of glass was placed at a 45-degree angle to the camera. The camera would be set up to film a set, and any image in the glass would then appear superimposed on the main image the camera was filming.

Although there is little point in using this effect now; with the advent of superimpose edit functions, its best use is to show an object on fire. By filming a house and then having a fire burn so it is reflected in the glass, the overall effect will show real flames on the house.

Remember this

Warning: Needless to say, working with fire can be very, very dangerous, so only attempt something like this if you put in place the appropriate precautions.

With this technique you must also pay attention to two factors – there needs to be a black material behind the fire otherwise other elements of the reflection could confuse and spoil the shot. Also, make sure that the fire is of the right size (either in intensity or proximity to the glass) or else the fire may look ridiculously small.

Despite the special effects technology available to the *Lords of the Rings* production, this fire trick was used in the final film of the trilogy.

The use of models, or miniatures, allowed film makers to move their cameras over desert landscapes or the streets of ancient cities without the need for aerial photography – which years ago was an expensive, imperfect and hazardous feat. It also allowed them to bring about spectacular catastrophes to vehicles or areas of a city. In this regard, miniatures still perform the same function they did decades ago.

One aspect of miniatures filming, which has almost totally been supplanted by the digital revolution, is stop-motion animation. There used to be a time when the only way you could show a huge dinosaur or monster moving was to create an articulated model of it, move its head, arms, legs and mouth by a tiny amount, and then film it one frame at a time. Numerous films over the years such as the first *King Kong* (dir. Merian C. Cooper and Ernest B. Schoedsack, 1933) have incorporated this technique. Perhaps the most famous exponent is the film maker Ray Harryhausen whose small models captivated film makers with their stunning movements on films such as *Jason and the Argonauts* (1963) and *Clash of the Titans* (1981).

Despite their appeal, filming models in such a way will always create unrealistic movement. Even in the most carefully planned and filmed stop-motion sequence of the best-known films, the movements of the miniature creatures will always look jerky and unrealistic. It also presents the issue of influencing the film maker in their choice of camera movements. Since the camera often needs to be in a fixed position to capture the movement of the model, having it move around the miniature set can further complicate things. Also, since these stop-motion sequences are often edited together with live action, they can have further limitations. Although these technical headaches can be worked around, they have often meant things had to be totally redone if there was a mistake. While digital effects have similar complexities and drawbacks, the process can often be worked backwards to the 'fix point' and then carried on again, whereas with miniatures, it may mean a model set rebuild and so on.

OLD VERSUS NEW

Although these techniques have been made either extinct or endangered, spare them a thought. Remember, their one big advantage is that they are mercifully free of the complexities associated with computer memory and can sometimes be achieved for very little money. Also, we will see shortly how these older techniques still have something to offer the modern film maker.

It is important to remember that all the effects we see today are really nothing new – the film makers of the 1920s and 1930s were essentially doing the same thing. Only now, it is a bit easier to achieve these imaginative effects.

The special effects department

'Special effects' is quite a large umbrella expression. In the modern age, there are distinctions within the discipline – there are those who deal with purely optical effects, those who build miniatures and those who work with digitally created images.

The interesting point to make is that these people can crop up at all phases of the film making process. There is not a distinct time when the special effects department takes the film and starts adding things to it. In fact, it will involve planning the shots in the pre-production phase of the film. Which shots will need miniature and optical effects and which will be achieved with computer-generated imagery (CGI)?

For using miniatures and other more traditional special effects techniques, this process is still very much part of the filming phase because it involves the use of cameras to capture the images. However, CGI work will take place sometimes purely in post-production as the images need to have been filmed before they can be worked on.

Special effects is quite a large yet subtle discipline. Without being too cruel to the practitioners, it is also at the geeky end of the film making spectrum. It is famed for enthusiasts' painstaking efforts to build some highly detailed model or work incredibly long hours on a computer graphic. In equal measure, it is perhaps a much-misunderstood part of the film making experience.

What are special effects?

Although we are frequently bombarded with talk of special effects used on films, very little discussion is dedicated to how such things are achieved. After all, these effects are not produced by some magic wand or special function key on software, automatically filling in the blanks or reading your mind. Instead they are crafted together after considerable planning, and more often than not, problem solving.

'Special effect' is a general expression given to the following things:

▶ something filmed in order to represent a larger object or area

▶ something done to enhance an existing piece of footage

▶ something added to a piece of footage

Filming miniatures

Although CGI seems to rule the roost when it comes to special effects, many large productions still use models, or miniatures, to achieve their special effects shots. Special effects-intensive films such as the *Star Wars* prequels and *The Lord of the Rings* trilogy used an impressive array of models and miniature sets to achieve various shots throughout the action.

Also, don't forget that the original *Star Wars* films used only miniatures and these effects still hold their own many years later.

So why use miniatures? For the low-budget film maker the answer is simple: they are cheap. If you want to blow up a car you can buy one from the toyshop, or model store, and (safely) detonate it without having to do it for real or rely on complicated software.

Next, it means a huge expensive object or area that would be impossible and dangerous to construct for real, can be created at a more practical level. The skyline of an ancient city could be constructed on top of a large table in a controlled environment, free from the effects of weather, or a catastrophe can be created without risk to anyone or anything.

Miniatures also tend to be relatively simple to film. By careful positioning of the camera in relation to the miniature, selecting the background and paying attention to the lights, you can achieve quite stunning effects. Another advantage is that you may only need yourself to carry out the shot, instead of other people who may be problematic to assemble in the same place at the same time.

Such optical effects will always have one advantage over their digital counterparts – they are a photoreal effect. In other words, it looks real because it is real. CGI – for the time being – suffers from not always looking totally convincing. Of course, CGI effects look impressive, fast moving and slick, but under closer scrutiny there is something a little artificial about them. This failing of technology will no doubt be rectified in the future, but present film makers will have the thought at the back of their minds that their CGI doesn't look 100 per cent convincing all of the time.

One disadvantage, however, of filming miniatures is also the above-mentioned advantage – it looks real. In fact, it looks so real that the human eye and mind will often process it for what it actually is: a small model. There is always an element of leeway depending on your camera's position and lighting, and so on, but if the audience is given a chance to look at something for long enough they may be able to see through things.

One way to offset this giveaway is to use large miniatures. Although this may seem odd, and contradictory, the larger the scale is, the less fake things will appear to be. In *The Lord of the Rings* trilogy the miniatures were so big that they were nicknamed 'bigatures'. One model for a fantasy city was actually bigger than a real-life house!

For those of you wanting to film miniature vehicles, whether they be cars, trucks, ships or spacecraft, the trick is to film them from close by and from as low an angle as possible. By using a low-angle shot you are making the object look big, and that's exactly where you want to be heading.

Filming your moving model can be another danger point. Seeing a small, highly detailed model car trundle over a miniature road can look ridiculous. Bumps and wobbles in direction can totally give the game away. Therefore, from a special effects point of view, static shots would tend to work best for the car example. However, like many things in film making, it is always a good idea to try out different set-ups and experiment to find out which method or combination of methods gives the best results.

Special effects in the post-digital age

There was once a time when special effects were limited by what could be achieved using actual objects, people and the practical skills of the film maker and special effects team. For generations, scenes that required a volcano eruption, a ship sinking or other fantastic event may have been done by using large models, fireworks, tanks of water and other such tools. A war film about fighter planes may have actually used real planes!

For cinemagoers, this was fine; it was more than fine, it was great. It was great because some films used to be judged by their special effects just as much as their story and the actors involved. Also, when done well, these effects looked brilliant, impressive and weren't something you saw every day. The disaster film craze of the 1970s would use huge models of buildings or entire city districts and then burn or flood them to suit the story. Audiences marvelled at the sheer spectacle of a huge and intricate model being destroyed; there was a kind of thrill in seeing such a spectacle. Yet, even then you could tell that the building or whatever wasn't real: the water droplets looked big, the flames were too big compared to the building, or you could just tell on instinct that the models were just that – models.

In 1968 the film *2001* (dir. Stanley Kubrick) and then, a decade later, *Star Wars*, set the bar very high with their ground-breaking special effects. The sight of planets, spaceships and lasers made many jaws hit the cinema floor. Yet, despite the realism that these effects gave the film, they were still essentially using the same general techniques as earlier films – namely, models, fireworks and hand-drawn artwork. Yes, they were filmed better and the models were of a size that made them work very well against the mock-up space backdrops, but everything was at the practical level. Real objects were being used. Plus, in one or two places, you can tell that a model was being used or a scene's backdrop was actually a painted image.

And so things continued: any film that had a large number of special effects scenes was doing these same things, either to a high or low standard depending largely on budget. The 1979 *Star Wars* rip-off film *Starcrash* (dir. Luigi Cozzi, 1978) almost matches the special effects scenes of its counterpart shot for shot. Yet, because the models used were smaller, they are hardly as convincing.

After 1993's *Jurassic Park*, digitally animated images started creeping into films. These CGI images instantly appeared to do away with the need for practical special effects. Giant dinosaurs didn't need to be clumsy stop-motion animation figures; they could now be drawn and animated with a huge degree of flexibility without the associated challenges. Spaceships could be created in the same way, dispensing with the need for model makers to construct, film and, in some cases, blow up their lovingly made creations. The film *Independence Day* (dir. Roland Emmerich, 1996) featured an aerial battle consisting of completely CGI F-18 aircraft, whereas the 1994 film *True Lies* (dir. James Cameron, 1994) features actual US Marine Corp Harrier jump jets. Which do you think looks the more convincing?

The man behind *Star Wars*, George Lucas, drove the technology and abilities of this new CGI revolution. He added many new scenes to the special-edition releases of the Star Wars trilogy, many of which consisted of CGI. In many ways, a new standard was set, as well as an expectation that, if you were able to, you should use CGI due to all the cost-saving benefits it could give you – no model making department, no special camera effects department, no pyrotechnics and so on. Instead a few (powerful) computers and the people to use them would now do all the work.

Plus, as time went on, and computers became even more powerful, the graphics and rendering capabilities became ever more sophisticated. Films bought into the movement big time and used the technology as a first choice. Using CGI became the new norm. Yet, over time something happened. Audiences started to become a little bit jaded with more and more CGI. What had once wowed the audiences of years before just became yet another CGI spectacle, with all and sundry knowing that what they were seeing was just a load of computer images, some of which was clearly of poor quality. Ultimately, there was a slight backlash against it all. The novelty of it had long wore off. It just didn't seem that believable any more.

Thus, there was a demand for a return to practical effects, as many high-profile effects-heavy films making much out of the fact they were minimizing their use of CGI in favour of real things.

Case study: *Dunkirk*

Out of recent releases, one of the high-profile examples of this return to practical effects has been *Dunkirk* (dir. Christopher Nolan, 2017). With *Dunkirk*, much mention has been made of the use of real aircraft for the air battles. Instead of computer-generated images flying over the skies of France, there are actual replica World War Two fighters, actually flying! Who would have thought it? From a film making perspective, nothing will look better than actual aircraft flying through the sky; CGI won't even come close. Likewise, some shots featuring the actors have them really up in the air in an aircraft that's manoeuvring around. Nothing can top the way the light and shadows move as the plane moves. Nothing can beat the way an actor will look shifting in the cockpit with the ground moving below.

Now bear in mind that the cost, danger and sheer hassle of arranging a real aerial battle, strapping film cameras to the side of an aircraft and putting you actors up in the air is a huge undertaking. It's a worry that some directors wouldn't even entertain. Yet, with *Dunkirk*, the director knew that the only way to achieve the realism and to maximize the emotional impact of certain shots was to use practical effects.

Even for shots where actual life-sized aircraft were not available, the film still used practical effects in the form of large remote-controlled models that were filmed from the air.

It just goes to show that, even in today's very high-tech film making landscape, using the methods of the past still holds many advantages.

A lesson in spaceflight

Objects that are supposed to be many times larger, such as a spacecraft, ocean-going vessels or aircraft, need some motion to make them impressive. Surprisingly, this is often achieved by moving the camera, not the model.

First, let's take this step by step and examine what elements you need to make this kind of shot work to a reasonable degree on a minimal budget:

▶ A model spaceship

▶ Some thin clear fishing line for hanging the model

▶ Something to hang the model from – hooks in the ceiling or some kind of frame

▶ A well-positioned light

▶ A totally dark room – this is supposed to be space after all!

▶ An actual, or improvised, camera track

Other things you may want to consider:

▶ A prop to look like a distant planet – a suspended basketball perhaps?

▶ Some small Christmas-tree lights on a far wall to represent the stars of deep space.

At many levels, the lighting here is key to the effect. The room needs to be totally dark to start off with otherwise people will be able to see that this is being filmed in a garage or wherever. Since space is supposed to be pitch black, you need to replicate this as best you can. This may mean covering any windows with a thick drape or covering some of the walls in a dark fabric. Next you need to place your light. In the context of this shot, it will serve a dual purpose – it will illuminate your miniature and it will represent the light of a star.

Another important lighting consideration is to be minimalistic with the amount of light that falls on the miniature. Too much light, and too much detail on the miniature will be revealed, which will in turn ruin the illusion; too little, and it will be invisible. You should aim towards showing less of the object as this will make the miniature appear more mysterious and real.

Next comes the camera move itself. In a professional studio there would be camera tracks, a special tripod and so on to hand, or even a special camera mount that can be programmed to move accurately around the miniature. But, without these tools, how can you improvise? Providing you can move smoothly across the floor, a tripod on top of a skateboard may work, or inside a small shopping trolley, wheelchair or other object on wheels. Just as long as you are able to move across the floor smoothly and at a constant speed, it really doesn't matter how you achieve this.

Some classic moves are to have the camera 'grazing' the side of the miniature or to have it looking up and moving under the model so it appears that the vessel is flying over the camera. The essential thing is not to move the camera too fast, otherwise the illusion will be destroyed. In addition, shots such as these are often slowed down in the edit so that they give the effect of huge mass.

Be advised, though, shots like this are often very troublesome. The line holding the miniature can break mid-shot to produce a bizarre 'special effect' of its own. Often the model can swing back and forth throughout the filming or the line can be seen in the final edit. These are things you just have to counter and find solutions for. Yet, the feeling of having successfully filmed a special effects miniature shot like this is immensely satisfying.

Case study

When using this technique to film a submarine for a war film, we used a blue light shining from the ceiling and filled the room with smoke which was allowed to settle. The effect was 100 per cent convincing and was achieved for an incredibly small budget. By adjusting the lighting and smoke, this technique is good for filming aircraft, too.

Destruction

Often with miniatures, the whole reason they are built and filmed is so they can be destroyed in some fantastic manner. This usually involves an appearance of fire or water as their means of destruction. One problem with using these two elements is they are another danger point for giving the game away and compromising your efforts to trick the audience with regard to the actual scale of your miniature objects.

Since flames and water droplets are of a constant size, seeing huge sized water droplets crashing into a house, or seeing tiny cigarette-lighter type flames coming out of the windows of an aircraft can turn a decent film into a comedy. If this is the effect you are after, then fine. Yet, if you want to maintain the emotional level of your film, it may be worth looking at some software-assisted options – more on this later.

Once again you can offset this by camera positioning, especially in the case of water – the further away it is from the camera, the less the size of the droplets will come across. Although sometimes with miniature filming you may just have to say, 'That is as good as we can get it!'

Even in the biggest movies, some of the miniature shots can look far from convincing. Once more looking at *The Lord of the Rings* trilogy, there is a scene where a flood destroys Saruman's base. The huge size of the water droplets 'destroying' buildings and walls does spoil things a bit. However, if it's good enough for a multi Oscar award-winning film, then it is good enough for a low-budget film.

It is also possible to 'destroy' your miniatures without harming them, using blue- or green-screen effects. More on this later.

Key idea: Compositing – it's the name of the game

When special effects professionals talk about their work, they frequently use the word 'compositing'. Compositing is special effects-speak for adding layers of different visual elements to your original footage. Therefore, when the finished effect is viewed it is composed of things such as the actual filmed footage and the special effects such as graphics or computer-generated images.

The best way to visualize compositing is to think of placing clear plastic sheets over a picture. The picture represents your footage, and by drawing things on the sheets you can then overlay them on the picture so that all the elements can be viewed together. In practice, this means having extra video tracks in the edit – each extra video track can represent a new effects element. Simple!

Enhancements

This is probably the subtlest form of special effects and appears in films ranging from period dramas to science-fiction horrors. It is the way in which panoramic views of otherwise normal landscapes can be given a fabulous sky full of darkened cloud or tinges of colour can be added to an otherwise unremarkable scene.

Many edit software packages today have functions that allow you to 'colour correct' any piece of footage. At the basic level, it means you can adjust the amount a certain colour dominates a piece of footage so that it becomes more blue or more yellow, for instance.

Initially, these functions were put in to allow editors to fix shots that had suffered from some kind of white balance issue. However, over time they have evolved into a useful effects tool that enables the editor to impart more mood on a shot or heighten the environment. For example, a bright shot of someone walking through a graveyard on a sunny day may not look very good in a horror film, but if the image is 'pushed' towards the blue end of the colour scale, it may take on a more doom-laden and spooky mood. You may also be able to slightly wash out the colours and give it even more ghostly connotations or darken it altogether.

Nowadays this editing tool is very important. It's so important, in fact, that there is a job role in itself called a 'colourist'. This is the individual who tweaks the colours, hues and tones of every shot in the final edit in order to impart a special mood to the film. If you were to see the raw footage from some of your favourite films or television shows you would probably be encouraged to learn that they sometimes don't look too dissimilar to your own camcorder footage.

The Coen brothers have used colour software extensively on their recent films. Take a look at Apple.com for an interview in which they sing the praises of the software they use with their Final Cut software.

Slicing and dicing – 'cropping'

Enhancements are not limited to adjusting the colours of a shot; you can replace parts of a shot, too.

Some of the more sophisticated edit systems available on the high street have 'crop' functions which allow you to slice off part of a shot along a horizontal or vertical axis. This means you can then replace the cropped part of a shot with another. For example, you may have a shot of a flat-roofed building that you filmed in daylight. By using the crop function, you could remove the bright sunny sky and replace it with a field of stars or a planet.

For those of you not completely familiar with the concept of cropping, the best way to describe it is to compare it to playing around with pictures drawn on paper. By cutting off parts of one picture and placing another picture underneath you can see parts of both. Cropping is exactly the same.

The important thing to consider when using this feature is to film your shots very carefully. Since this effect requires an element of precision when you reconcile the different images together, if you film something inaccurately it may be impossible to make it work with your other shot, or shots. Above all, since cropping only allows you to cut a picture either vertically or horizontally you have to plan out your filming along those lines.

For example, if you are filming a hill from side-on, it will be impossible to crop the diagonal slope. Also, if you are filming something that was filmed on an uneven tripod you may have the same problem.

Key idea: The oldest trick in the book – how to make an appearance from behind a broom handle

Stand a tall broom or pole upright in the ground. Film it so that it is in the middle of the frame with plenty of room either side. Without moving the camera, next film a shot and have someone walk from one side of the frame to the other, making sure they pass behind the pole. In the edit, use the crop function to remove the side of the shot when the person is walking towards the pole. With the other shot, crop it so the other side of the image from the pole is removed. Edit these two images together. When done properly, it will create the illusion that someone has just (somehow) walked out from behind the pole.

Cropping has found its way on to many ultra-low-budget films as a way of creating masses of people, such as at demonstrations or in battle, for no cost. If you are able to film a large area, such as a field or empty car park from a decent height, you can place the same group of people at various locations in that space. Next you can film them in the top corners, bottom corners and then the middle. In the edit you can use the crop tool to slice off the empty bits of the screen so that the finished shot shows several groups of people standing in the same area. With this effect, it is important to make sure the faces cannot be made out too easily, and also the groups of people are not always standing in the same order otherwise things may look a bit odd and give the game away.

Blue- and green-screen explained

After cropping, the next step in special effects awareness is the often mentioned blue- and green-screen. Just like cropping, this effect is essentially doing the same thing – removing part of a shot and replacing it with something else. However, there is much more flexibility with this effect.

When something is filmed using this process, the actors (or even miniatures) will be filmed with some blue- or green-coloured fabric or partition behind them. In post-production, the colour of the screen is completely removed. Midway through the process it looks as though the actors are standing in front of a black void. Next, the black part of the picture is replaced with a pre-selected image, giving the illusion that the actors are somewhere else. That's it!

Some of today's commercially available software allows you to achieve this effect. Believe it or not, they are very simple to do in the edit stage; the difficult part is getting it right when filming.

The biggest challenge is to ensure that the lighting all over the screen is of a uniform brightness and that there are no imperfections (creases or tears) on the material. It is important to understand that you need to have two separate lighting set-ups for any blue- or green-screen shot – one for the actors and another for the screen itself. You must also make sure that there are no shadows falling on the screen from the actors. This is because your software will only be able to handle one hue of blue or green at a time. If one part is partially in shadow, the software will not be able to compensate for this and you will only be able to remove part of the screen. The other imperfect part will 'ghost' into the finished shot and utterly ruin things.

Key idea: What material is best?

Anything that is uniformly blue or green will work. Ensure the material isn't too reflective otherwise you will have 'hot spots' which you will be unable to work around in the edit. Commonly used materials are appropriately coloured walls, a clear blue sky, some big pieces of paper, a green noticeboard or some fabric. You can improvise using almost anything that's blue or green for a minimal price.

Blue- and green-screen special effects filming and editing can really create even more wonderful and fantastic shots when used in conjunction with other edit functions. One of the assumptions some people make when using blue- and green-screens is to think only in terms of the image that will replace the screen area. Although this may be what you want, sometimes spare a thought to consider that the actors in your screen set-up may be only a small element of the completed shot.

Once the blue- or green-screen shot is in your edit, it can be further manipulated. The image can now be resized (shrunk) and repositioned so that your actors, or miniatures, can be placed as part of some fantastic scene. For example, they could be walking in front of some large elaborate country home, or perhaps you could film your spacecraft miniature in front of a green-screen and then edit it so it is dwarfed as it flies past a giant galaxy.

The possibilities are limited only by your imagination and by how much work you want to put in to your film making.

Importantly, don't think that the special effects filming and editing are separate entities. Try to get in to the habit of combining them to produce some really unique sequences. Don't just consider miniatures filming as a standalone element of film making. Add green-screen filming to miniatures, and vice versa, so that you can get both things to work together. Imagine building a miniature model of some underground cavern and then adding in your actors using blue- or green-screen. This is a common technique used in feature films and you don't have to be a rocket scientist to understand the concept and use it for yourself.

Have fun and go for it!

Case study: Going for a car ride

A great blue- or green-screen effect you can achieve is to simulate someone driving a car. Although putting a camera in a car and filming the driver and scenery going by does not sound too difficult, you have to remember that you may distract the driver, there will be lots of bumps and also the lighting can be changing all the time as the car keeps moving in and out of shadow. An easy fix is to put a screen next to the driver's window (and other windows according to your needs) and then put in the required footage during the edit. This way you can control the lighting and camera settings to your preference. However, don't forget to rock the car from side to side and maybe have a fan blowing in from an open window otherwise things may look odd in spite of your special effects editing skills.

Computer-generated imagery (CGI)

Computer-generated images are the 'big boys' of the special effects world. Although over the years there have been appearances of computer images in films, it has only been since the 1990s that they have truly taken over from other more traditional methods. The first big production to use them was *Jurassic Park*, in which the dinosaurs were given life by way of this new and improved film making technique. Then a few years later, they further caught the public's eye in *Titanic* (dir. James Cameron, 1997).

Even though there were one or two miniature and model shots in both of these films, it was the CGI that convinced moviegoers that the dinosaurs had been resurrected after millions of years or that RMS *Titanic* had been recreated.

WHY CGI?

The answer is straightforward. CGI can make anything – absolutely anything. Although miniature models may be able to hold their own with certain set-ups, there is no way they can compete with the sheer scope of objects, creatures, spacecraft, landscapes, robots, movement and worlds that CGI can create.

If a film like *Jurassic Park* had been made before the 1990s, then the chances are the creatures would have been the product of the previously discussed stop-motion animation, people wearing dinosaur suits or even pet iguanas with a few horns stuck to their heads. Although fine for its time, the jerky unrealistic motions of perhaps fake-looking dinosaurs would not have fooled anyone. Likewise, having various scale models of the *Titanic* float back and forth in a large tank of water may have given the game away. It is only with CGI that the film maker can be free of such constraints and considerations.

However, the big downside to all of this is the complexity, expertise, hardware and expense needed to create something that will pass muster within a film. Film fans are getting more and more demanding in what they see and will show merciless cruelty when an effect looks fake or out of place. As a consequence, there is an almost insatiable need for CGI-intensive films to be better than those that have gone before.

CGI AND THE LOW-BUDGET FILM MAKER

Let's not kid ourselves here. The kind of CGI effects you see in a major feature film are going to be out of reach for lots of reasons. So, what can you hope to achieve? There are some budget software packages that may allow you to produce simple creations and then add them to your film, but you must consider the impact that having a cheap-looking CGI image will do to the rest of your film. The last thing you want is to have people laugh when some monstrous creature is destroying a city.

One common method is to set your CGI sequences during the night. The simple reason is that the darkness of the setting, and in which the images have been created, will be hard to distinguish and will perhaps soften the blow of your CGI being on the cheap side. Very similar to the miniatures adage of 'the less you see the better it is', employing a similar technique with any moving CGI effects may be worth thinking about.

However CGI does not always have to mean elaborate movement; it can be just as effective to create still images or graphics and then superimpose them on your footage. A simple shot of an unremarkable part of town can be transferred to a fantastic futuristic cityscape, or huge snow-capped mountains can be placed on shots of fields. You could also film a simple-looking interior set and make that shot part of something larger by placing it in the midst of the graphic representing a gigantic industrial complex. Once again, the possibilities here are quite limitless.

After Effects – the aspiring low-budget sfx junkie's best friend

Just as cameras and editing software have become more accessible in terms of availability and price, the same is true of special effects products. Perhaps the best-known, and most used, software package at the low-budget film maker level is After Effects by Adobe. In recent years, it has created a small revolution within film making and turned a lot of heads with its sophisticated capabilities and wide appeal.

Like all good things its main selling point has been its simplicity, or relative simplicity, to use. There is no need for huge drives or expensive add-ons to your computer in order for this software to start delivering results. It has very much been aimed at the bedroom film editor and has found quite a large niche with colleges, universities and independent film makers.

WHAT DOES IT DO?
After Effects is something you can do compositing with, as well as other effects. Lightning bolts can fly out of people's eyes, magic-looking orbs can float in the room and chase people, fires can be virtually added to cars and buildings. It can even add snow and

rain. Graphic sequences can be added so giant constructs can be animated and superimposed on your footage.

Due to this wide range of capability, After Effects is a very cost-effective way of achieving special effects without any of the hassles that occur during the actual filming stage. Some of the effects filming described earlier in the chapter may end up taking a lot of co-ordination and resetting the components to get right. They may require special materials, a certain amount of space and so on. Like many things digital, this package can essentially give you the same results (or even better) but it allows you a lot more flexibility to add and play around with.

However, one of the dangers with using a package like this is overuse. Many who choose to use such compositing software within their film making can easily sleepwalk into creating something bizarre and full of unnecessary effects that distract from the story and generally make the presentation seem odd.

When you are thinking about using such software with your film making, remember that you need to plan things at a very early stage. It may be possible that some of your shots do not work very well with some compositing effects due to camera movements, brightness levels or objects/actors in the foreground.

Think very carefully about how you want to use software such as this or you may be seriously disappointed during the post-production phase of your film.

Remember this

Special effects are there to help you make a film more interesting. Don't overuse them just because you have the capability. Think carefully about how you are going to use special effects in your film (if at all) and remember that some of the effects you produce may not look totally convincing. As with many things in film making, sometimes less is more.

Focus points

* Critically assess if your film needs any special effects at all.
* What is the better option for you – miniatures or CGI?
* If using miniatures, be prepared to spend a lot of time building them, and possibly rebuilding them after you have blown them up.
* If using any pyrotechnics with your miniatures, ensure the appropriate safety precautions have been taken. Don't risk injuring yourself or anyone else for the sake of a shot.
* Always be prepared to accept that some of your shots may not be totally convincing.
* Think about what special effects capabilities are open to you by using the simple tools included with your editing system.
* If you are set on using CGI, do you have the software already, can you afford it, will it run on your computer and do you know how to use it?
* Be prepared for lots of extra work, above and beyond the main filming, when making special effects shots.
* Think about reusing the same special effects shots, or graphics, within your film to save on effort and expense.
* Don't expect everything to work well first time round.

Next step

You've scripted, filmed and edited your masterpiece. It was a long, challenging, but rewarding process, but you're still not there yet. Now you need to get the film out there to the public, your audience ...

14

Showing your film

In this chapter you will learn:

▶ *some straightforward ways of exhibiting your film*

▶ *how to go about 'getting noticed'*

▶ *how not to be sued by a global entertainment company*

There is not much point in making a film if you are not prepared to show it to people. Luckily for today's low- and no-budget film maker there are a multitude of outlets for informing people about and exhibiting your visual talents. These can range from the World Wide Web, to a popular monthly film magazine, to the screen room at a local conference centre.

Finding an outlet

Brainstorming and lateral thinking will allow you to think of places to show your film, but don't just think about getting it shown, think about getting it – and yourself – noticed. See if a few of the local film agency, film office or arts board people can come to the screening. But don't stop there. Call up a few television stations and try to get hold of someone who you think may be interested in your talents – drama, comedy or documentary – depending on the subject matter of your film. Make copies and send them off to everyone you can think of. It's all part of the process of going on to bigger things. This is how the system works.

Depending on the faith you have in your film, and your ambition, you may want to try your hand at contacting some major film and distribution companies. They may tell you to get lost, give you a large amount money to make another film or put you in contact with someone who may be able to develop another project. Look in the *Yellow Pages* or on the Internet. Just phone people and see what they say.

UPLOADING AND SOCIAL NETWORKING

The Internet has become the biggest outlet for new talent these days. Anyone can upload their song, film or art to the web. Although this is a great tool for showing off your work and attempting to get some publicity or recognition, you will be just one of thousands, or millions, trying to get some attention for your film. It is certainly true that some people have been very lucky using the Internet as a platform for publicizing their film ideas and have achieved large deals as a result.

It is important to be realistic about the power of the Internet. Although you may have worked incredibly hard on your film, be proud of it and think it great, there are plenty of people uploading their work and thinking the same. Although your film's URL may be at the forefront of your mind, it is just one of millions available.

At the very least, having a film, or parts of a film, available to view online gives you the ability to direct others to your work. It gives your film a presence that may gain a following. Its biggest strength is to show others in the industry what you can do and perhaps enable you to gain work or further projects from it. Who needs a résumé when you can show your work instead?

However, uploading your film is just the beginning. Another web-based tool many now use is social networking sites in which dedicated pages promote your planned or finished film. This method allows more depth to be added as, instead of just having the film with a bit of descriptive text, you can make things a bit more lively by adding photographs from the filming, updates on progress, biographies of cast, making of videos and so on. By using social networking you may find that you get some kind of following from various random people all over the place signing up to be fans or friends. It is another way of getting noticed.

The follow-on from all of this is to get a website in support of your film. With this option you can have total flexibility, although, depending on how you go about things, you may have to pay someone to make it for you. The first two options are free which is great for the low-/no-budget film maker.

FILM FESTIVALS

Although you may think film festivals are the preserve of the glamorous and mainstream film makers, there are in fact thousands of film festivals all over the place that cater to independent film makers.

Every year, film festivals take place all across the globe dedicated to all genres of factual and fiction film making. Others may be local or national events intended to showcase new talent without the need for a previous track record in film making. The process usually goes along the lines of submitting some details about yourself and the film, and maybe paying a small submission fee. Not only is this another method of trying to get some recognition for your work, but it is great to have complete strangers look at your films and hopefully enjoy them.

Remember this

'The best money I ever spent' – *Clerks* director Kevin Smith on the small submission fee he had to pay to enter his film at a festival, which gave him a lot of exposure. If you have identified a festival relevant to your film, then go for it. Who knows where it may lead?

Copyright laws

Copyright is something that may not concern most of you. However, there may be times when covering yourself over the use of other people's images, words and music is a wise policy.

If you intend only to show your film privately, for example to friends, your local movie club or in a film class, then it may not matter if you have a soundtrack courtesy of The Beatles and film clips taken from *Apocalypse Now* (dir. Frances Ford Coppola, 1979). If, however, you have arranged to show it in a location where you plan to make a charge, such as a local community hall, 'art cinema' or wherever, then you could get into serious trouble. The reason for this is that you are using someone else's work (music, film, television clips) without their permission or acknowledgement, in a production that will legally be considered commercial. If you are caught you could face a massive fine that will change your hair colour.

The same rules apply if you upload a film to YouTube or Facebook that contains uncleared third-party material – you could find that it is taken off the web or the soundtrack is muted. So be careful.

If you are making a film that you intend to promote commercially and you want to include third-party material, then my advice to you is don't! The cost of obtaining permission to use a song, or a film or television clip for whatever rights you require is very, very high – usually thousands for a few seconds.

If you are able to get your film on a television talent series, new film makers' showcase or a festival, they will probably first ask for documents proving that any extra material you have in your film is cleared for use by you. The same goes for Internet independent film sites. If this isn't the case then they will refuse to accept and screen it.

If you want a soundtrack, then ask a friend to play their guitar, drums or keyboard to ensure you don't get into big trouble in the event of your film becoming successful. However, first make sure that the terms and conditions are agreed in writing otherwise your 'friend' may resurface in a couple of years asking for a few thousand in backdated royalty payments. Alternatively, you could compose something yourself using one of the many music creation software packages available such as GarageBand.

Copyright-related matters don't stop here. For the more commercially minded, watch out if there are radios or televisions in your scenes. You may inadvertently end up with a popular song or programme in your film. The same goes for logos of brands and companies. They may not agree to 'appear' in your film and thus may sue you or make some kind of complaint. Something else to consider are release and consent forms. These are forms that people sign stating that they agree to appear in your film – it's just another safeguard against future problems.

Be careful out there. Don't think that your film will go unnoticed by the company who owns the music rights to a song you are using. Many low-budget film makers have been ruined, or had their work shredded into unrecognizable pieces, by making this assumption.

Key idea

If in doubt, leave it out. If you are ever unsure about a piece of music, or some other material, then don't include it in your film. Otherwise your film may be making some headway on YouTube or wherever when it gets taken down and loses its publicity momentum – disaster.

Focus points

* Be prepared to make lots of copies of your film to send to festivals and/or people working in the film and television industry.
* Research the film festivals relevant to your film and target them.
* Pay attention to the submission guidelines. Certain festivals insist that the film must not have been shown anywhere, including the Internet.
* Be prepared to pay a submission fee to be considered for some film festivals.
* When uploading your film ensure there is no third-party material, otherwise your film may be taken down.
* Don't expect overnight success.
* When uploading your film make sure you have encoded it in the best possible format.
* People's attention spans can be very small when viewing online content.
* Create as much hype as possible using a combination of social networking and video sharing sites – it's all free, after all!
* Be prepared for at least some negative reaction to your work.

Next step

Nothing tells us more about the democratization of film making than vlogging – the usually home-produced creation of short video logs (whence 'blogs'), video diaries or other filmed commentaries for distribution over social media platforms like YouTube. This is the subject of Chapter 15.

15

Presenting and filming logs

In this chapter you will learn:

▶ *basic technical considerations such as lighting and sound*

▶ *how to present an effective vlog*

▶ *how to put together a professional-looking company vlog*

The appeal of vlogs, for many, is the no-frills way in which the presenter talks to their audience. That almost intimate feel created by the vlogger looking directly into the camera, in an often-unassuming location, is a very powerful bond between the content creator and viewer. If your average vlogger was to come across as a slick and polished presenter akin to the news anchor of a major news network, then that bond might not be so special. It would look just like, well, regular TV.

And that's one of the appeals of vlogging. Having a peer lay it on the line about a variety of subjects from the serious, controversial and plain bizarre in their own particular way is the key attraction. Anything goes.

So how can you make your vlog a cut above the rest? Well, it's a subtle combination of technology and presentation. Sometimes the two are one and the same thing, but don't worry – it can be very simple to inject some stylish professional polish into your own BBC (Bedroom Broadcasting Corporation) productions. The simplest vlogs out there usually consist of a person just talking into the laptop or tablet camera about a subject. There's nothing wrong with that, but a lot of the time very little thought has been given to the sound, lighting or set-up.

Many vloggers will default towards speaking directly to the in-built camera for a one-take shot, as it's a very simple thing to do. There is no editing required, as what's recorded is what's uploaded. It can't get simpler than that – no music, no titles, done. However, there are pitfalls with this approach. Depending on the capability of the camera and microphone on your laptop, tablet or smartphone, then your image and sound quality can vary wildly and, in many instances, be distractingly awful.

While such things may seem less than important in light of the subject matter, they can make your audience scratch their heads and wonder what's going on. In turn, any message you are trying to get across may be compromised in a morass of amateurish oddness.

While the actual content and the details of what you are saying will be around half of what people are clicking on your videos for, there are some other considerations worth thinking about. They can be split into two main categories:

- the environment
- the delivery

The environment is where the filming is taking place. Be it your bedroom, kitchen or garage, the issues will be the same – distractions and other factors that make your presentation less than great. This isn't to say that you have to reconfigure your filming space to resemble a modern studio environment. Rather, you should pay a little bit of attention to what else is in the picture besides your good self. Now, this is going to be common sense and very obvious, but a quick view of YouTube for vlogs will reveal of host of bizarre and humorously inappropriate backdrops that can have an audience focusing on the wrong part of the presentation. Let's face it, there's no point having a pumped-up vlog dedicated to the types of swords used in *Game of Thrones* if there's a huge My Little Pony poster in the background.

Props and set-up

So, have a look around the space you will use and maybe think about the stuff that is 'off message', distracting, bizarre or maybe just a bit embarrassing. This is particularly a hazard if you have set up your camera at one end of the room, giving it a wide field of view that potentially shows things you hadn't thought about.

To flip this situation on its head, why not have some simple easily available props that reinforce the message or subject you are getting across? Again, this is a really basic consideration but it will give your vlog some extra impact and almost creates a brand image for yourself and your videos. Just having one item in shot, and clearly visible, makes a big difference and automatically elevates things into another bracket of quality.

So what things can you use? Just like other aspects of film making you don't always need be literal – think abstract. So, if your vlog is about politics, why not have a photo or souvenir of a famous government building in shot. If you are reviewing film releases, then any iconic film poster will do the trick, or simply a coffee mug with a film logo on it. If it's about food, set up in the kitchen. You get the idea.

Lighting

While it's all very good having one or two props placed judiciously, if no one can see them owing to poor lighting then it defeats the point. Given many vloggers tend to operate in the darker hours, no doubt on account of work or study commitments, sources of illumination are often overlooked.

Lighting, or rather lack of it, is a common problem with vlogs. Many vloggers film in the evening after work or studies, meaning that the available light is at the mercy of whatever light bulb, or bulbs, are in the room. Now, not all cameras are the same and each will respond differently in the same lighting conditions. If you are using an actual video camera, you will probably get better results than the in-built camera of your iPad, for example. Also, some cameras, when filming in poor lighting, will automatically kick in their low shutter speed and gain functions in an attempt to brighten the image. The result of this is a grainy washed-out picture and an almost spooky slow-motion feel to any movement. This is definitely not the kind of video quality to aspire to if you are talking about decorating tips.

Remember this

Clever use of available lights or cheaply and readily bought items can inject a serious dose of quality into vlogs.

The first choice for many will be the in-built light on their laptop, mobile device or video camera. There's nothing fundamentally wrong with this, but their output and effective range will vary from device to device, meaning in some cases that you have to be rather close to the light, and in turn the camera, with the result that your head is uncomfortably large (and close) on screen. Even the most photogenic vlogger will not be doing themselves any favours if viewers can look straight up their nostrils or can see nothing but their eyebrows and forehead.

Arranging reading lights and switching on the main room lighting can often be very effective, depending on their wattage. Again, however, the quality of your in-built camera can let you down, as it may not be able to white-balance (see Chapter 3) different lighting sources accurately, giving your picture strange hues of blue or orange. Fortunately, cheap and widely available LED lighting picked up from local discount stores can boost your illumination and vastly improve your picture quality. No, don't worry, I'm not suggesting that you go out and purchase some elaborate chandelier or party lighting – rather USB-powered LED reading lights that can be powered by your laptop itself. Just angle them at your face, preferably having one on each side, and you are ready to go. Or

LED strip lighting can be arranged in long or short sections and stuck on to things. If so inclined, you could stick it around the outside of your laptop screen giving you an instant mini studio lighting set-up. These simple lights can be very strong, help give a defined picture and make a big and positive difference.

Remember this

The bottom line here is: the more light you have pointing at you, the better your picture will be. Remember that basic adage and you won't go far wrong.

Sound

The next piece of the technical pie for vlogging is your sound recording. Like other aspects of film making, the audio quality is something that is often ignored or given scant concern.

The one-shot vloggers using built-in microphones contained in their mobile devices or laptops can often have the worst sound quality. While they do indeed record sound, they are often afterthoughts that can leave your video sounding like a bad Skype call. While it's true that the nearer you are to a mic the better the audio quality will be, this can create the same aesthetic problems mentioned above if you put your head too close. Some people get around this issue by using microphone headsets. While giving good sound quality these can look rather stand-offish and create a subtle barrier between vlogger and viewer. So what can you do?

Those readers blessed with an iPhone can simply use the headset mic. While it's not necessary to plug it into your ears, you can still use the mic function, as this will give you great sound quality that will be a cut about the rest. Plus, it's entirely possible that such microphones are compatible with your laptop.

For the truly techno-minded, you might want to use exotic devices such as Bluetooth mics, separate audio recorders and so on. That's up to you, and many do go down that route, but so long as you are recording audio that can at least be understood then there's no reason to reinvent the wheel.

The camera

The prime camera for vlogging is the inbuilt camera of your smartphone, tablet or laptop. If such a device is available to you, that's great. Such devices dispense with the need for recording media, transferring files, digitizing material, and editing on another computer, and generally prevent you from getting bogged down with fiddly technical considerations. You film, you upload, you're done. However, such cameras do have limitations in that they are automatic, with no scope for making manual adjustments ahead of your shoot. Likewise, smartphones may have little or no possibility for you to make adjustments, leaving you to settle for whatever it decides to do.

For this reason, you need to pay very close attention to your set-up and lighting. In fact, the lighting is in some ways going to be your surrogate way of making camera adjustments, so pay close attention to it and take on board some of the tips mentioned above.

While some vloggers do indeed invest in expensive capable cameras and dedicate themselves to producing some very slick videos, I'd personally start out slow and see what you can achieve with what you've got. Understand what your inbuilt camera's limitations are and work around them. Then, if you become some vlogging mogul with a highly monetized YouTube account, then, fair enough, buy a Sony 4K camera.

To conclude things at the technical level, vlogging is perhaps the simplest form of film making. It can be a single shot lasting for many minutes, in excess of an hour, or longer. Pay attention to the technical basics and you can't go far wrong – after all, you're not exactly making a blockbuster!

Presenting

So what are the key personal requisites for taking the plunge and hitting that record button? Having a thick skin is part of the deal, as it's inevitable some of the interest you create will not always be positive, and the haters and trolls out there will be making their views known volubly and in quite visceral ways. However, you probably knew that anyway.

Just like the technical considerations discussed earlier, it's important to get your message across clearly and without distractions. What this doesn't necessarily mean is that your delivery needs to resemble a well-rehearsed speech; rather, it should be an honest one. The difference is subtle but important. People viewing will accept you stuttering, forgetting what to say or having a brain freeze every few moments, as it's a vlog, not regular TV. However, you do at least need to retain your train of thought and stay on subject, otherwise your presentation will become a rambling stream of consciousness that may stray a long way from your original message.

This is a common problem with any presenting or on-camera, role. It's easy to either freeze every few moments in tongue-tied stupor, swear while in a panic or start a confused, rapid ejection of fragmented ideas while your face turns increasingly red. Here's the thing: presenting isn't as easy as many believe it to be. It's perhaps seen as a no-skill-required job where you can just breeze in front of your camera, speak for a while, and then head home. However, it's anything but that. All too often when a camera is pointed at someone the effect is like a party balloon having its air released from the knotted end – everything comes out in a mad gushing babble. All of a sudden, the presenter looks wide-eyed into the camera and any thoughts they had prepared in their head disappear.

This panic is something I've frequently seen while filming aspiring or new presenters. Yet there's a fundamental difference with vlogging. Most of the time – though not all of the time, depending on your eventual set-up – it's just you. There's no crew pointing cameras, lights and microphones and staring at you expectantly and increasing the pressure you're feeling. No, it's just you and your device. Also, you are in a familiar environment – usually your bedroom or some other location in your home. You are not delivering a piece to camera in the midst of a busy downtown area with all sorts of people pointing and giggling at you, nor are you in a professional studio with all manner of high-tech torture equipment (i.e. huge cameras) pointing in your direction. No, you are somewhere safe and familiar.

That said, even though it isn't live TV being watched by millions, it can have its own anxiety-creating pressures.

So, what comes first when thinking about what to say? Although a simple device, introducing yourself and what you're about to talk about goes a long way in helping the audience know what's about to happen. All too often the vlogger just launches straight into things without any kind of introduction and this can create a slight psychological barrier in terms of understanding what's going on. Moreover, an introduction can ease you into the subject you are about to discuss. You don't have to explain or justify *why* you are talking about a certain subject or anything like that: a simple 'Hi, my name is Alonzo Chavez. Welcome to my vlog. Today I'm going to be talking about so-and-so's facial hair' will suffice. Try it out!

What about the rest of the presentation? Some vlogs can go on for a considerable amount of time, so if you plan on having a video of several minutes, maybe think about having a few cue cards or yellow stickies with key phrases or words stuck around the camera lens or your laptop. After all, professional and highly paid TV presenters are often doing exactly the same thing with a teleprompter or 'idiot cards'. Or, if notes are not practical, write it down on a pad in front of you. It doesn't matter if the viewers can see it, too – it's a vlog, that's part of the attraction.

Don't feel you have to look into the lens every moment of your vlog. Just like speaking to people in real life, sometimes your eyes can look away elsewhere as you consider what to say or collect your thoughts. Plus, it can make things more natural and that is something that any audience will appreciate. For this reason, you may want to avoid reading off a script, as this can seem very unnatural and forced, making the audience lose that unique emotional connection they may have with you, the presenter. It's much better to be yourself.

Another aspect that can affect the quality of your vlog is the start of the recording process. Those using a standalone dedicated video camera may have to start the vlog within a few seconds of them pressing the record button and stepping back a few paces to start their presentation. Others may use a remote control, but even so this can mean that the first thing the audience sees is the vlogger pointing a remote at them. OK, that isn't something that will destroy the integrity of a vlog, but it's a detail you should think about editing out as it will make things that little bit better and smoother-running. Likewise, the end of some vlogs can have the same awkward moments of pointing the remote or walking towards the camera. By contrast, those using laptops, smartphones and other mobile devices can surreptitiously press the record start without skipping a beat.

Although editing a vlog is something you shouldn't worry about much, unless you want to do something simple at the start and end ('topping and tailing', as it's known), editing can be a way to greatly enhance vlogs, especially those describing objects and technical processes or how-to guides. In these circumstances, editing should be considered as a way to enhance your message and video. If you want to take about some film merchandise – for example, if your latest vlog is dedicated to an action figure of Finn from *Star Wars Episode VII* – there will be times when you want your audience to have a closer look at things. This is where things can get very tricky. If you just shove the object close to the camera lens, a couple things will happen: the camera will lose focus and your audience will squint in confusion. It's at times like this when you need to think about cutaways.

Remember this

Just as in larger and longer films, cutaways can serve an important function in the humble vlog and add some brilliantly important detail to an otherwise simple video.

Those unfamiliar with film making and editing can often use cutaways clumsily. Either the vlogger will suddenly hold it up to the lens, or they may stop filming the vlog, film the object, then go back to filming themselves. Neither of these is ideal. As mentioned, one method can create focus problems while the other can seriously affect the pace and coherence of your vlog. It's better to record your vlog as normal and then film the cutaways separately. So, if you say, 'Just look at the detail on the figure here', you should film a close-up of the detail you are referring to afterwards and then add it to the edit at the appropriate spot. In the completed vlog your cutaway will seamlessly fit into the presentation and make things a bit more interesting and, dare I say it, professional.

Of course, if you are using a basic in-built camera you may struggle to film in close-up on account of there being no zoom function available or by losing focus on close objects. You may just have to take a photo and edit that in instead or set up some kind of pack shot (a term used for some objects arranged nicely in a separate area). In a television studio, this pack shot area can often be a special raised platform with its own dedicated lighting rig and camera set-up. For the vlogger, it could be a small table with a white paper background and reading light shining on it giving illumination to whatever is placed there. Simple! Again, forget about perfection but concentrate on getting your message across with clear visuals.

The company vlog

For those of thinking about using a vlog, or some other kind of video, for the purposes of marketing or representing your company in some way, the stakes are rather higher. While many are posting videos talking about their companies, or how to install or use items from their product lines, things can be fraught. Quite often there is a huge gulf in the quality between a company's website and the videos it creates. It's a sad fact the democratization of video-making has led many to believe they can make a video. This is a moot point at best and one that will cause a professional videographer to facepalm upon hearing.

Nothing will make your company look cheap and amateurish like a poorly made video. It's often heart-breaking, or mirth-inducing, to visit an otherwise professional and slick-looking website only to click on their video content and see their CEO badly lit in some dark basement, while they inaudibly talk about their business activities over the sound of traffic and dogs barking.

If you have a company, no matter how big or small, then please realize that producing bad videos will turn people away just as much as a cheap-looking website or poor advertising. It's another thing representing you and your company, so it needs attention and some care in the making.

Many feel that they have no option but to make their own content due to the price of hiring a professional. If you are a small company with a limited turnover, then this is understandable. Thus, many look around them, realize that their smartphone shoots video, and so decide to make a couple of little presentations for no cost. The trouble is, without basic skills, knowledge and awareness of how to make a video presentation, the content produced can often be a bizarre video filmed as a selfie. At best, these will make great comedic viewing but will probably have a negative impact on sales and reputation.

Let's stop a moment. This isn't a precursor to saying you need to hire a studio, expensive cameras or talent if you want your plumbing or car hire business to make some decent videos. Instead, this is a slight extrapolation of what's been written earlier in this section – just think about what your message is, how you want to say it and where you want to say it. Instead of filming in some random location, how about setting up at your desk, at a workbench, or some other area of your company. Simple touches like this reinforce the message. What are you wearing? If your business is a car repair shop, then wearing a smart suit and tie may be counterproductive. If you run a law firm, then something too casual may likewise give the wrong message. If you want to deliver a simple message telling people what you do, then you could just deliver a few lines to the camera from a static location. If you want to want to highlight specific products or activities, then you may need to consider filming in multiple locations and taking the time to film pack shots or cutaways of some kind.

Then there are the technical considerations. Do you have sufficient lighting? What camera will you be using? What about microphones and sound recording. Will you edit your film or will it be a one-shot take? Have a holistic concept of what you want to achieve and take your time planning it.

Remember this

Don't make the common mistake of thinking that just because you have the latest smartphone you can make a good video. Remember, technology doesn't make the film for you; *you* make the film using the technology. There is a difference, so it's important you know how to use things.

Focus points

* Have a clear idea of what it is you want to say in the vlog.
* It makes a big difference if you introduce yourself and the subject.
* If you don't think you can remember everything, use cue cards or yellow stickies.
* Give thought to your location. Is it appropriate to the vlog?
* What's in the background? Certain objects and decorations could be off message or distracting.
* Are there any simple props that can reinforce what you are talking about?
* Do you have enough light to be seen clearly?
* Can people hear you?
* What are the limitations of your camera? Know what they are and work around them.
* Consider editing for certain subject matter.

Next step

In the final chapter I will pass on some of my own personal experiences from my early film making career. The point is to show you that even professionals have to start somewhere. We all learn by experience and by making mistakes (sometimes big ones). You won't get anywhere just by dreaming and doing nothing ...

16

Confessions of a first-time film maker

In this chapter you will learn:

▶ *what not to do*
▶ *how to avoid disaster*
▶ *how to remain in control*

Two exploded 800-watt lights, smashed bottles, spilled beer, an actress crying hysterically, a drunk lead actor, 30 moaning and bored extras and a caretaker telling me to get out of the building – not exactly how I planned on finishing my first ever day's filming. But you can never predict how these things will go.

If, at the end of your filming experience, you don't have one single amusing story, then you have been doing something very wrong. I hope my tales of woe/amusement will serve to highlight some of the ways not to make a film.

Obtaining sponsorship from a brewery was quite a coup on a number of levels: the film had official support, the production received genuine and much-needed props, plus beer is a good way of paying cavalier and feisty actors.

Unfortunately, having about 40 people hanging around a set all day drinking alcohol can lead to circumstances that are not conducive to the making of a film. People got drunk and every so often the sound of breaking glass and a drunken expletive was heard right in the middle of a take.

Having the lead actor drink real vodka and beer for all the takes was probably not too wise either, as by the time he was on the cusp of getting the lines right – he just sighed, swooned and fell to the floor from all the alcohol he had consumed.

This was nothing in comparison to one of the other actors in the pub scenes who had also been absorbing a steady stream of vodka. By the time he had to say his lines, a stream of vomit came out of his mouth instead of the words I had written. He then passed out and had to be taken home in a wheelchair.

Adding to the festival of inebriation, a meek and mild-mannered extra drank one beer too many and turned into a psychopathic lunatic. After he had attacked a cast member and knocked over some lights, he ran out of the set and went on a crime spree in the local liquor store. I heard he was arrested later that night.

To add to my misery, one of the actresses, who was top of her drama class at college, suddenly got an attack of the nerves. Instead of walking over to the tables and serving drinks, she froze in the middle of the set and dropped a tray of alcohol on the floor. At the exact moment beer came into contact with floor, two of the 800-watt lights blew up. The caretaker of the building came in and told us to get out as he was closing up. I had not even filmed a page and a half of script. I had two scenes to get through and I wouldn't be able to hire the hall again for another two months!

Through the smell of stale beer, vomit and burning I suddenly realized how hard all this could be. Having beer flowing freely on the set was probably not a great idea, especially for actors as it seriously affected their performances. But it was all part of the learning process, I suppose.

That first day was a bit of a disaster as numerous things went very wrong. Thankfully, from there on the production found its pace and the cast and crew learned how to work together until they were a 'well-oiled machine'. The rule here is: try to keep everyone in line on set. Without a bit of order and, dare I say it, discipline, a large group of people can soon turn into a rabble of maniacs (see boxed text on 1st assistant directors in Chapter 11). Have fun, but don't let things get out of hand.

Health and safety

The general health and safety of your cast and crew should also be something to which you pay particular attention. However, no matter how diligent you are, there will always be something that goes wrong. Once, while filming an interrogation scene, we were in a long bare room with a window at the far end. I had framed the mastershot so that the entire length of the room was at an 'arty' oblique angle and tilt, and the actor and two actresses were in frame. The set-up was simple enough: the interrogation victim was between the other two actors, and I had told her to wriggle about on the bar stool on which she was tied up. Unfortunately, she wriggled so much that she lost her balance, and in the process of falling off her perch knocked over a very large and heavy bronze sculpture that was on a pedestal behind her. The bronze bust then fell against the window but, amazingly, just bounced off the glass and fell harmlessly to the floor. Since this room – and window – were four storeys up, a potentially nasty accident, and possible legal headache, was averted. Luckily the actress was not harmed by the fall – and it made a great end of shot.

The rule here is: try to look at what could happen on your set that might result in someone getting hurt. Try to figure out everything so that you can avoid an accident. As mentioned earlier, wires and cables are probably the biggest potential source for accidents.

Safety is something that can be gauged through a recce, as is the overall state of the location where you want to film. Avoiding a recce may lead to unfortunate surprises...

The importance of a recce

When filming in the southern Czech Republic, I decided that it would be great if we could film something in the not-too-far-away Austrian capital of Vienna. I had some 'stand-by' pages of script in the event that we made it to Austria (this was low, low budget remember). We hopped over the border and, as we all neared the beautiful and elegant eighteenth-century Schönbrunn Palace and its equally breath-taking gardens (used in a James Bond film), I was telling the cast and crew about the sheer magnificence of the place and how it was a unique location at which to film. We then turned the corner and went through the palace grounds gates and I was rather upset to discover that the entire building was covered in scaffolding, weatherproof sheeting and all the gardens were being dug up by crowds of workmen and bulldozers.

Although we managed to film the scene I had written, my original shot sequence was seriously limited due to the sheer scale of renovation work going on. The rule here is: go on a recce, otherwise when you turn up for filming any number of obstacles to your film may be waiting for you.

People

Another important thing to highlight is the people factor. People – actors, crew or whoever – can hinder your film in all manner of ways. These can range from a cast member starting to get all cocky and too big for their boots just because they have a bit more experience than the other actors, to perhaps a camera operator who wants to film things in their own special way. Although many of the comments that actors and crew make can be innocent suggestions to help out a certain scene of your film, sometimes they can be a bit more awkward and meddlesome. A common one is actors improvising a tad too much or adding new lines in the middle of filming a scene. Sometimes these things can really change the focus of a scene and dilute the film from what you want it to be.

Another people factor is to make sure people are happy when being filmed. Some actors, while great at delivering lines, can suddenly freeze when they see a camera on them. They may even say their lines and from time to time look into the camera. Do try to avoid situations like this. You may find out that although someone is a very talented actor, they become extremely self-conscious when filmed, and it may take a bit of time to get over this slight difficulty (see Chapter 3).

Also, if you are out filming in the street or in another public place, it is very annoying when passing people shout and wave into the camera or suddenly get embarrassed and deliberately look away. So, bear this in mind. People react in strange ways when they see a camera. I've often been held up shooting a scene due to some passing lunatics offering to strip off in front of the camera, generally shouting random abuse or beeping car horns.

While on this subject, there was a Greek film company in the 1970s and early 1980s that constantly made big-budget films about glamorous women who became mixed up in international espionage. In every single film there were several scenes where the heroine was seen running through the crowded streets of Athens. In these shots you could always see people in the street smiling and pointing at the camera as they ambled on by, eating a sandwich or drinking a beer. It was ridiculous to see the actress looking all forlorn when next to her was a group of locals pulling faces and giving the thumbs-up sign to the camera.

I also had an interesting situation in a hotel in Prague: after all the cast and crew had settled into their rooms on the first night, a Russian woman who was also staying in the hotel and who spoke very little English, got talking to us in the lounge and asked us what we were doing in Prague. After a while I suddenly decided to improvise a scene in which one of the characters meets up with a lady of the night as a follow-on from a scene we had filmed back in Britain (low-budget is about capitalizing on available resources, remember). So, I explained to the Russian woman what we wanted to do. She agreed to take part and so we went ahead. The scene was simple enough: one of the actors and the Russian woman walked down a corridor, into an open doorway and out again, and that was that – or so I thought. Later that evening as everyone was going to bed, the Russian woman came up to me and stated that she had not realized what we wanted her to do due to her poor English, and that if anyone saw this film in Russia then people could get killed, so would we please destroy the footage of her!

Remember this

The rule here is: if you have any 'tertiary actors' make sure they agree to be filmed. Some people can be very vocal about not wanting to be filmed and you must respect their feelings. For film and television there are 'release and consent' forms that people have to sign that state they agree to be filmed – something to think about (see Chapter 14). Try to balance fun with responsibility and you won't go far wrong.

Closing thoughts

I hope this book has entertained as well as informed and that you have a good idea of what is involved in making a film.

Remember this

'There are now more ways for more people to show other people how bad they are at making films.' Director Terry Gilliam, on the downside to the proliferation of digital film making technology

In the time it has taken you to read this book there has probably been some other piece of technology or computerization invented that means it is a bit easier, and even more accessible, to make a film. A low-budget film maker ten years ago could not have dreamed up some of the things that are now sold on every high street. However, do remember that despite all the technology and gadgets out there, making a film is about harnessing your creativity and translating this into a story of moving images. No amount of gadgetry can do this for you, it's got to come from within.

There are two kinds of people in this world: those who talk about doing things and those who do things. Those in the latter category make films. But remember, the best anyone can do is try ...

Get out there and make your film happen!

Good luck.

Glossary

ambient sound Background sound that is picked up by the microphone in addition to dialogue.

aperture Opening which controls the amount of light that eventually hits the film or video. Its size can be altered to vary the amount of light coming through.

audio channel See sound channel.

backlight Light placed behind the actor.

blonde Popular professionally used light.

boom A 'pole' with a microphone on the end that allows the sound recordist to get the microphone close to the actors without appearing in shot.

call sheet Simple document showing the arrangements for a day's filming (*also called* the schedule).

close-up A shot that will make the subject, for example a face, fill the screen.

crash zoom A very rapid zoom done for dramatic effect; *see* zoom in *and* zoom out.

cut The instant when one shot joins another in the editing process.

cutaway A shot that reveals some detail that is not filmed via the mastershot, yet has relevance to the scene. For example, two men are in a room, one is seated at a desk, the other is standing in front of the desk opening a drawer. A possible cutaway could be a close-up on the desk drawer being opened to get out a gun. In a busy pub, with two people speaking at the bar, a possible cutaway might be of some of the other people seated around the pub having a drink.

depth of field The distance from the lens that objects will be in focus.

dissolve An edit effect in which two shots are joined by means of fading out of one shot while simultaneously fading into the next.

drop-out or degeneration (of image) Reduction in the quality of the image and sound as it is copied from tape to tape.

edit controller Machine of varying size and complexity which links a player, or video camera, to a recorder for the purposes of assembling and editing shots together.

edit script An idea of the intended chronology of the footage, and any effects and soundtrack, etc., written out in the form of a plan. Sometimes it is only used as a guide. Also known as a paper edit.

exposure A camera control to set how bright or dark a picture is.

external microphone A microphone that is plugged into the camera.

fade A method used, either via the aperture controls (*see* aperture) or in editing, where the image fades from or fades into black. The former might be done with a countryside scene to signify daybreak, while the latter might be done as a character's eye view to indicate falling asleep or dying.

field of vision The 'visual area' your camera will record and film at any one time.

fill light Complements the key light.

focus A camera control to ensure an image is sharp and clear – 'in focus'.

frame The filmed shot.

frame-accurate editing Editing that allows editors to stop and start cuts exactly where they want.

gag A method, and object, for reducing the amount of wind sound a microphone picks up.

gel Coloured transparent plastic 'paper' that can be put in front of lights to change their colour, or in front of windows to maintain the white balance (*see below*) of the picture.

hook The feature of your script or story that gets people interested.

jump cut A cut in which some of the action disappears and will cause a jolt in continuity.

key light The main light on a set, which lights everything up. Other lights may be used to film cutaways, etc.

linear editing Editing using a tape-to-tape method where the film is edited in the order in which it will be viewed.

log sheet A record of all shots made during filming to be used for reference during editing.

long shot A shot taken a long way away from the subject or building.

low-angle shot A shot made when the camera is placed low to the ground facing upwards. This is very effective in making someone look domineering or huge. The opposite, having the camera high up and facing the ground, will make someone look very puny or insignificant. Remember the scene in *Oliver* (dir. Carol Reed, 1968), when Twist says, 'Please sir, can I have some more?' to Harry Secombe's Mr Bumble? Harry Secombe is filmed in a low-angle shot, while Oliver Twist is filmed in a high-angle shot.

mastershot The main shot of a scene, filmed continuously with the same camera. Extras such as cutaways and close-ups, etc. are filmed later and then put in via the editing process. Some film scenes are simply mastershots with nothing else, but this can be boring for the viewer.

match funding Process whereby funds are received to equal and match those you already have.

non-linear editing A flexible form of editing where shots can be edited in a manner that does not conform to, or affect, the planned story order.

overexposure When too much light has got on to the film or video during the filming process. This has the effect of making people's faces, and other reflective surfaces, look exceptionally shiny and radioactive. In film and television it is commonly called 'flare' or 'bleach'. It is usually caused by the sun coming out from behind the clouds, having lights that are too bright or having the aperture/iris of the camera too wide open. Overexposure is a good and popular way to film flashback or dream sequences in a film.

pan Moving the camera around horizontally on a tripod or shoulder for the purposes of filming someone walking, a car driving, a dog running past the camera, etc.

paper edit *See* edit script.

partners A person, or persons, with whom you may be required to form an organization or group, for the purposes of obtaining funding.

plug-in microphone Another term for an external microphone.

reaction shot A shot showing someone's reaction to something in the action. For example, a wife is speaking to her husband. The wife says, 'I used to be a man.' There would then be a reaction shot of the man's face (usually in close-up), filmed as cutaway.

recce Short for reconnaissance. Having a look at a potential location.

redhead Popular professionally used light.

reflector A hand-held object made of reflective material which is used to increase the light illuminating a subject.

reverse cut This is when something has been filmed from two opposite angles. If someone is walking it will give the effect that the person has suddenly changed direction. However, it has its uses: if two people are sitting at a bar, there may be a reverse cut to show the view from behind the bar.

roll back A mechanical feature of a video camera or VCR. When 'record' or 'stop' is pressed, the tape can physically roll back slightly which means it has not stopped at the intended place. With a video camera this can mean the few final moments of a take can be clipped when the record is stopped and then started again. When using a video camera, always keep it recording for a few seconds after you have finished recording your subject. When editing with a VCR it can mean that a few moments at the end of a shot can be recorded over.

scenic projection You've all seen this in films, usually employed when someone is driving in a car and you can see the road going behind them at impossible speeds and turns. A film or slide projector is used to project an image on to a screen while the actors perform in the foreground. Make sure, however, that the projector is between the actors and the projection surface, or behind it, otherwise the results will look awful! Watch the film *Natural Born Killers* to see how effective scenic projection can be in a contemporary film.

schedule Another name for the call sheet.

set The place where you film a scene. Can be decorated to the guidelines in the script, such as a room, or left as it is, a city, for example.

shot Something that is filmed in one continuous run of the camera, i.e. between the director saying 'Action!' and 'Cut!'.

sound channel 'Space' allocated via an edit system, and then in turn on the film, for each different type of sound, e.g. dialogue, sound effects, music.

strobing Digital editing method in which images sourced on a video format are altered to appear more 'film-looking' in texture.

third-party material Material such as music, film clips or text used but not owned by the film maker.

tilt Like pan but in a vertical direction, for example, to tilt down the height of a tall building.

time code Numeric display in a camera viewfinder, or tape player, used to reference where shots are.

transitions Effects used to move between shots (see dissolve and fade).

treatment A concise synopsis of the intended film script outlining its story and characters. Usually on no more than one A4 piece of paper.

two shot A shot where two people are shown dominating the frame.

underexposure The opposite of overexposure. Caused by the sun suddenly going behind clouds, having the aperture iris closed too much or by using ineffective lighting. Underexposure can be a good way of simulating twilight or night.

whip pan Like a pan but much faster. So fast in fact that the images are all blurred. A very popular method of jumping from scene to scene in television spy spoof/superhero series of the 1960s – usually accompanied by some equally rapid bongo drumming.

white balance A camera control to set the correct colour tone for a shot in a given lighting situation.

wild track Recording of the natural sound of a location to use as a background track in the edit.

zoom in Makes the subject progressively larger in the frame. Also see crash zoom.

zoom out Makes the subject progressively smaller in the frame.

Taking it further

Useful contacts

Here are the contact details of some groups and organizations in UK, USA, Australia and Canada who may be able to give you practical advice, funding guidance or even grants and bursaries. The list starts off with the regional arts boards, which are often the first calling point for aspiring film makers.

THE REGIONAL ARTS COUNCILS

Arts Council of Northern Ireland

1 The Sidings

Antrim Road

Lisburn BT28 3AJ

Tel: +44 28 9262 3555

Fax: +44 28 92623560

Website: www.artscouncil-ni.org

Arts Council of Wales

(Central Office)

Bute Place

Cardiff CF10 5AL

Tel: +44 845 8734 900

Website: www.arts.wales

(Regional Offices)

Princes Park II

Princes Drive

Colwyn Bay LL29 8PL

Tel: +44 149 253 3440

Website: www.arts.wales

The Mount 18 Queen Street

Carmarthen SA31 1JT

Tel: +44 845 8734 900

Website: www.arts.wales

Scottish Arts Council

12 Manor Place

Edinburgh EH3 7DD

Tel: +44 131 226 6051

Fax: 0131 255 9833

Website: www.scottisharts.org.uk

Arts Council England, Cambridge Office

24 Brooklands Avenue

Cambridge CB2 8BU

Tel: +44 161 934 4317 or +44 845 300 6200

Website: www.artscouncil.org.uk

Arts Council England, Nottingham Office

Rooms 005 & 005A, Arkwright Building, Nottingham Trent
University, Burton Street

Nottingham NG1 4BU

Tel: +44 845 300 6200

Website: www.artscouncil.org.uk

Arts Council England, London Office

21 Bloomsbury Street

London WC1B 3HF

Tel: +44 845 300 6200

Website: www.artscouncil.org.uk

Arts Council England, Newcastle Office

Central Square

Forth Street

Newcastle upon Tyne NE1 3PJ

Tel: +44 845 300 6200

Website: www.artscouncil.org.uk

Arts Council England, Manchester Office

The Hive

49 Lever Street

Manchester M1 1FN

Tel: +44 845 300 6200

Website: www.artscouncil.org.uk

Arts Council England, Brighton Office

Unit A, Level 4, New England House

New England Street

Brighton BN1 4GH

Tel: +44 845 300 6200

Website: www.artscouncil.org.uk

Arts Council England, Bristol Office

Third Floor, St Thomas Court

Thomas Lane

Bristol BS1 6JG

Tel: +44 845 300 6200

Website: www.artscouncil.org.uk

Arts Council England, Birmingham Office

The Foundry, 82 Granville Street

Birmingham B1 2LH

Tel: +44 845 300 6200

Website: www.artscouncil.org.uk

Arts Council England, Leeds Office

1st Floor South, Marshall's Mill

Marshall Street

Leeds LS11 9YJ

Tel: +44 845 300 6200

Website: www.artscouncil.org.uk

NATIONAL ORGANIZATIONS

The British Academy of Film and Television Arts (BAFTA)

195 Piccadilly

London W1J 9LN

Tel: +44 20 7734 0022

Email: info@bafta.org

Website: www.bafta.org

BAFTA have central offices in London, but they have regional centres around the UK. They can offer advice and a wide range of support to film makers.

The British Film Institute (BFI)

21 Stephen Street

London WIT 1LN

Tel: +44 20 7255 1444

Website: www.bfi.org.uk

The BFI exists to promote and help the production of films in the UK. Although it has a limited funding capacity and runs a few schemes from time to time, it mostly advises and acts as a resource for film making information, be it other organizations or individuals, who may be able to help you.

Pro8mm (USA)

2805 W. Magnolia Blvd

Burbank

CA 91505

USA

Tel: +1 818 848 5522

Email: sales@pro8mm.com

Website: www.pro8mm.com

This company (as the name suggests) specializes in services, cameras, film and accessories to do with 8 mm film. They are used by professionals and amateurs alike and also deal with 16 mm film. A great place to start if you want to look into this format of film a bit more closely.

A GENERAL DESCRIPTION OF SOME OTHER ARTS AND FUNDING BODIES AROUND THE WORLD

Finding funding (and information) to help make your film is something that is never too far away no matter where you live. Arts boards are not only regional organizations in the UK, but they exist in other countries. For example, around the world there is Americans for the Arts, The Australian Council for the Arts and The Canada Council for the Arts to name only three.

With regard to charitable trusts (or philanthropic societies as they are sometimes known), these exist around the globe and there is always a publication, be it an almanac or directory, that lists them for a particular country. Likewise, every major town around the world will have some manifestation of community film and video. In many cases they co-exist with commercial companies. In addition to having bursaries available, they also often run training days in the use of film and video making equipment. Just like community film and video organizations, there are film agencies all over the world for most major towns and national districts. Even if you don't know it, there is probably one in your area.

Lotteries around the world vary a great deal in terms of the way they are organized and what they do with the revenue they make. Some may have a percentage that they pay into charities or other organizations. For example, the Lotteries Commission of Western Australia pays money to the Western Australia Film Industry as well as to other arts bodies. However, some of you may be in a part of the world where the lottery has no provision for film or arts and money is given to education or health programmes instead.

Australian Council for the Arts

PO Box 788

Strawberry Hills

NSW 2012

Street address:

Surry Hills

372 Elizabeth Street

NSW 2010

Australia

Tel: +61 29 215 9000

Toll Free: 1800 266 912 (charges may apply for mobiles/international calls)

Email: enquiries@australiacouncil.gov.au

Website: www.australiacouncil.gov.au

Screen Australia

Head office:

Level 7, 45 Jones Street

Ultimo

NSW 2007

GPO Box 3984

Sydney NSW 2001

Phone: +61 2 8113 5800

Toll Free: 1800 213 099 (charges may apply for mobiles/international calls)

Fax: +61 2 8113 5888

Melbourne Office:

PO Box 404

South Melbourne VIC 3205

Street address

Ground floor, 290 Coventry Street

South Melbourne VIC 3205

Phone: +61 3 8682 1900

Toll Free: 1800 213 681 (charges may apply for mobiles/
international calls)

Fax: +61 3 9696 1476

Website: www.screenaustralia.gov.au

Americans for the Arts

Washington Office

1000 Vermont Avenue NW, 6th Floor

Washington, DC 20005

Tel: +1 202 371 2830

Fax: +1 202 371 0424

Website: www.americansforthearts.org

New York Office

One East 53rd Street, 2nd Floor

New York, NY 10022

Tel: +1 212 223 2787

Fax: +1 212 980 4857

The Canada Council for the Arts

150 Elgin St, 2nd floor

PO Box 1047

Ottawa

Ontario K2P 1L4

Tel: +1 613-566-4414

Toll Free: 1 800 263 5588 (charges may apply for mobiles/
international calls)

Fax: +1 613 566 4390

Website: www.canadacouncil.ca

National Film Board of Canada

Operational headquarters:

Norman-McLaren Building

3155 Cote-de-Liesse Road

Montreal

Quebec H4N 2N4

Tel: +1 514 283 9000

Toll Free: 1 800 267 7710 (charges may apply for mobiles/international calls)

Postal address:

National Film Board of Canada

P.O. Box 6100

Station Centre-ville

Montreal, Quebec, H3C 3H5

Website: www.nfb.ca

Websites

www.cyberfilmschool.com

Website which goes into some depth and detail about the processes and stages involved in making a film. Also features news and reviews on new film making technology as well as links to related sites.

www.filmmaking.net

Website that acts as a forum for film makers, a trading post, a resource for information about techniques and tips, and a general database of knowledge about film making.

www.indiewire.com

Not totally dedicated to low budget film making, but it does contain numerous articles and features of the craft, gadgets and world of low budget and guerrilla film making.

www.nobudgetfilmschool.com

A reassuringly stripped down and raw looking website that points users to its classes and other events, but it also contains other info including a long list of low budget websites, vlogs and blogs.

www.nofilmschool.com

Site packed solid with techo reviews, gadgets, best practice and general features of those engaged in no and low budget film making. Also has community and social media pages.

Disclaimer: The publisher has used its best endeavours to ensure that the URLs for external websites referred to in this book are correct and active at the time of going to press. However, the publisher has no responsibility for the websites and can make no guarantee that the site will remain live or that the content is, or will remain, appropriate.

Further reading

Raymond G. Frensham (2010) *Break into Screenwriting*, Hodder Education.

Raymond Fielding (1985) *Special Effects Cinematography*, Focal Press – although this version is dated, it gives some great practical instruction on how to use miniatures and camera effects.

Barry Hampe (1997) *Making Documentary Film and Reality Videos: A Practical Guide to Planning, Filming, and Editing Documentaries of Real Events*, Owl Paperbacks.

Michael Hyatt (2012) *Platform: Get Noticed in a Noisy World*, Thomas Nelson Inc. A guide to raising your personal brand and/or profile. Has a few insights into the use of video and could be useful for someone trying to raise their film's profile for the purposes of finance or promotion. Also for someone wanting to generate popularity for their vlogs.

Nicolas Kent (1991) Naked Hollywood. *Money, Power and the Movies*, BBC books. A decent overview of the business side of the movie industry with a few technical insights too.

Kris Malkiewicz (1992) *Film Lighting*, Simon & Schuster – a 'bible' for anyone wanting to learn how to light their film.

Robert B. Musburger (1998) *Single-camera Video Production*, Focal Press.

John Boorman (1985) *Money into Light, The Emerald Forest, A Diary*, Faber & Faber – a beautifully written, personal account of all the stages of production connected with the film *The Emerald Forest*. It weaves the technical, creative and logistical together wonderfully.

Index